Facilitating Learning with the Adult Brain in Mind

Facilitating Learning with the Adult Brain in Mind

A Conceptual and Practical Guide

Kathleen Taylor
Catherine Marienau

JOSSEY-BASS™
A Wiley Brand

Published by Jossey-Bass

A Wiley Brand

One Montgomery Street, Suite 1000, San Francisco, CA 94104-4594—www.josseybass.com

Library of Congress Cataloging-in-Publication Data Available at:

ISBN 978-1-118-71145-3 (Hardcover)
ISBN 978-1-118-71149-1 (ePDF)
ISBN 978-1-118-71159-0 (ePub)

Cover design by Wiley
Cover Illustration: © agsandrew/iStockphoto

Printed in the United States of America
FIRST EDITION

HB Printing 10 9 8 7 6 5 4 3 2 1

CONTENTS

For Anna Marienau Roth and Ken Miller,
for their love, insights, and forbearance.
(Someday there will be cleared table-tops.)

PREFACE

Once upon a time, like Goldilocks, we went searching for a book about the brain and adult learning that was just right—neither too abstract nor too technical. Such a book would describe in language accessible to nonneuroscientists (like us) how the adult brain works and also how to use this understanding to construct more brain-aware approaches that help adults learn and perform more effectively in diverse settings.

Having worked for many years with adult learners in various contexts, we had been avidly following the growing literature on the brain and learning. But most implications for practice seemed to focus on school-aged learners, and much of the technical, scholarly literature overwhelmed us with anatomical detail. In addition, we weren't satisfied with the how-to lists that regularly popped up in print and online of the latest so-called brain-based teaching strategies. To devise approaches that would better serve adult learners, we needed to boost our repertoires in more robust ways. We wanted more than new tools in our tool kits: we wanted to know with greater clarity why a certain model, technique, or facilitation approach was more aligned with how the brain learns yet not get lost in brain geography and architecture.

As we researched we discovered that many long-standing theories and models of adult learning—some of our favorites, in fact—could be viewed from the perspective of emerging brain science, though the connections were rarely explicit. Sharing our early findings in faculty development sessions, as consultants to organizations focused on teaching or training adults, and with colleagues around the globe confirmed for us that the information and ideas we had cobbled together about brain, practice, and theory were meaningful and useful to others. We finally realized that the book we wanted to read was one we would have to write.

This is not the book we first envisioned.

That book would have been built largely on our years of practice embellished with our explanations of neuroscience for nonscientists. It would have been a meaningful contribution, but would have posed little or no threat to our familiar ways of doing things. Looking back at how things appeared to us then, neuroscience seemed mostly to affirm much of what we already knew as best practices.

Our further researches opened us to additional perspectives such as cognitive science, psychology, artificial intelligence, and philosophy of mind. As we tried to visualize or diagram what we were learning about the brain's learning process, so that we could more easily explain it when we wrote about it, we found ourselves going around in circles.

After many frustrating attempts at categorization and association—defining and redefining the elements, processes, interconnections, promoters, and inhibitors—our eureka moment occurred when we realized that we had conflated what was going on inside and outside the brain. Learning involves two separate but interwoven areas of activity; the external environment, typically constructed and directed by someone else, and the internal environment, constructed and directed by the brain.

Sketching out this multifaceted relationship illuminated for us an unexpected disconnect between how the brain engages in learning and how we engage in facilitation. It also prompted us to think about new approaches, so as to better align with how the brain learns when no one is telling it what to do and how to do it. We invite you to preview the visual analogy and storyboard we call the *Theatre of Knowing* (further explanation follows later in the book).

For now it is enough to consider the four major areas; contrary to expectation, the story flows from right to left. First there's a neuron next to indicators of the five senses; then the silhouette of a head within which rests a body labeled to represent what brains do silently and inwardly; in the middle of the page is both a gauzy curtain that separates the images on the right from those on the left and, above it, a bridge connecting them, from which emanates a spotlight; on the left, indicators of things brains do visibly and verbally.

This visual metaphor and storyboard may prompt your own reflection. We will describe in detail the significance of our epiphany and the application to practice in the introduction to part 2. First, however, part 1 provides the background information needed to make sense of those descriptions

As our understanding of the learning process grew, so did our appreciation of how adult learning could promote adult development. Brain-aware facilitation seemed likely to contribute to the very kind of learning that enables adults to make more informed choices and act in more deliberate and impactful ways. Learning about how the adult brain learns underscores the role that we and other practitioners can play in fostering these developmental outcomes both for individuals and toward the greater social good. (See "Citations.").

Citations

Although our earlier book, *Developing Adult Learners: Strategies for Teachers and Trainers* (K. Taylor, Marienau, & Fiddler, 2000), did not touch on the brain, we now find that much of what we said there accords with brain-aware practice; we just didn't know it yet. For more recent development-related or brain-related material, see K. Taylor (2006), K. Taylor and Marienau (2008), K. Taylor and Lamoreaux (2008), and Lamoreaux and Taylor (2011).

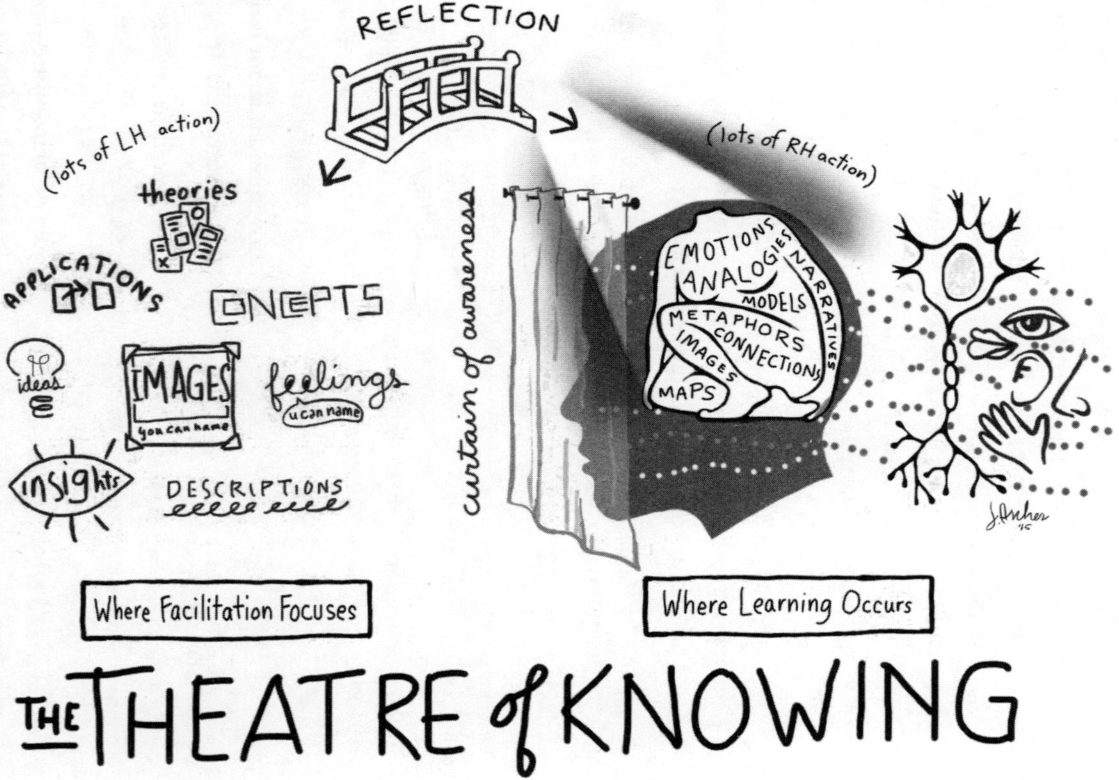
REFLECTION
(lots of LH action)
(lots of RH action)
theories
APPLICATIONS
CONCEPTS
ideas
IMAGES
you can name
feelings
u can name
insights
DESCRIPTIONS
curtain of awareness
EMOTIONS
ANALOGIES
NARRATIVES
MODELS
METAPHORS
CONNECTIONS
IMAGES
MAPS
Where Facilitation Focuses
Where Learning Occurs
THE THEATRE of KNOWING

What Colleagues Shared

Early in our process of planning this book, we invited dozens of experienced practitioners on five continents to share with us their persistent questions with regard to working with adults. Their wide-ranging responses included observations about their own felt limitations as well as what they perceived as challenges many adult learners face. Here is our synthesis of their questions, concerns, and desires:

- How do we effectively encourage learners to explore and engage with new perspectives and unfamiliar ideas?
- How can we help adults more readily value and build on their experience for learning?
- How do we help learners become more invested in their own learning?
- How can we help adults discover and work effectively with connections between theory and practice, concepts and application?
- How do we best approach socially sensitive issues—for example, diversity and inclusion—that may challenge long-standing assumptions and beliefs?
- How do we deal with our own assumptions about learning and our value judgments as adult educators?
- How might we become aware of and reconcile incongruities between our rhetoric and our practice?

We believe the dozens of examples of brain-aware practice that form the heart of this book offer creative ways to approach these issues.

Who, Where, and When?

It's often said that adult learning happens anywhere and at any time. This book is therefore designed for adult learning facilitators in any setting; in this book, we're calling them ALFAS for short. We intend this work to be equally useful to experienced ALFAS and those just entering the field who want information that is both evidence and theory based—for example:

- *In college settings.* Whether credit or noncredit courses, in brick-and-mortar classrooms or online, this may include academic advisors, learning assessors, counselors, faculty mentors, instructors, instructional designers, professional community advisors, academic administrators, and professional development specialists.
- *Learning professionals in other organizational settings.* This includes facilitators, coaches, corporate trainers, designers, managers, designers of learning management systems, and chief learning officers, as well as consultants working with individuals and groups.
- *ALFAS who are consultants to colleges and other organizations.* Those who counsel about particular aspects of adult learning, such as student success services, prior learning assessment, and competency-based approaches, will find it useful.
- *Graduate students.* This book will be a rich resource for graduate students, both facilitators and learners.
- *Any adult learner.* We believe adult learners in general will find this book valuable.

We invite you to join our exploration of this exciting terrain.

Our Intentions

As practitioner-scholars, we interpret and interweave what scientists and theoreticians in various relevant disciplines and fields have been saying for some time—but rarely, it seems, to one another. Having in this way discovered similar themes that also relate to our own primary field of adult development and learning, we now seek to translate those wide-ranging but overlapping perspectives into language that can better inform the practice of ALFAS.

How the Narrative Is Organized

We first provide background information about the brain that will help you make sense of the approaches to practice that follow. To maintain accessibility and flow, we avoid peppering the page with citations and unneeded scientific jargon. We instead include additional explanations, suggestions for further reading, and more technical material in boxes. These are particularly informative for graduate students and practitioners who want to dig a bit deeper. They are not essential if your primary purpose is to expand your repertoire toward more brain-aware approaches.

How the Book Is Organized

This book is presented in three parts. The science in part 1 is grounded in brain research; however, we frequently use stories and metaphors to illuminate technical ideas. In similar fashion, we often describe the brain and its functions in analogical rather than anatomical terms, sometimes speaking as though it has a mind of its own. Chapter 1 introduces the notion of two states of mind and how they affect adult learners. We then briefly examine how the human brain developed over eons, why it works as it now does, and how it continues to change. In chapter 2 we describe the significance of experience and the body (embodiment) to how the adult brain learns. Chapter 3 emphasizes the essential role of analogy and metaphor in the brain's process of association and categorization and examines current findings on how hemispheric differences affect learning.

Part 2 focuses explicitly on practices that encourage and strengthen adult learning in a variety of settings. It reintroduces the visual metaphor and storyboard for how learning occurs: the *Theatre of Knowing*. Then, drawing on contributions of experienced practitioners, chapter 4 sets the stage with approaches designed to overcome adults' initial anxieties and spark their curiosity; chapters 5, 6, and 7 progress toward greater integration of embodied and analogical approaches; and chapter 8 spotlights approaches that emphasize reflection and feedback. (We use *approaches* to mean activities, exercises, and strategies.)

In part 3, we tie together theory, practice, and our overall intentions. Chapter 9 explores selected theories and models of learning through the lenses of brain research and analogies highlighted in the previous chapters. Rather than begin our book with theory, which is typical, we first illuminate practice in part 2 because (*brain-aware alert!*) theories are more meaningful when the brain can connect them to concrete experiences. Chapter 10 returns to our overarching theme: how learning with the brain in mind can cultivate in adults a greater capacity to deal meaningfully and effectively with the complexities of modern life and commit to action for the greater good. The epilogue describes our personal journey of integrating brain-aware facilitation into our own practices.

To spark rather than direct your reflections, every chapter ends with a *Pause for Reflection*. At the end of each informational chapter (parts 1 and 3), we revisit *Key Ideas*.

A Gentle Suggestion

It may be tempting to skip part 1 entirely and thus get quickly to the "useful stuff" in part 2. Please try to resist. You will be more masterful in both adopting new approaches and enhancing those you already employ if you have a broader understanding of why they are effective. You will also be more likely to successfully generalize many of these approaches to other applications or situations beyond the specific setting described. But please do scan the approaches to practice to see what piques your interest. Here's another brain alert: Having particular issues or questions in mind as you read the introductory chapters is likely to enhance your learning and deepen your understanding. We hope to be companions and guides for you as you continue that journey.

By the way, when we say *we* or *us*, referring to Catherine and Kathleen, it could be either or both of us. At other times we may mean ALFAS or people in general. We trust the latter distinctions will be clear from the context.

Facilitating Learning with the Adult Brain in Mind

Part I

Brain: Then and Now

WE BEGIN with a brief overview of the brain. Rather than focus on anatomical detail, we use stories and analogies to explore how it came to be what it is today.

Chapter 1 first describes the brain's activity metaphorically, in terms of two states of mind that can affect how learning happens. We then explore what sociobiologists have inferred about the development of brain structures and function over time, culminating in what now resides in our twenty-first-century skulls. Finally, we briefly touch on an admittedly touchy subject: our currently aging brains.

Building on this backdrop, chapter 2 explores in more detail what we know about what the brain does as it learns—specifically, what supports and enhances adult learning. We more closely examine the embodied brain's fundamental learning process—analogical categorization and association—and the role that emotions play.

Chapter 3 looks more closely at how analogy and metaphor shape experience and conceptual understanding. We also examine current understandings of the differences between the left hemisphere and right hemisphere and how they affect learning.

1

Brain Basics

The biological mind is, first and foremost, an organ for controlling the biological body. . . . Minds are not *disembodied logical reasoning devices.*

— ANDY CLARK

THE BRAIN'S prime directive has always been to keep the organism alive and functioning optimally, whatever the situation. It does so by monitoring everything going on in and around the body. In fact, your brain can do a lot of things sophisticated medical diagnostic systems can do—and some they cannot. For example, in addition to continuously analyzing all body systems and states, your brain also responds instantly when those readings are out of whack, working to put things back in balance, called *homeostasis*.

Now, imagine what might have happened way back at the beginning when the brain had to face a saber-toothed tiger. In such situations, it is designed to go into survival mode: adrenaline rushes through the body, extra blood flows to muscles, and respiration rate increases. Though our current brain has ways to keep our more primitive emotions at bay, fear-based systems still affect much of our conscious and unconscious behavior. More than anything else, the brain wants *out of there*! The parts of the brain that can focus on problem solving and rational reflection are on hold. For many adults, taking a test is just about the modern equivalent of the tiger.

This is also true, though less intensely, in any new learning situation. Fortunately, adults have two competing states of mind: whereas one says, "I'm anxious," the other says, "I'm curious." Negotiating this ongoing tension is a major factor for adult learning facilitators in any setting (ALFAS) seeking to facilitate meaningful, lasting learning—but in our experience, it is one that is not sufficiently addressed in many learning environments.

Two States of Mind

It makes perfect sense that the brain's most basic imperative is self-preservation because if it can't manage that, nothing else much matters. We are constantly on the alert for potential threats. In fact, the brain suffers from *negativity bias*; that is, it is many times more likely to focus on and remember negative interpretations of experience.

Negativity bias affects thinking, feeling, and acting. Daniel Kahneman (2011) also describes this in terms of negativity dominance, in which "negativity and escape dominate positivity and approach" (p. 300). We see and respond to visual threats (a scary picture) or verbal threats (words like *war*) more quickly than we do to positive stimuli (happy faces, pleasant words). Furthermore, when presented with positive and negative stimuli (such as words or photographs on a screen), we unconsciously—and almost imperceptibly—lean our bodies toward the positive and away from the negative. And in interactions with others, we may dwell more intensely on what we perceive as negative input than on positive.

Anxious Brain

Here is a metaphorical description of our threat-anticipating, defensive, certainty-seeking, anxious, ready-to-fight-or-flee, no-time-to-think-about-learning brain figure 1.1. Its response to the basic question, "What do I have to do to save myself?" is:

- I have to *know* what's happening.
- I have to *focus narrowly* on the immediate potential danger.
- I have to be *certain*.
- I have to be *right* (uncertainty or ambiguity can mean annihilation!).
- I have to *avoid threat*.
- I have to be *always prepared to react*, just in case.

Figure 1.1 Anxious Brain

Curious Brain

Fortunately, a few hundred million years ago, our brains began refining and elaborating the systems designed to respond to threats. We now also have a very well-developed novelty-seeking,

Figure 1.2 Curious Brain

pattern-constructing, cause-seeking, meaning-making, analogy-directed brain figure 1.2. Its major focus is still and always self-preservation, but it comes at it in a completely different way:

- I have to *seek* experience.
- I have to *categorize and associate* by comparison (analogy) what's happening now with what happened before.
- I have to *construct and elaborate* patterns.
- I have to *determine* cause and effect.
- I have to *reward myself* for figuring things out with "feel-good" hormone release.
- I have to *focus more widely*, on possibilities beyond the immediate.

To be most effective, our practice as ALFAS has to account for both of these states of mind. But unless we first attend sufficiently well to threat mediation, adults may literally not have enough presence of mind to learn. They may dutifully try to memorize and

> **Mezirow on Learning**
>
> "Learning is understood as the process of using a prior interpretation to construe a new or revised interpretation of the meaning of one's experience in order to guide future action" (Mezirow, 1996, p. 162). This is especially relevant in the context of adult learning and the brain because it (1) frames learning as a process rather than merely an outcome; (2) places meaning making, which is the essence of adult learning, at the core of the process; (3) includes the role of prior experience and interpretation of that experience; (4) refers to the brain's construction and reconstruction of knowledge, key to literally changing one's mind; and (5) alludes to the relationship between reflection and action, which is the essence of praxis. (For more on Mezirow, see chapter 9.)

follow procedures, but until the brain can pull itself together, it is likely to have difficulty with more substantive learning.

Learning and State of Mind

We must be attuned to situations likely to trigger the always-on-alert anxious brain to go into threat overdrive. People in a state of heightened anxiety, such as during tests or performance appraisals, are on brain overload. They may not see or hear correctly, "which causes them to misinterpret and give the wrong answer.... Their brains are so busy dealing with the [intensity that the brain can't] perceive accurately. Our brains are not infinite. They run out of space, out of gas, as it were," as worry and anxiety leave less room for perceiving (Ratey, 2002, pp. 61–62).

Most ALFAS intuitively realize this—but not all of us and perhaps not consciously. Moreover, we may not recognize that some of our favorite strategies for enhancing learning, such as detailed feedback and group activities, need to be carefully reviewed with the anxious brain in mind. (More on this in chapter 8.)

Think of it this way: In terms of learning, when the brain is scared, it has a foot on the brake; when it is curious, it has a foot on the accelerator (figure 1.3). With a foot on the brake and none on

Figure 1.3 Foot on Gas and Foot on Brake

the gas, such as at a stoplight, the car idles. Many adults, including those with impressive experience and credentials, start off a new learning situation that way. Even if they have willingly chosen to participate (sometimes they are there for other reasons), stress inevitably is associated with a new setting, new facilitator, and perhaps new approaches to new ideas. As Julie Willans and Karen Seary (2011) found in their study of adults returning to formal learning environments, they may feel bombarded from all directions. As they settle in and become more familiar with what will be required of them—and, one hopes, some thoughtful intervention by the facilitator—foot-on-brake can start to relax. By itself, though, that slight letup still doesn't get anywhere. The car needs some foot-on-gas as well. A skilled facilitator provides this by focused attention on motivation and engagement. But unless similar attention has also been paid to the potential for threat, there may now be a foot on each pedal. The car may be revving yet still not moving.

Once that foot-on-brake lets up, though, *zoom*! In other words, these two states of mind are not simply the inverse of one another. Increasing curiosity doesn't ensure less anxiety; lowering threat doesn't guarantee curiosity. This is why many of the approaches described in part 2 feature effective responses to both imperatives.

We now briefly examine biology. The brain is a relentless, whirling, ongoing, multifaceted process. Its fundamental activity relies ultimately on electrochemical signals at the cellular level. Most people are familiar with the basic structure of a typical brain cell, often drawn in a way that appears treelike (see figure 1.4).

The cell body of the neuron, which contains the nucleus, is analogous to the crown of the tree, with bushy *dendritic* branches. The trunk is the *axon*, and the roots are the *axon terminals*. Dendrites receive stimulation from other neurons, which causes an electrical impulse to travel down through the cell body and along

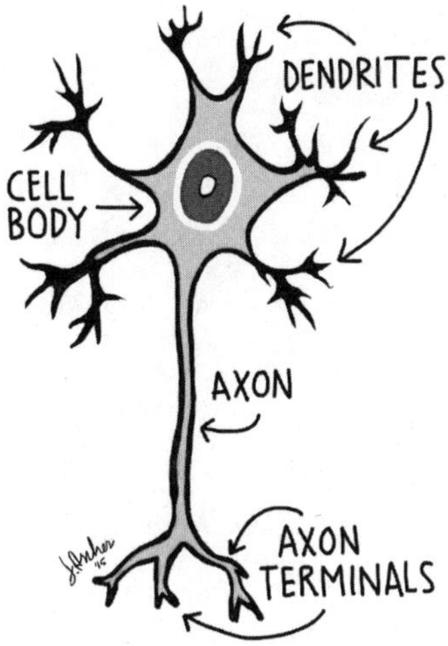

Figure 1.4 Typical Neuron

the length of the axon. When the impulse reaches one of the axon's terminal buttons, it triggers the release of chemical messengers (*neurotransmitters*) that cross a tiny space (*synapse* or *synaptic cleft*) to the dendrites of another neuron. That stimulates specialized receptors on the dendrites of the next neuron, thus passing along the message. This process continues from neuron to neuron, usually requiring only milliseconds from one to the next.

The words we commonly use to name what the brain does—*think, identify, feel, understand, imagine, decide, know, plan, distinguish, believe, remember*—are descriptions of what we experience when vast networks of neurons are activated in ever-changing patterns of connection. Neuroscientists currently studying microscopic activity along these neural pathways are attempting to unpack the anatomy of particular brain functions. As ALFAS interested primarily in the activity called learning, which involves millions of neurons engaged in various combinations of tasks, we find it more meaningful to tell the story of brain history and function from a more macrolevel.

The Brain Then

Brains eventually emerged from the basic stimulus-response mechanisms that all animals share. Even one-celled organisms swim toward nutrients and away from danger. As life-forms crawled out of the ocean and evolved into various creatures, these responses evolved along with early brain structures. The modern brain took hundreds of millions of years to evolve. Much of what we understand about human brain development has been inferred from changes in the prehistorical skeletal evidence and comparative studies of the brains of other species. In our case, the gradual increase in the size of the most frontal portion of the brain—which we identify as its more "civilized" part—led to less sloped foreheads. (The increasing proportion of the brain's *white matter* also contributed to pushing hominid foreheads toward the vertical.)

We can also think about changes in our brain as similar to an archaeological dig, where more recent structures were built on top of earlier ones. But in contrast to the built-over remains of civilizations that had died out or been destroyed, the older structures of the brain had to keep operating. Evolution can't suspend current activity while it goes back to the drawing board; neurobiological economy requires building on whatever is working at the time. Over eons, as modifications emerged that were better suited to the environment, the updated versions had the edge in the ongoing evolutionary process. The brain's additional and increasingly complex capacities enabled still further development within progressively more varied surroundings.

A well-known model that attempted to account for the historical development of major brain structures refers to the *triune*, or three-part, *brain*. Though it was later critiqued as being oversimplified, Paul MacLean's model (1990), first developed in the 1960s, became widely known because it seemed to account for human nature, such as our tendency for both primitive and civilized ways of thinking and acting. More recent analyses of brain architecture focus on other spatial relationships in the brain. We will later look more closely at the right and left hemispheres.

Using the triune model in figure 1.5 as our framework, we're going to borrow a time machine to observe how early hominid brains probably functioned about 2 million years ago. Here is Mr. Oog (*Homo erectus*—not the earliest hominid, but a long way from *Homo sapiens,* who appeared only 200,000 years ago), walking through the primeval savanna. *Wait!* He hears noises up ahead but can't determine the source. His brain is on high alert. Is this situation, *I can eat that?* or is it *That can eat me?* Either

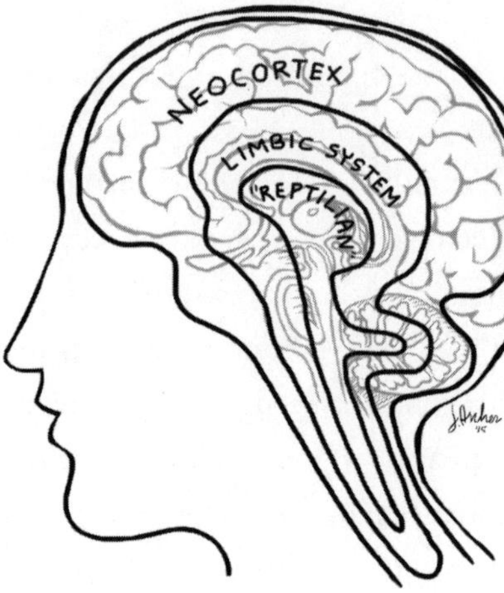

Figure 1.5 Triune Brain

way, his life may hang in the balance. If there is food ahead (or a potential mate), continued existence is enhanced; if not, it could be the end of him.

It is unknown whether Mr. Oog's group was capable of what we now call *reflection*, but two pointers suggest the capacity for language. The first is the brain structure of early hominids. Endocasts—molds made of the inside of ancient skulls—seem to reveal brain areas we know to be associated with language. The second is archaeological evidence that their toolmaking was a communal process, hence one that required fairly explicit communication.

Brain Stem

Just as it is now, the brain's primary task was to keep the organism alive and functioning optimally, whatever the circumstances. The part of Mr. Oog's brain that controlled his reflexive fight-or-flight response, the *brain stem*, still has the same job it did then: to continuously monitor and react to internal and external environments. The brain stem is located at the hindmost part of the brain and looks like a tail as it extends down to become the spinal cord. It regulates the functions of internal organs, blood vessels, and activities such as heart rate, breathing, and blood pressure, over which we usually have little conscious control.

The earliest version of the brain stem (about 500 million years ago) was essentially the entire brain of primordial fish, followed by amphibians and, eventually, reptiles. It is sometimes, and rather inaccurately, referred to as the "lizard brain." Just as the brains of lizards continued to evolve, the brain stem has also evolved. Nevertheless, it is still focused on what sociobiologists call the 4 Fs: feeding, fighting, fleeing, and mating.

The brain works unnoticed most of the time, quietly and effectively controlling homeostasis, but it also springs into heart-thumping action if danger threatens or appears to. ALFAS need to be aware that when the reflexive brain is sharply stimulated—perhaps when an adult is suddenly put on the spot (especially if everyone else is watching)—the capacity of the rest of the brain to reflect, reason, or learn is severely curtailed.

Limbic System

Mr. Oog pauses. As he remembers that the place he is approaching is a good source of food, his threat level decreases. Rather than responding only reflexively, he can intentionally seek pleasure and avoid pain. The *limbic system,* the second major brain component, gives him the basic capacity for memory, learning, and emotion (see "Limbic System Structures").

Mr. Oog and his mate are members of a small community of hunter-gatherers. The men make tools and hunt together; the women care for children and gather nuts and berries. Whereas the earlier brain was focused primarily on individual survival, the limbic system helps enable the emotional and feeling responses

Limbic System Structures

Sometimes referred to as the *mammalian brain,* the limbic system is not a single organized system; it is a group of structures related by their location and functions. For our purposes, the most important structures are those critical to memory and emotion, the hippocampus and amygdala. They exist bilaterally (in both hemispheres) in the inner side of the temporal lobes (between and just a little behind the temples). Their names, *hippocampus* (seahorse) and *amygdala* (almond), are derived from the Greek words for the objects they are thought to resemble. A major criticism of the triune brain model is its identification of the limbic system as the emotional brain. We now know both that the limbic system has functions other than emotions and that emotions involve much more than just the limbic system.

needed to cooperate and form communities as part of an evolutionarily stable strategy. It also appears to act as a mediator or brake on the harsh survival-focused behaviors of the more primitive structure that would otherwise dominate.

With the limbic system as moderator, Joshua Greene (2013) says, we are less likely to engage in violent behavior toward those we consider part of our group. It also contributes to altruistic behavior in mammals, such as self-sacrifice for the good of the collective or a mother's fight to the death when her young are in danger. If our brains had not developed the capacities to bond with and nurture our young, we would not have survived as a species. In fact, Matthew Lieberman (2013) claims, establishing and maintaining connection with others is the "*central problem of mammalian evolution*" (p. 99). As we will later describe, these bonds depend in part on the brain's ability to interpret what someone else is thinking or feeling. Whether we know it or not, we all need to read others' minds; fortunately, most of us do so relatively easily. Indeed, social connections are so essential to our survival that their loss can cause physical pain; at the same time, intense connection can cause enormous pleasure.

Neocortex

Arriving at the hunting ground, Mr. Oog lifts his axe and signals to his fellow hunters. The third, and latest-to-develop and most complex part of the primate brain, the *cerebral cortex* (or new cortex: *neocortex*), makes possible more complex responses to the changing environment. (See "Social Complexity.") For example, the discovery of fire and learning to clothe themselves in animal skins will ultimately allow Mr. Oog's descendants to expand his tribe northward, out of Africa.

Seen from the top, the cerebral cortex is what we tend to visualize as *brain.* A lump of matter appears to have been messily pushed together into a walnut-shaped pile of soft bulges and valleys with a ridge running down the center between the left and right hemispheres. From this view, we cannot see that the cortex, composed of cell bodies, or *gray matter,* is only about one-eighth inch thick; it covers the *white matter* beneath it, like a rind.

Social Complexity

The growing complexity of social groups may have been a major factor in the dramatic increase of the frontal part of the brain (Dunbar, 1998). Individuals had to develop behaviors of mutual assistance and cooperation, which required understanding potential trade-offs between short-term costs and long-term gains. Although the limbic system is the source of direct emotional response, the complex calculus of ongoing social give-and-take occurs in the newer prefrontal cortex, which therefore expanded over time. Social evolutionary models further suggest that three group-focused capacities probably coevolved: social intelligence (understanding and using one's connection to others), environmental intelligence (figuring out how things work), and language (sharing and exchanging with others what one knows, thinks, and feels) (Deacon, 1997). As each developed incrementally toward greater complexity, that put pressure on the other two to develop in tandem. The physical locations of parts of the brain facilitated such interactions. Roughly speaking, the reactivity of the brain stem, at the bottom, is mediated by the limbic system, located above it and below the cortex, where thinking is processed.

White matter is composed of axons insulated with a fatty white substance, *myelin*, which improves the transmission of signals to and from various centers of brain activity. The higher ratio of white matter to gray matter (along with the wrinkling and folding of the cortical surface, allowing more cortical neurons to fit inside the hominid skull) has greatly increased the brain's capacity to make new synapses, thus the potential for creativity and complexity. As we will see in chapter 2, this is a factor in memory and all that implies for learning, planning, and assessing.

The cortex as a whole accounts for 80 to 90 percent of the weight of the adult brain and endows aspects of ourselves that we consider uniquely human, such as language (spoken and written), rational analysis, imagination, and self-understanding. These capacities give rise to art and science; they also enable us to review the past in ways that change over time and to imagine a future rich with possibilities. Although most of our attention as ALFAS is directed toward the cognitive functions that the cortex facilitates (especially the prefrontal cortex, the part closest to the forehead), we are likely to be more effective when we take into account the influences of other aspects of brain function, as well.

The Brain Now

Despite all the amazing changes that the last several hundred million years of evolution have wrought, our brains have never forgotten where they came from. When pressed, they are likely to revert to their more primitive responses. The unconscious in-the-moment default mode of the earliest hominid brains was simply reflexive. They *acted*! That historical imperative is still very much with us.

Right and Fast

To survive in that long-ago environment, brains had to be right and fast. "What's up ahead?" requires immediate action.

Brains that over (lots of) time began to compare this moment to some other moment had an edge in the Darwinian sweepstakes: staying alive longer allowed them to pass that capacity on to their progeny. Thus, the speed and accuracy with which one could identify and connect new experiences with earlier experiences profoundly affected the course of human development.

This may also account for our modern brain's negative bias. For most people, anxiety about possible bad outcomes strongly outweighs the positive potential of a good outcome. As they say, the tiger has to be right once, but you have to be right all the time. Our brains are geared to flash warning signs, and the brain is several times faster at arriving at a negative appraisal than a positive one. Then, when something bad does happen, negative bias is confirmed; unfortunately, when a negative prediction does not come true, the brain is likely to assume it was just lucky that time.

An offshoot of the desire to be right is the need to know. Not knowing creates anxiety. Unfortunately, the desire to avoid that discomfort can encourage us to take risky choices rather than remain undecided. When these are well-calculated risks based on sufficient experience and thoughtful assessments of potential losses and gains, there may be positive outcomes. But less informed adults may also rush to arrive at far less considered decisions. Moreover, when we feel, "Whew! that's taken care of," the brain rewards itself with a rush of feel-good hormones such as *dopamine*. (That is why some folks play bridge, do Sudoko, and solve crossword puzzles.)

To be in a state of not knowing is to venture out in the wilds without self-protection. Anything could be out there, just waiting to pounce. Most of us therefore avoid ambiguity and what researchers call "ill-structured" or "messy" problems (Schön, 1983)—terminology that seems to suggest the problem is poorly framed. In reality, for our species to survive, our modern brains have to figure out how to address just such increasingly complex and multifaceted problems.

Because an open-ended problem sparks anxiety and stress, our brains do their best to construct stories that appear to account for the evident facts. In seeking to resolve the ambiguity, the brain will also fill in missing details, such as finding relationships and patterns where there aren't any. The brain effectively counters its discomfort by projecting certainty—or at least cause-and-effect explanations—onto the environment. People especially prone to such behavior are likely to be superstitious, believe in conspiracies, and be gullible about the supernatural. Shermer (2011) also draws connections between 9/11—the anxiety and uncertainty that it created—and the bumper crop of conspiracy theories it engendered. Furthermore, once people have decided that there is a causal relationship between two phenomena, they will subsequently consciously or unconsciously seek out confirming data, thus demonstrating *certainty bias*.

What's more, if two things happen in rapid succession, we are likely to assume, even if only momentarily, that the earlier one *caused* the later one—thus being right, fast, *now!* The following is an instance of the brain creating an immediate story around an unexpected feeling of threat that one of us experienced. A friend was on a ladder organizing a high shelf containing dozens of greeting-card-sized boxes, when he accidentally knocked a small stack off the shelf. I was standing below him, and in the first startled moment they rained down on me (I did not see them start to fall), my brain told me that he had unaccountably started slapping my head and shoulders. "Stop it!" I cried and backed away, shaking the ladder in a reflexive attempt at self-protection. (Fortunately, he didn't fall.)

That instantaneous associative response is the brain doing its job of self-protection: "The brain evolved to detect patterns of immediate significance in do-or-die, fight-or-flight situations" (Geary, 2012, p. 36). It would much rather react defensively in a situation that turns out to be safe than not react in one that turns out to be dangerous. In addition, the brain does not, without prompting, think in terms of correlation. The associative process does not consider, "Hmm, these two things may have occurred more or less together, but does that mean one caused the other, or can there be some as yet unknown third element, that causes both?" Nor is it geared to consider whether it is reasonable to ascribe every perceived effect to a particular cause. It wants to *know*!

We are capable of thinking in terms of correlation only when we become aware of the connections our brain is making. But most of these associations never reach consciousness. If someone we have just met reminds our brain of an experience that involved strong emotions, we almost instantly connect those emotions with the new acquaintance without knowing we are doing so. Of course, whatever similarities the brain thinks it found can be based on only superficial criteria.

The brain's tendency is to construct a plausible story. Daniel Kahneman (2011), a Nobel Prize–winning behavioral economist, observed, "We are prone to exaggerate the consistency and coherence of what we see" (p. 114)—or think we see. Daily changes in the financial indexes, for example, are sometimes occasioned by current events or new economic data, but more often they are random fluctuation. But even when nothing noteworthy has happened, the evening news is likely to present a rationale, however tenuous: *Markets moved lower[higher] on news of ________ in Somewhereville.* Nor are experts immune from believing their own stories (see "Experts Pick Stocks").

Left to its own devices, the brain will be the decider. Many people have experienced a version of the following scenario. An electrician had been working on the wiring in our ninety-year-old house. The job was more challenging and time consuming than expected because we did not want to break into the original six-inch-thick lathe-and-plaster walls. He had to thread new wires

> **Experts Pick Stocks**
>
> In the 1990s, the *Wall Street Journal* conducted a study in which stock picks carefully selected by experienced professionals were compared over time to those "selected" by throwing a dart at a list of stocks (http://www.investorhome.com/darts.htm). On a week-by-week basis, sometimes the experts were ahead, and sometimes a lucky dart throw proved more profitable. However, the results over many months revealed no significant difference between the stock pattern–picking experts and random dart throws. (*Coincidentally*, the experiment was discontinued shortly there after.)

down from the attic inside the existing walls, then move to the crawl space under the floor to complete the connections. At the end of the day, I walked back into the home office and switched on the overhead light. A computer screen suddenly went black! *Oh no!* I thought. *He miswired something!* That made perfect sense, given that he had worked by touch more than by sight—except, as soon as I touched the keyboard, the screen came back on. It had merely gone into sleep mode at the same moment I flipped the light switch.

The brain is also very effective at constructing explanations that self-protectively leaves us blameless about whatever undesirable result may have occurred. "Mistakes were made" is a lot more tolerable than "I blew it":

> Even a small amount of ambiguity triggers increased activity in the . . . deep brain structures that play a major role in our response to threats. . . . The brain doesn't merely prefer certainty over ambiguity—it craves it. Our need to be right is actually a need to "feel" right. . . . When we feel right about the decision or a belief—whether big or small—our brains are happy. (DiSalvo, 2011, pp. 31–32)

This contributes to the *certainty bias* described earlier.

Need to Know

A corollary to *right and fast* is the need to *know*. Most adults are used to being in the know. Even—perhaps, especially—those with impressive professional credentials may be anxious about revealing or acknowledging what they do *not* know. However enthusiastic adults may be about the idea of new learning, being in a learning situation—whether in a classroom or boardroom—is cause for anxiety. A man who fits this profile revealed, "I went from an environment—my work—where I knew all there was to know, to an environment of feeling like I didn't know anything. This was challenging and scary!"

from having a property manager to being one.

On the positive side, the curious brain's drive to know—to figure things out, to come to closure—encourages us to continue learning. However, the period during which an adult moves from not knowing to coming to know and, finally, to understanding is uncomfortable at best. As one woman described it, "I was so worried about earning the points that I lost the focus of finding what was most relevant for my topic."

The Feeling of Not Knowing Robert Burton (2008) offers an interesting activity that will help you experience your brain's need to know. Read the following paragraph slowly and carefully; maybe even read it twice, paying attention to your feelings as you read. (Don't skip this paragraph. Once you understand the key, it will be impossible to go back to not knowing.)

> A newspaper is better than a magazine. A seashore is a better place than the street. At first it is better to run than to walk. You may have to try several times. It takes some skill, but it is easy to learn. Even young children can enjoy it. Once successful, complications are minimal. Birds seldom get too close. Rain, however, soaks in very fast. Too many people doing the same thing can also cause

> problems. One needs lots of room. If there are no complications, it can be very peaceful. A rock will serve as an anchor. If things break loose from it, however, you will not get a second chance. (Burton, 2008, p. 5)

As you read the quote, you almost certainly experienced the feeling of slight disorientation, perhaps even the frustration that comes when something just doesn't make sense. Maybe you even frowned a little. Clearly, there are no technical words or difficult concepts to contend with, so your brain may say, with some annoyance, *I ought to be able to figure this out!*

Now notice the shift in your experience at the introduction of the idea of a kite. As you reread the paragraph with that in mind, you may find yourself smiling or even chuckling out loud. As Burton describes it, "In an instant, without due conscious deliberation, the paragraph has been irreversibly infused with a *feeling of knowing*" (p. 5). You may also relax as the tension you felt on first reading dissipates with the explanation of the kite: your brain once again feels secure and in charge, its preferred state.

Highly creative people may be an exception to the brain feeling anxious in the face of the unknown. According to Gregory Berns (2008), rather than run from not knowing, those he calls *iconoclasts* respond with increased curiosity and greater energy to explore further. Their brains appear to delight in novelty and avoid default patterns. Because they seem to perceive things differently, they are likely to make the creative leaps of imagination that can lead to significant discoveries others failed to consider.

Knowing "Facts" Adults are also dismayed to discover that even their certainties may be up for grabs. New learning can challenge long-held beliefs. Occasionally new facts can simply be swapped for old facts. But even something as seemingly uncontroversial as how fast water freezes may be connected to one's sense of "who I am" and "how thing are." Such beliefs are not easily challenged, as the narrator of the following incident discovered:

> We stopped for coffee in a roadside café near the Donner Pass in midwinter. The conversation turned to freezing water. People assured us that they had lived here a long time and knew, for certain, that hot water freezes faster than cold. Our protests were rejected. Because it was snowing heavily and we had time on our hands, we suggested a test: taking a cup of boiling water and a cup of refrigerated water outside to see what would happen. When the cold water froze first, the locals' reaction was to stubbornly—and testily—insist that it had been a trick.

It turns out that in rare circumstances, hot water does freeze more quickly. When we first heard this, our immediate reaction (including that of an engineer husband), based on a lifetime of assumptions was, *It can't be!* Then we looked on the Internet: the Mpemba effect exists, though scientists are uncertain why. Our subsequent reactions after learning this changed to acceptance, interest, satisfaction. Why so different from the folks in the diner? We were not committed to our initial belief; we *sort of just* knew. Being told otherwise—first by a friend (who had heard of the unusual Mpemba effect exception), then confirmed by an authoritative Internet source—was intriguing rather than distressing. We even felt a little smug, because now we knew more and might be able to tell someone else this fascinating tidbit.

Why didn't it work that way for the folks who lived near the diner? Given the special conditions required for hot liquid to freeze faster, it seems likely that most of them had never actually seen it; they also *just knew*. Having some city slicker contradict them did not go down well; it had become less about the objective phenomenon than about the brain's need to know (and be right).

Not knowing had become a source of anxiety, and anger is one response to fear.

We do not intend to overemphasize the brain's capacity for anxiety, but based on what experienced ALFAS and adult learners have shared with us over the years, in general too little attention is paid to this reality. Our concern is that well-planned approaches to facilitation and meaningful learning may still fall flat if we have not taken into account adults' emotional responses to having their beliefs and certainties challenged.

Adults are especially anxious about being wrong. As one observed, "I grew up seeing mistakes or doing something wrong as failure." Such vulnerability can lead to insisting that what they already know is all there is to know or to not speaking up when they are confused and have questions that might reveal their lack of knowledge to their peers and the facilitator. Or they might apologize in advance: "This is a dumb question, but . . . "

Similarly, when asked to consider a situation or idea from an unfamiliar perspective—which, as far as the brain is concerned, may be like walking into a dark, unknown jungle—adults may adamantly not want to go there. The history of science and medicine is littered with disastrous examples of such resistance (see "Certainty and Tragedy").

The anxious brain resists change for many reasons. In the case of childbed fever, aside from the threat to their established ways of doing things, doctors simply could not accept they were the cause of the problem, even in the face of compelling evidence. Brains that want to be certain and right will do their utmost not to acknowledge, "I did it. I caused all this tragedy." In the early twentieth century, resolution of another scientific issue, the cause of pellagra, a disease characterized by dermatitis, diarrhea, and sometimes mental disturbances, was delayed for socioeconomic and political reasons. Most victims of pellagra were sharecropping African Americans in the Deep South of the United States. It took

> ### Certainty and Tragedy
>
> In the mid-nineteenth century "childbed fever" killed many poor women in hospitals but far fewer wealthy women, who gave birth at home. Also at that time, demonstrating active interest in dissection elevated a doctor's status among his peers. Many went directly from dissecting corpses to examining women in labor, their hands and medical aprons soiled with evidence of their scientific pursuits. However, when one young doctor required his medical staff to disinfect their hands before attending laboring mothers, the death rate in his hospital plummeted. He was quickly shunned and reviled by the medical establishment, which *knew* that all disease was caused by a "miasma"—an invisible cloud of pestilence that hung over hospitals and where poor people lived. Physicians were affronted at his demand that they change their practice and refused to participate; they even sabotaged his experiments. Not until the discovery of microscopic pathogens two decades and thousands of maternal deaths later was Ignaz Semmelweis's insight accepted.

decades to accept that the cause of pellagra was neither infection nor bad agricultural practices but a nutritional deficiency caused by diet. Accepting that reality shone an unwelcome spotlight on inequality and poverty.

What the brain is willing to accept is also deeply and invisibly influenced by *what I want* (or *don't want*) *to be true*. As philosopher of science Thomas Kuhn (1962) famously said, significant scientific advancement often requires a paradigm shift. Such a major break in continuity is needed for scientists to accept a radical new framework. Of course, even when many do recognize the new reality, others can still discount overwhelming evidence if the implications require them to change both their minds and their behaviors (a good example is climate change).

Cultural norms and expectations of all kinds can limit openness to new thinking. As one adult reflected, "When I have to get out of my comfort zone, . . . I tend to focus on getting the task done rather than understanding the concepts or rationale." Both of us frequently see this tendency demonstrated by our doctoral students as they start to design their dissertation research. They almost always begin with the tacit notion that they will prove what they already know or believe. It takes considerable effort to wrap their minds around a lengthy project based on questions to which they do not already have answers.

And the Brain Still Changing

As Darwin noted, when ordinary variations within a species prove to be more successful than others, especially with regard to matching the demands of changing environments, creatures with those variations are more likely to survive and reproduce. Many improvements in brain and brain function over eons are evidence of this. However, some early adaptations have proven less advantageous in the long run.

Maladaptation

Though serial brain enhancements have managed to get us to now, a feature that enabled our primitive ancestors to survive in that earlier environment may, in this vastly different environment, have become a bug (Buonomano, 2011), and thus now be deemed maladaptive:

> Although we currently inhabit a time and place we were not programmed to live in, the set of instructions written down in our DNA on how to build a brain are the same as they were 100,000 years ago. Which raises the question, to what extent is the neural operating system established by evolution well tuned for the digital, predator-free, sugar-abundant, special-effects-filled, antibiotic-laden, media-saturated, densely populated world we have managed to build for ourselves? (p. 16)

And this is to say nothing of a world in which the possibilities for both instantaneous (nuclear) and longer-term (climate change) annihilation are a reality.

Furthermore, given the current rate of change, an increasingly pressing question is whether our brains can develop fast enough to keep pace with it. As one example, it was crucial that our early forebears quickly distinguish between those whom we considered like us (our community or tribe, therefore presumably safe) and not like us (therefore possibly dangerous). Our modern brains still make such discriminations, subconsciously and more or less instantly, but these can be unhelpful assessments in our modern global village. And because we don't realize what our brain is doing or why, we cannot challenge the highly questionable criteria it uses to determine who is us versus who is them, nor do we realize how easily we can be manipulated.

Our early ancestors were benefited by establishing groups of "our kind" in terms of mutual defense or allocating scarce resources. Since making such distinctions conferred a greater chance of survival, brains with those tendencies persisted. However, though our brains (and that of other primates) are wired to distinguish between us and them, which Greene (2013) calls *tribalism,* we have to *learn* to make distinctions on the basis of racial characteristics. Early on, there was no racial diversity, so this was not wired into the brain's distinctions. Our modern tendency to use race as a mark of difference is an outgrowth of cultural rather than brain-based distinctions—and something that modern demagogues consistently exploit.

An important question therefore is what role we ALFAS can play in improving the brain's set of instructions and thus contribute to developing more effective responses. Fortunately, we are not limited to evolving in geological time; plasticity enables our brains to adapt within our lifetimes.

Plasticity

It was once thought that we were born with all the brain cells we would ever have. Actually, after a spurt of neural growth in the first two years of life (which is also severely pruned soon after), we can continue to grow neurons throughout the life span, though relatively few in number. The bad news is that we continually lose neurons throughout the rest of our lives. The good news is that at the rate of about one-millionth of the total per day, even with a life span of 100-plus years, the cumulative loss is inconsequential in terms of our capacity to learn and change.

From the standpoint of brain function and learning, dendritic connections are far more important than total number of neurons. Because each neuron may make up to 10,000 synaptic connections to other neurons, "the theoretical number of different patterns of connections possible in a single brain is approximately forty quadrillion" (Ratey, 2002, p. 9). These connections make up the neural networks that enable your brain to examine, reflect on, and evaluate your current experience while also constructing your remembered past and imagining various possible futures.

As we age, our brain cells continue to generate such connections, thus increasing our capacity for interpretation of experience and therefore imagination and insight. Plasticity also means these connections are adapted, elaborated, and reorganized as new experiences strengthen or weaken existing synapses. Put simply, *experience consistently and continuously changes the brain.* (We explore this more fully in the next chapter.) The challenge for facilitators is to design experiences that take full advantage of this capacity for change.

Learning While Aging

Average cognitive capacity reaches its peak around forty years of age and begins a slow decline thereafter (Hertzog, Kramer, Wilson, & Lindenberger, 2009). Since we two are decades past

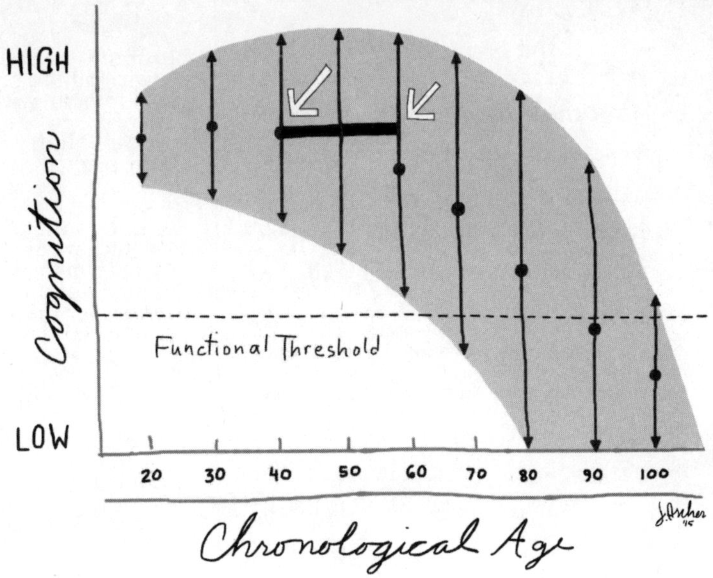

Figure 1.6 Brain Function over Time
Source: Adapted from Hertzog et al. (2009, p. 5).

that point, we want to underscore how *not* predictive of adequate brain function that single statistic is! More important is the range of capacity. As demonstrated in figure 1.6, the upper ranges (top curving line; vertical arrows within the shaded portion mark the top and bottom of each range) in one's seventies and even eighties are above the average capacity (dots) in one's forties. Therefore, as the angled arrows (pointing to the dark horizontal line) indicate, a sixty-year-old operating somewhat above average is just as cognitively effective as an average forty-year-old.

Many factors contribute to where in the range any individual may be located. Though genetics plays some role, there is clear evidence that what one starts with is profoundly affected by what happens next. Certainly good nutrition and overall health are significant factors, as is ongoing physical activity. And so is ongoing learning: being a lifelong learner is likely to enhance one's cognitive capacities (see "The Nuns' Story.")

Though there may be optimum periods of brain development with regard to specific kinds of learning (language learning is one example), the curtain does not fall when that period is over. Older brains are not as fast, but they are likely to have a broader, more varied experience base to draw from. More experienced adults are likely to have the edge in the pattern-recognition department, which, we will see in the next chapter, is the fundamental brain process associated with learning and knowing. The final bit of good news for aging brains is that normal, healthy brains retain substantial *neuroplasticity*—the ability to change and adapt neural connections.

The Nuns' Story

A long-term study of over four hundred Catholic sisters, several of them centenarians, has demonstrated that consistently challenging one's brain—for example, many continued to teach well into their eighties and nineties—led to far fewer clinical symptoms of dementia than postmortem analysis of their brains would have indicated. Though not all the nuns had been teachers, those who demonstrated the fewest symptoms were generally those who had more formal education or kept their minds busy with other cognitive challenges, such as debating politics (Ratey, 2002).

Key Ideas

- Unless ALFAS attend sufficiently well to threat mediation, adults may literally not have enough presence of mind to learn.
- Increasing curiosity doesn't ensure less anxiety; lowering threat doesn't guarantee curiosity.
- When the reflexive brain is sharply stimulated—perhaps when an adult is suddenly put on the spot (especially if everyone else is

watching)—the capacity of the rest of the brain to reflect, reason, or learn is severely curtailed.

- Our brains are geared to flash warning signs, and the brain is several times faster at arriving at a negative appraisal than a positive one.
- To be in a state of not knowing is to venture out in the wilds without self-protection. Most of us therefore avoid ambiguity.
- The brain will fill in missing details, such as finding relationships and patterns even where there aren't any. The brain effectively counters its discomfort by projecting certainty—or at least explanations—onto the environment.
- The period during which an adult moves from not knowing to coming to know and finally to understanding is uncomfortable at best.
- Well-planned approaches to facilitation and meaningful learning may fall flat if we have not taken into account adults' emotional responses to having their beliefs and certainties challenged.
- What the brain is willing to accept is deeply and invisibly influenced by *what I want* (or *don't want) to be true.*
- Experience consistently and continuously changes the brain. The challenge for facilitators is to design experiences that take full advantage of this capacity for change.
- Because we don't realize what our brain is doing or why, we cannot challenge the highly questionable criteria it uses to determine who is us versus who is them, nor do we realize how easily we can be manipulated.
- Older brains are not as fast as younger ones, but they usually have a broader, more varied experience base to draw from. More experienced adults are likely to have the edge in the pattern-recognition department.

Pause for Reflection

Consider using this space to comment on, question, or freewrite any thoughts and reactions to this introduction to knowing more about the brain. You may even wish to doodle or sketch your feelings about the material.

1. Did the readings confirm what you already understood about the brain? Were you able to elaborate on that understanding? Did you make any unexpected connections?
2. Did the readings contradict your understanding? How will you reconcile the differences?
3. Does any of the information seem to apply to your sense of yourself as a learner, and/or to your practice?

1. yes. I did not know about a sense of threat from learning. however.

2

The Learning, Changing Adult Brain

The source of cognition is not just the naked brain, but the brain in concert with the sensing, acting body . . . [as it] intervenes with the environment.

— ANDY CLARK

HAVING explored the historical and functional background of the brain, we now hone in on what the adult brain does when it is learning. At the synaptic level, all brains learn the same way. However, because experience is the basis of all learning, adults' greater variety of life experiences sets them apart from younger learners, as well as from one another. This chapter explores how the adult brain works to turn experience into learning.

The Embodied Brain

The fact that the brain is embodied is crucial to understanding how brains function (see "Further Reading"), as well as an essential focus for adult learning facilitators in any setting (ALFAS).

Further Reading

Berns, G. (2008). *Iconoclast: A neuroscientist reveals how to think differently.* Boston, MA: Harvard Business Press.

Edelman, G. M., & Tononi, G. (2000). *A universe of consciousness: How matter becomes imagination.* New York, NY: Basic Books

Edelman, G. M. (2006). *Second nature: Brain science and human knowledge.* New Haven, CT: Yale University Press.

Varela, F. J., Thompson, E., & Rosch, E. (1991). *The embodied mind: Cognitive science and human experience.* Cambridge, MA: MIT Press.

Wilson, M. (2002). Six views of embodied cognition. *Psychonomic Bulletin and Review, 9,* 625–636.

The brain is not just inside the skull like a walnut in a shell. It is a *body-brain,* connected with and responsive to every part of the body by extension of the peripheral nervous system. And every part of the body contributes to all the functions of brain we commonly call *mind.*

In describing this body-brain, we choose to avoid the common phrase *mind-body,* because it carries additional connotations. Ever since philosophers of the European Enlightenment established the primacy of mind, indicating literal superiority over the body, Western philosophy—and therefore the Western cultural narrative—has focused on the mind as the source of knowing and rational action. Indeed, these are often conflated. Rational action is associated with and presumably due to cognition—essentially, mind; *ir*rational action is associated with and presumably due to emotion—essentially, body (as in "gut feelings" or "heart versus head").

Because our cultural assumptions have for so long distinguished between mind and body, it is difficult to find words that effectively capture how they are inseparably one—in anatomy as well as function. The definition of *mind* in almost every dictionary is synonymous with *brain, understanding,* and *reason. Brain,* however, is defined merely as an organ of the body that enables and coordinates various physical and intellectual functions—the estate manager, as it were, to the mind's superior position as lord of the manor (and most definitely not lady of the manor; see "Women's Minds").

> **Women's Minds**
>
> Women were long assumed to be incapable of rational thought because they were at the mercy of their bodies, hence ruled by emotion. *Hysteria*, supposedly a condition of women, was first named by Hippocrates; its etymology is the Greek word for *uterus*. As recently as the early twentieth century, physicians advised that a woman not be allowed too much mental stimulation (see Charlotte Perkins Gilman's *The Yellow Wallpaper*, originally published in 1892) or education, because an overstimulated brain could shrivel her uterus, making her unfit or unable to carry out her natural functions.

Note also that mind/body is often written to emphasize separation: mind-*slash*-body. In such definitions, *mind* is the more encompassing term—more conceptual, as it were. The further implication that *brain* is essentially a physical, almost mechanical entity consigns it to an ambiguous space in the mind/body duality. By contrast, when the terms *mind-body* and *body-mind* are hyphenated, indicating connection, they tend to be associated with psychological and spiritual pursuits. Such approaches are considered by some as less than rational (and in certain circles, notably behaviorism, which has no use even for the concept of *mental*—*ir*rational). Thus, once the terms are conjoined as equals, mind loses its aura of intellectual superiority.

Descartes' Error

Meanwhile, the term *cognitive* also focuses on *knowing* through perception, awareness, and reason. Hardly ever acknowledged (except in the "seat of cognition" sense) is what else the brain is doing to achieve those outcomes. We acknowledge that brain is where perception happens and awareness emerges. Missing from this narrative is the piece that Descartes discarded the body:

> This is Descartes' error: the abyssal separation between body and mind . . . the suggestion that reason, and moral judgment, and the suffering that comes from physical pain or emotional upheaval might exist separately from the body. Specifically: the separation of the most refined operations of mind from the structure and operation of a biological organism. (Damasio, 1994, pp. 249–250)

> ### *Think* or *Experience*?
>
> Descartes' famous phrase, *Cogito ergo sum*, means, "I think, therefore I am." Our claim for embodiment is more in line with what Marton and Booth (1997) prefer, *Cognosco ergo sum*, "I experience, therefore I am" (p. 114), because "learning . . . is an ongoing exploration of the world as experienced" (p. 156).

Between *perception* and *knowing* is the embodied brain busily constructing what we eventually recognize as thought—that is, meaning we are aware of and can attempt to articulate. What we call thinking, therefore, is just the final step in a long process of knowing that goes on within the body—the body-brain—before we can discover that we know something. Learning is a whole-body experience (See "*Think* or *Experience*").

Activities that focus almost entirely on conscious process—reading, writing, speaking—ignore aspects of *somatic* (body based) knowing that precede awareness. By contrast, intentionally and planfully involving the body-brain earlier in the process can provide opportunities to counter established patterns by tapping into construction of meaning before it rises to awareness fully formed. *Situated learning* is an offshoot of somatic learning or knowing. Initially, situated learning was defined as taking place in natural settings (or "communities of practice"), involving "authentic" tasks and tools—learning *to* rather than learning *about* (Lave & Wenger, 1991). Many ALFAS now use variants of this approach (theories focused on embodied learning are discussed in chapter 9) in settings from classrooms to boardrooms, without realizing the role of embodiment.

The Motor of Cognition

Indeed, rather than assuming that cognition is the highest intended product of brain activity, some neuroscientists posit that the overarching intention is movement. In this formulation, the purpose of thinking is to figure out what the body is supposed to do next, based largely on reviewing what it did at some earlier time. "Sensory and motor processes, perception and action, are fundamentally inseparable in lived cognition . . . [and] evolved together" (Varela, Thompson, & Rosch, 1991, p. 172; for an example of what happens when they disconnect, see "The Thoughtless Sea Squirt").

The Thoughtless Sea Squirt

"Movement is fundamental to the very existence of a brain," Ratey (2002, pp. 155–156) observes, and offers the sea squirt as a striking example. Moving around the ocean early in its life cycle, the sea squirt has a brain. Once it attaches itself to the coral where it will spend the rest of its life, the sea squirt resorbs (digests) its own brain and nerve cord because it no longer needs them.

Granted that the executive functions of the frontal cortex also play a major role, many processes we tend to regard as purely cognitive—evaluating, decision making, planning, predicting—are in fact directed by parts of the brain devoted to motor activity. "Cognition is embodied," Kahneman (2011) states unequivocally, "you think with your body, not only with your brain" (p. 51).

Experience, Association, and Learning

To understand the importance of Kahneman's claim, we must examine the process of association. All knowing (therefore all learning) begins with experience—not just current, this-moment-in-time experience but all our previous experience. (See "The Moses Illusion.")

> **The Moses Illusion**
>
> Ask someone, "How many animals of each kind did Moses take into the ark?" The answer, of course, is *none*. That was Noah's job. But most people know the biblical story about the ark and the animals, plus *Moses* is a two-syllable biblical name with a similar initial vowel sound. So in the vast majority of cases, the brain's prior experience kicks in with a ready—but wrong—association. The response is so consistent that the example is known as the "Moses illusion."

Edelman (2006), in discussing the foundation of what he calls a brain-based epistemology, says: "It is important to recognize the *priority of experience* in giving rise to the descriptions that illuminate the bases of that experience itself" (p. 150, emphasis added). To learn, the brain must associate any new experience with what it already "knows."

Michael Polanyi, renowned for his contributions to philosophy of mind, says we tend to "overlook things that are *unprecedented.* Having no clue to them, we do not see them" (Polanyi & Grene, 1969, p. 113). He therefore argued against the possibility of value-free, "objective" science, since all perceptions are colored by beliefs and expectation. Polanyi also said, "We know more than we can tell," which he called learn more

tacit knowledge, an example of what the body-brain may know but cannot verbalize. (For vivid examples of tacit knowing, see "X-rays and Bonesetters.")

> **X-rays and Bonesetters**
>
> Despite having access to textbooks and instructors who describe the distinctions, professional radiographers learn to interpret the vague shadows on an X-ray only through experience over time. Even more startling is the tacit knowing of traditional bonesetters, who serve poor or rural areas of India and many countries in Africa and Latin America where Western medical facilities are lacking or unaffordable. These non-medically trained "specialists" accurately diagnose bone fractures by touch, without any X-rays, having learned from similarly "trained" experts.

Children's Learning

Though this chapter is about adult learning, the following brief example concerns early school-aged children. Can you recognize what they are trying to say in the following passage?

> I led the pigeons to the flag of the United States of America and to the republic for Richard Stands. One nation under guard, invisible, with library just down the hall.

what I was doing helping Isaac read

After listening closely to young children reciting the Pledge of Allegiance, someone compiled their various mistaken interpretations of the words and phrases that were unfamiliar to them (Safire, 2004). To first graders, *allegiance* and *indivisible* might as well be nonsense syllables. Upon hearing words they were required to repeat, their brains had to interpret the sounds in terms of words, phrases, or images they understood.

This illuminates the brain's associative approach. In order to make sense of something, the brain must find a connection to what it already knows—and it has no way of knowing that the association is incorrect, since it also cannot know what it doesn't know

Intentionally associating something we know with something we want to remember is the basis of mnemonics, or memory aids. For example, the first letters of the phrase "every good boy does fine" stands for the notes—E, G, B, D, F—of the treble clef. But rote memorization is not understanding. Children could perhaps be drilled in the sounds of *a-lee-gens* and provided a definition. But pronouncing it correctly and even reporting the definition would not signify they understood the concept. One must be able to draw on experiences that give meaning to a concept. A thoughtful adult might even offer a concrete example—perhaps involving stories (which are descriptions of experience) about friendship and loyalty. But that will not work unless the young person had acquired experiences and understandings that made it possible to interpret those stories in the way the adult intended.

For example, after assigning his class of seventh-grade boys a story about a wimpy kid being picked on by his peers, a teacher was surprised when the class validated the bigger kids' behavior rather than express sympathy for the victim. Their reasoning was that an even wimpier new kid will eventually show up, at which point the previous owner of that unhappy distinction will then rightfully be able to pick on someone else!—clearly the sum of the boys' life experiences thus far (Kegan, 1982).

Young children can also create highly original metaphors, largely because their imagination knows few bounds, yet they are not adept at interpreting figurative language. If a character in a story is spoken of as "hard" or "sweet," they will most likely imagine that a hard man must be athletic and a sweet woman makes desserts (Geary, 2012). Not until adolescence does the brain develop the capacity to work with figurative language and understand conceptual metaphors

Adults and Experience

Seeing how children's understanding is limited by their experience underscores the difference that adults' rich store of life experiences can make. Adults have more, and more varied, raw material from which to extract, interpret, and ascribe meaning. Unfortunately, there is also a downside to this wealth of experience. What we already know, or believe, affects how we interpret new experience—in other words, what we are prepared to learn.

Similarly, people evaluate factual evidence based on how comfortable their brains are with the proposed solutions. Conservatives are more likely to deny climate change if it is framed in terms of a need for greater government regulation but less likely if the response focuses on free-market solutions. In the same vein, liberals are likely to downplay the problem of violent home invasions if it is presented as a rationale to facilitate gun ownership (Campbell & Kay, 2014).

Elaborating Networks

The fundamental process of learning at any age is based on creating and elaborating networks of neural associations. Once a stimulus (experience) has passed the threshold of attention, the brain immediately categorizes it by comparing the unknown to the known. It seeks similarities between this experience and previous experiences in order to connect it to existing patterns. Obviously the brain must also have a way to engage with unfamiliar experience, or there could be no new learning. Neuroscientist Gerald Edelman (2006) describes it this way: "Brains operate . . . not by logic but rather by pattern recognition . . . . It is likely that early human thought proceeded by metaphor . . . which, continues to be a major source of imagination and creativity in adult life" (p. 58).

Metaphor's contribution to language development is analogous to how the brain itself functions (and the brains of our simian

> **Gorilla Analogies**
>
> Koko, the gorilla famous for having learned to communicate in sign language, vividly demonstrated the contribution of metaphors to language development. When presented with an unfamiliar object, she created a new word by combining familiar signs, thus describing the item metaphorically. A sleep mask (a formerly unseen object and not in Koko's vocabulary of signs) became an "eye hat," a ring was a "finger bracelet," a zebra was a "white tiger," and so on.

cousins as well; see "Gorilla Analogies"). Geary (2012) cites a historian who looks back to Aristotle for an explanation: "When a new thing or new idea comes into the consciousness of the community, it is described not by a new word, but by the name of the pre-existing object which most closely resembles it" (p. 20), for example, *horseless carriage*. In essence, the brain cannot recognize (*re-cognize*: literally, know again) that which it does not already know, at least by analogy.

Saving Energy The brain uses existing patterns wherever possible to save energy. The waking brain, which accounts for only 2 percent of our body weight, can demand more than 20 percent of the available energy. That's why people working on a challenging problem tend to reach for a snack: thinking takes effort. The brain needs to replenish its store of energy and wants to reward itself for working so hard. (Practice may not make perfect, but over time, it definitely makes easier.)

When we learn to drive, for example, we have to be constantly aware of what is happening at every moment. Even with an automatic transmission, the inexperienced driver must be alert to each step of the process: step on the gas, steer, scan road, check mirrors, read signs, step on brake, anticipate changes, and so on. Trying to carry on a conversation while driving can feel burdensome and distracting. Eventually such skills effectively become hard-wired; at that point driving takes up far less conscious processing.

Adults' many years of experience means they have well-established synaptic patterns in all areas, not only motor skills. The more often a given pattern is reactivated, the more efficient it gets, because as the synaptic spaces shrink, that route requires less energy. This is commonly referred to as "fired together, wired together"; it is the process that establishes and elaborates neural networks. In a kind of self-fulfilling prophecy, the more frequently a connection is made, the more likely it will be made in the future. As one result, though neural networks are constantly being revised and refined, well-established patterns are far more difficult to change.

Here's an analogous example of how existing pathways, once established, can be difficult to alter. Looking at the map of current-day New York City in figure 2.1, you notice at the tip of Manhattan island short, jumbled streets once typical of European villages and, a bit above that, a strict lattice-work pattern of right-angled streets and avenues. And then you notice

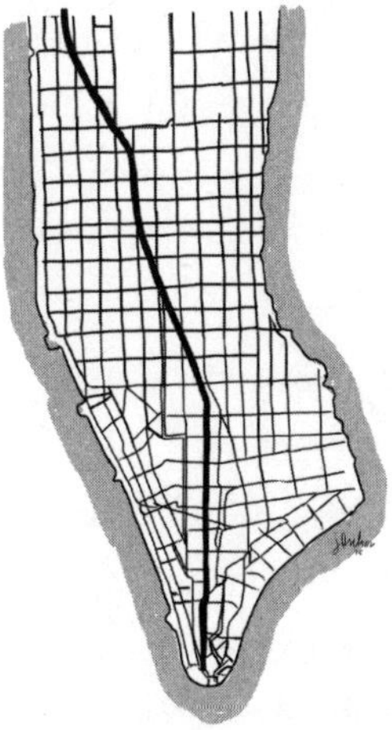

Figure 2.1 Broadway: The Road More Traveled

the anomaly of Broadway, initially a thoroughfare through the disorder, which then continues for several miles in a meandering diagonal through half the grid.

Within the early settlement, Broadway was the main road. Beyond that, grazing cows made their own route through the hilly and rocky places to greener pastures. Once cows had created a trodden-down path, horses, oxcarts, and then coaches followed it, as settlement pushed farther north. Long before the grid system was imagined, Broadway had become the established route to the wilds of upper Manhattan and couldn't be shifted.

Default Patterns Although the brain is plastic and constantly changing, deeply rooted patterns become not just the Broadways but the Grand Canyons of neural networks, where the rivers of experience have cut deeply into the bedrock. Anthropologists and sociologists call these patterns *culture;* psychologists call them *identity, life-scripts,* and *mental models*. They act as filters or routers as the brain seeks to establish associations and categories. Thus we have two early brain imperatives—*save energy* (by reinforcing often-used neural patterns) and *seek safety* (by discriminating between "our kind" and "not our kind")—that make absolute sense in the primeval savanna but can be problematic for adult learners today. The neural networks that establish such cultural norms and expectations may also limit adults' openness to new learning (figure 2.2).

When people encounter ideas that depart from well-established ways of thinking, especially if the patterns are connected to strong emotions, new experiences may be treated as insignificant or, as we saw in the case of freezing hot or cold water, perhaps actively rejected. Under the right circumstances, however, they may contribute to learning, as Piaget described in his model of cognitive development.

Figure 2.2 Two Pathways: Familiar or New?

Learning, wrote Piaget (1955), results from two complementary ways of interacting with new ideas, or thought *schemas*: assimilation and accommodation. When we assimilate, we expand our current understanding by incorporation. The existing schema can do this if it is flexible and roomy enough. By contrast, when we accommodate, we relinquish the former perspective, which is limited and more rigid, in order to reconstruct one that is more comprehensive and can account for the new understanding. Learning is thus a process of serially enlarging and redefining our existing schemas through these adaptations. This developmental description is clearly also a description of what the brain itself is doing as it enlarges and reconfigures existing neural networks. However, Piaget's model, based initially on research with children and adolescents, does not address adults' resistance to changing their existing schemas.

Nevertheless, given their established Broadway-like schemas, when adults encounter new approaches to topics about which they feel experienced and knowledgeable, they may be polite but dismissive, along the lines of, "That may be how it works in books, but that's not how it works in real life." New learning that contradicts their established beliefs also threatens to arouse unwelcome feelings of not knowing. As one adult learner described her eventual realization, "When I am uncomfortable, I tend to shut down and resist learning something new."

More problematic—because ALFAS can't address their unexpressed concerns—are situations where adults appear to actively engage with new material and may even seem to understand or practice it, yet have not altered their underlying assumptions, beliefs, or behaviors. When the session is over, they revert to their familiar (hence less anxiety-provoking), well-established ideas and patterns. A possible antidote to this kind of regression is explored in Mezirow's (1991) theory of transformative learning (see chapter 9). He identifies a series of facilitated experiences, beginning with a "disorienting dilemma," that can encourage changes that lead toward a perspective shift on the way to a more complex way of knowing.

Memory, Emotions, and Learning

Remembering is clearly an important aspect of learning. However, people tend to think about memory as if it is something stored whole in some brain space from which it can later be recalled. This subjective impression of the act of remembering is misleading and inaccurate. There is no *there,* there! Memory is neither a discrete thing, nor does it occupy a particular place in the brain; it is a process, not merely a subject of retrieval. By the time we become aware of, or intentionally bring to mind, that which we call *a* memory, the brain has been busily associating various prior and current *memory traces* located in far-flung neural networks.

Memory traces are not faint images of an entire experience; they are a record of changes in neuronal activation that result from a stimulus and include body-state responses (i.e., emotions). These traces of memory are stored in various networks based on association and categorization. Every "retrieved" memory is thus an accretion of not only the traces of the distant happening that you now "remember" (actually, reconstruct), but all the subsequent experiences that your brain has, unbeknown to you, associated with it.

Memory Begins with Experience

Here is a more detailed overview. As with all other potential learning, memory begins with *experience*—stimulus of the sense organs (see figure 2.3). The type of stimulus (e.g., auditory, visual, tactile)

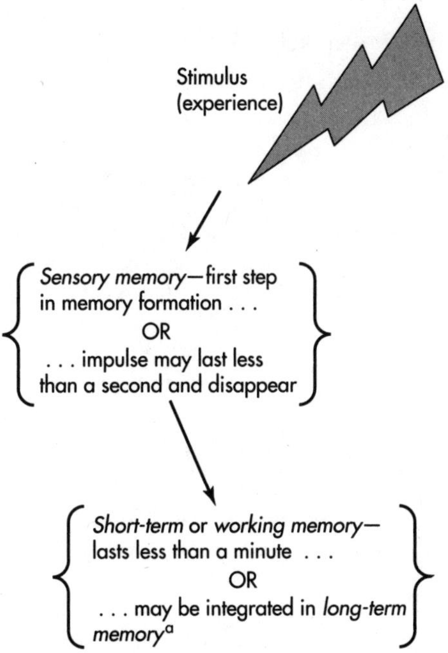

Figure 2.3 Memory Formation

[a]See figure 2.4.

will determine where in the brain it goes first. Sometimes these initial electrochemical impulses are ignored and quickly disappear; the brain does not keep forever every impulse generated by every stimulus.

Short- and Long-Term Memory Impulses that make it past that initial threshold enter *working memory* (commonly called *short-term memory*). Depending on how relevant the brain decides these new experiences are—a function of the association/categorization process described in more detail in figure 2.4—they may now disappear or they may be integrated and consolidated in long-term memory. Facilitation that encourages active engagement and involves conscious association and categorization early on can lead to more meaningful and longer-lasting learning. For example, when adults are asked to keep a reading journal, they pay more attention to the words that flow into their eyes and brains. This is also the basis of meaningful debriefing; discussing a

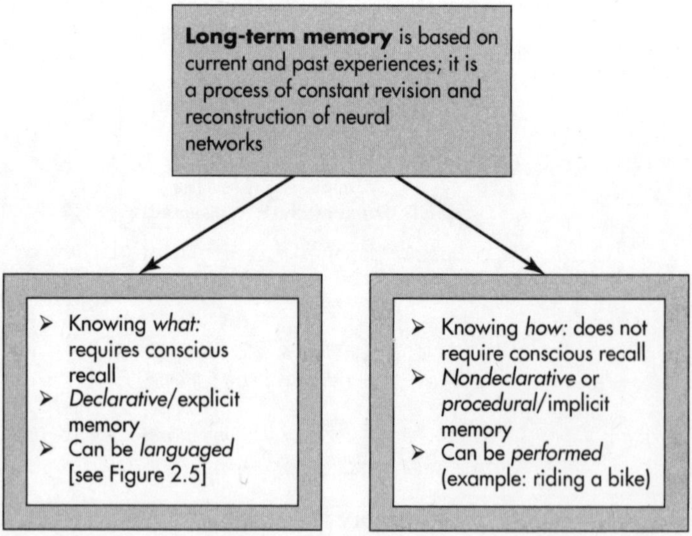

Figure 2.4 Types of Long-Term Memory

learning activity in which adults have just participated as a group can lead to broader and deeper understanding of the experience.

Long-term memory is affected by our attentiveness in the moment as well as the intensity of any emotions connected to the experience. Long-term memory may be *explicit* (declarative, can be languaged) or *implicit* (nondeclarative, expressed in ways other than language). For example, once mastered, motor skills are stored as nondeclarative motor memory and effortlessly and unconsciously recalled. (It's true: we never forget how to ride a bike. Whether we still have good balance or effective spatial discrimination is another matter.)

Episodic and Semantic Memory By contrast, we need to consciously recall explicit memories, which we can then describe verbally. Explicit memories are often *episodic,* or autobiographical. In other words, we appear in our episodic memories. They are also contextual, in that we remember not only what happened but also the setting, the sensory information, and the emotions associated with the event. These memories can be triggered in amazing detail by stimuli associated with a long-ago experience. In *Remembrance of Things Past,* Marcel Proust famously described the flood of vivid memories that returned to overwhelm his adult senses when he tasted again the madeleines that he had enjoyed as a child.

Semantic, as opposed to episodic, long-term memories involve words, concepts, principles, and so forth; they are the kinds of memories we typically associate with learning. We don't appear in these memories; we "have" these memories, or so it seems to us when we reconstruct them. (See figure 2.5)

The emotional content of earlier experiences is another important factor in their reactivation as memory. Overwhelming emotion, especially that associated with fear, violence, and trauma, can inhibit both formation and later recall, whereas pleasurable emotions can contribute to formation and recall. Furthermore,

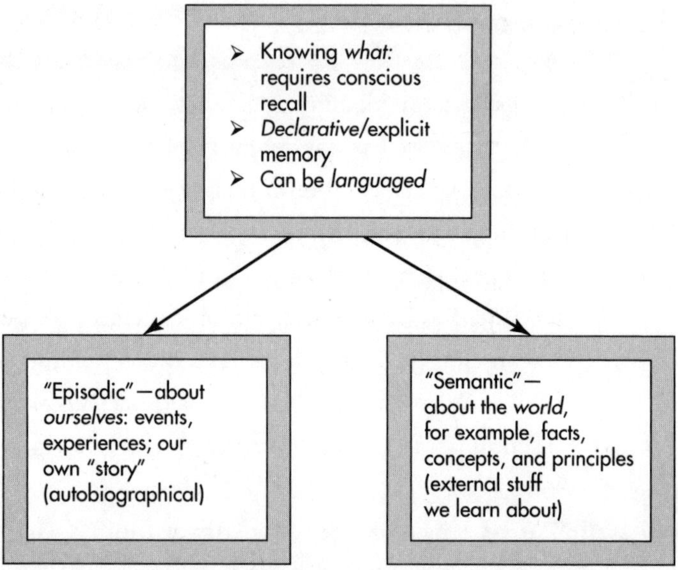

Figure 2.5 Types of Explicit Memory

based on knowledge drawn from existing patterns that are not conscious memories, the associate/categorize process leads our brains to construct models that affect our current emotional and behavioral responses. "Forming mental models is the essential manner in which the brain learns from the past and then directly influences the present and shapes future actions" (Siegel, 1999, p. 72).

Just as learning is dependent on memory, memory is also dependent on learning, in the sense that previous learning affects how we can know or may come to understand new experiences. As earlier impressions are reinterpreted in light of new experience, learning literally *changes the brain* at the neuronal level. Furthermore, as neural networks become more complex and interconnected, thus providing more options for interpreting and reinterpreting experience, the brain comes to know in more complex ways. In effect, what constructivists call development—or greater complexity of mind—is an outcome of this process. (Developmental models are discussed in chapter 9.)

Emotions and Feelings

Neuroscientists, though generally not social scientists, currently distinguish between emotions and feelings. According to Damasio (2000), *emotions* describe the brain's internal-to-the-body responses to environmental stimuli; *feelings* are our subsequent perceptions of these changes in body-state. Let's say you unexpectedly have to swerve your car sharply to avoid someone cutting in front of you. The brain's immediate reaction is to ramp up adrenaline and cortisol production, increase heartbeat, and in other ways prepare to freeze, fight, or flee. As you become aware of these physiological changes, you experience *feelings*. But how you then name those feelings is very much influenced by the filters (described earlier in terms of Broadways or Grand Canyons) created by the sum of your life experiences. For example, the casual Sunday driver is likely to respond by feeling terrified, angry, or both. A professional race-car driver, by comparison, might ascribe feelings of pleasure and exhilaration to those same changes in body-state.

fear vs excitement

Fear of Judgment

Researchers examining how emotions arising in various situations activate particular regions of the brain found that "in physical danger situations, the fear experienced was related to bodily harm . . . In social evaluation situations, the fear experienced was related to being judged negatively by another" (Wilson-Mendenhall, Barrett, Simmons, & Barsalou, 2011, p. 1121).

For many adults, being called on suddenly to answer a question or perform a task may trigger emotions more appropriate to a life-threatening situation than to learning. We may not only be anxious that we will not know the right answer or perform adequately; we may unconsciously be even more distressed that others might witness our vulnerability and failure (see "Fear of Judgment").

Stress and Memory Though a moderate amount of stress-related hormones can enhance attention and encourage the curious brain, too much affects the anxious brain in ways that make it difficult to either focus or remember. Emotions involve many distributed aspects of brain circuitry, but two parts of the brain most involved in fear reactions, the hippocampus and the amygdala, are also essential to memory formation. This underscores the fact that in attending to the cognitive aspects of adult learning, ALFAS must remain alert to their emotions, as well. As John Dirkx (2008), an adult educator and Jungian psychologist, observes, "In one form or another, emotional issues never seem very far from the surface in adult learning contexts. The social and relationship nature of these contexts fosters, elicits, or implicitly encourages learners to give voice or expression to this underlying affect or emotion," and that attending to these experiences in a way that is appropriate for the particular context is among "the most important and most challenging tasks for the [facilitator]" (p. 9).

Emotions Guide Thinking

Emotion is also the source of our motivation to think and learn, though we are generally unaware of that fact. Just as Mr. Oog did, we are driven to advance our well-being and ensure our survival. Understanding, making meaning, and problem solving all contribute to that goal, but emotion is also essential. Without emotional input, the brain may be able to solve discrete problems (such as during laboratory tests of cognitive function), but it cannot make evaluative decisions leading to appropriate action.

Damasio (1994) describes the unexpected changes experienced by a patient, Eliot, after brain surgery. Eliot's cognitive, motor, and language functions were unaffected; in fact, he continued to score higher than average on tests of reasoning and thinking ability. He nevertheless had problems with decision making that severely affected his everyday life. Eliot could not make simple decisions, such as which restaurant to eat in. He started businesses that were doomed to fail by any objective analysis and was married and divorced twice in a brief period. His reasoning in the social world did not accord with his reasoning on cognitive tests. The researchers ultimately discovered that surgery had affected Eliot's capacity for emotion. Without emotion, cognition has no grounding in values, and social decision making is fatally flawed. Siegel (1999) explains: "Generated by the value systems of the brain, these emotional activations pervade all mental functions and literally create meaning in life. In this way, we can say that emotion and meaning are created by the same processes" (p. 158).

Emotion contributes to meaning by giving us clues—anger, joy, sadness, surprise, fear, shame, disgust—as to what we want to approach and what we want to avoid, resulting in feelings of pleasure or pain. Thus, emotion contributes to forming or elaborating more intricate pathways for interpretation of experience—changes that become the substrate for development of increasingly complex ways of knowing.

David Gelertner (1994), a leading figure in artificial intelligence, has spent decades theorizing about how the human brain works. "Thought is usually confused with reasoning," he says, pointing to the preponderance of claims that conflate rationality, logical thought, and problem solving (p. 39). Although these examples of *convergent thought* (linear, search for one right answer) also tend to correlate with the results of most intelligence tests, he suggests that the capacity for *divergent thought* (nonlinear, searching for multiple possibilities) is more likely to lead to creative, inventive thinking (thus, we note, more likely to effectively address many of the seemingly intractable issues of the twenty-first century).

But as Gelertner suggested two decades ago, to acquire this more expansive capacity, people have to stop thinking they can separate the rational from the emotional: "Emotions are not [merely] a form of thought, not an additional way to think, not a special cognitive bonus, but are *fundamental* to thought"

(1994, pp. 46-47). Only recently has brain science caught up with him and verified the role of emotions in "rational" thinking (see "Thoughts and Feelings").

Thoughts and Feelings

For an extended interview in which neuroscientist Antonio Damasio describes his research on emotions and the brain, see http://library.fora.tv/2009/07/04/Antonio_Damasio_This_Time_With_Feeling

Without emotions, intelligence has no anchor. A problem might seem to have a rational solution based on presumably objective criteria such as a cost-benefit analysis, but that may prove inadequate without an underlying value system that can look beyond a spreadsheet. And values, by definition, evaluate: they encompass both judgment and emotions. Thus, the most significant problems adults face—generally those with a human dimension—require emotions as an integral part of thinking and acting rationally.

Though the modern brain's capacity for sustained, ever-narrowed focus has bought our culture the achievements of logic, analysis, and rationality, the cost has been to the more broadly focused capacities of creativity and intuition. The former relies on precise words, abstraction, and deduction. By contrast, bringing seemingly unconnected ideas together—perhaps metaphorically and for no apparent good reason—is a source of outside-the-box thinking, or what Daniel Pink (2005) describes as seeing the big picture with a whole new mind. Gelernter sums up the implications: "Emotions are fundamental to thought; but the body, inconveniently enough, is fundamental to emotions . . . . [It therefore] becomes inescapable that you don't think just with your brain; you think with your body too . . . [and that] intelligent thinking per se is itself impossible without the body" (p. 47).

Unfortunately, the emphasis on learning and thinking primarily as rational, cognitive, activities effectively diminishes the powerful potential of intentionally learning with and through the body—which is, ironically, the only way the brain can ever learn!

Aspects of Basic Brain Functions

- The brain's prime directive is to keep the organism alive and functioning optimally, whatever the circumstances. It does this by continually monitoring and responding to internal and external environments.
- Maintaining the body's internal environment, that is, homeostasis, is primarily the task of parts of the brain over which we have little conscious control.
- The embodied brain responds to external environments by taking in and reacting to stimuli—information received through the senses.
- Unlike a tape recorder or camera, where everything audible or visible in the viewfinder is recorded, not every potential stimulus in the environment passes the brain's threshold of attention.
- Once the brain has attended to a stimulus, it processes that input so that it can be useful in the brain's pursuit of the prime directive. This processing is based on analogy: every new experience is compared to prior experiences, including the emotions that accompanied them, that have been stored in various neural networks, essential by asking, *How is this experience like what I already "know"*?
- Filters play a pivotal role in this associative process. Over a lifetime of experiential interactions, adults build up associative patterns colored by family, community, and society about, among other things, who we are as individuals within our group and how our group stands in relation to other groups. This tacit knowledge (beliefs and assumptions) of which we are unaware also continuously informs subsequent experiences of every kind.
- Well-established neural networks offer processing efficiency, thus saving energy. Since the actively engaged waking brain demands a lot of energy, such shortcuts are essential.
- Many of the brain's default systems, such as seeking shortcuts and using long-established filters, may prove counterproductive to engaging in the kind of learning currently demanded of us by the increasing complexity of the world.
- Adult education can play a vital role in creating environments in which adults' brains can challenge their own existing patterns and thus develop greater complexity of mind.

Key Ideas

- What we call thinking is just the final step in a long process of knowing that goes on within the body—the body-brain—before we can discover that we know something. Learning is a whole-body experience.
- To learn, the brain must associate any new experience with what it already "knows."
- Once a stimulus (experience) has passed the threshold of attention, the brain immediately categorizes it by comparing the unknown to the known. It seeks similarities between this experience and previous experiences in order to connect it to existing patterns.
- Though neural networks are constantly being revised and refined, well-established patterns are far more difficult to change.
- Anthropologists and sociologists call many established neural patterns *culture;* psychologists call them *identity, life-scripts,* and *mental models.*
- We have two early brain imperatives—save energy (by reinforcing often-used neural patterns) and seek safety (by discriminating between "our kind" of people and "not our kind" of people)—that make absolute sense in the primeval savanna but can be problematic for adults in the twenty-first century.
- As earlier impressions are reinterpreted in light of new experience, learning literally changes the brain at the neuronal level.
- Memory is neither a discrete thing nor does it occupy a particular place in the brain; it is a process, not merely a subject of retrieval.
- Without emotions, intelligence has no anchor. Without emotion, cognition has no grounding in values and social decision making is fatally flawed.

- Emotion contributes to forming or elaborating more intricate pathways for interpretation of experience—changes that become the substrate for the development of increasingly complex ways of knowing.
- People have to stop thinking they can separate the rational from the emotional: "Emotions are not [merely] a form of thought, not an additional way to think, not a special cognitive bonus, but are *fundamental* to thought."
- "You don't think *just with your brain*; you think with your body too. . . . Intelligent *thinking per se* is *itself* impossible without the body."
- Unfortunately, the emphasis on learning and thinking primarily as rational, cognitive activities effectively diminishes the powerful potential of intentionally learning with and through the body—which is, ironically, the only way the brain can ever learn.
- ALFAS can play a vital role in creating environments wherein adults' brains can challenge their own existing patterns and thus develop greater complexity of mind.

? Pause for Reflection

Please comment on, question, freewrite, doodle, or sketch any thoughts and feelings about the reading. Also:

understanding my own learning
understanding older people in class

1. What in this chapter was most surprising, intriguing, or provocative? How did you feel when you came across that idea or example?
2. Please continue to consider: How might any of this material relate to your own practice? To your own learning?

encourage members to correlate their new freedom to past experiences.
"Remember when you waited forever to hear from your landlord?"

3

Metaphors, Embodiment, and Hemispheres

The mind is inherently embodied. Thought is mostly unconscious. Abstract concepts are largely metaphorical.

— GEORGE LAKOFF AND MARK JOHNSON

WE HAVE emphasized that learning begins with experience and experience stimulates the embodied brain. Now we ask, How does embodied experience lead to learning? Neuroscientists are attempting to work out those details at the cellular level and from the viewpoint of brain function. As ALFAS (adult learning facilitators in any setting), we approach the question through analogy—indeed, that's a big part of the answer!

The Analogical Brain

Brains link current experiences with prior understandings through association and categorization, that is, analogically. (Linguists and grammarians may shudder, but we will use terms such as *analogy, metaphor*, and related figures of speech more or less interchangeably to describe the nonliteral, associative aspects of how the brain works.)

Think of the facial recognition systems common to police procedural dramas. We see a fuzzy, grainy photo of an unidentified suspect taken by a security camera. Next to that photo, comparison images whiz by in a blur until—freeze!—a matching image pops up from an official database such as a mug shot, military ID, or driver's license. This works because details of facial characteristics can be reduced to mathematical specifications that are then statistically analyzed for a probable match. "Recognition" becomes a matter of quickly crunching enough data, a task at which computers excel. (We note that in the real world, after the computer finds a probable match, a human brain is still necessary to decide if it's accurate.)

Though comparison between an unidentified image and a database of stored images is analogous to what the brain does to determine what to make of a new experience, there are major differences. The brain's comparison data are not crisp, clear images that have been reduced to precise specification. Most crucial, the brain has no external programmer to first construct and then test the accuracy of its analytical process against objective data before putting it to use. Instead, the brain has been continuously constructing and using its experience recognition systems since infancy—in other words, starting with what is, metaphorically speaking, a version 1.0 brain. Though new experiences and further development continually update earlier association patterns, outdated versions may still be reactivated.

Over the life span, the brain consistently refines and elaborates neural networks as it searches for the best response to the current circumstance. And every refinement or elaboration of dendritic connections effectively changes the meaning the brain makes. In this way, we also update and revise aspects of our own narratives, thus changing how we see ourselves and the world around us. Such changes can enable us to reach beyond our familiar but often limiting ways of thinking toward more complex and creative approaches to the issues we face, individually and collectively. As Mary Catherine Bateson (1994) points out,

> Metaphors are what thought is all about. We use metaphors, consciously or unconsciously, all the time, so it is a matter of mental hygiene to take responsibility for these metaphors, to look at them carefully, to see how meanings slide from one to the other. Any metaphor is double-sided, offering both insight and new confusion, but metaphors are unavoidable. By recognizing similarities, metaphors bring different kinds of knowledge together. (p. 34)

Comparison and Association

To further explore the potential of brain-aware facilitation, we look more closely at the brain's process of comparison and association, again through an analogical rather than neurological description. It is a word picture of a process that does not involve words—though words may arise after association and categorization have occurred if the experience rises to the level of conscious awareness.

Since everything we learn begins with experience—data that enter the brain through the portals of our senses—we start with the first opportunity we can observe. Figure 3.1 is a photo of a two-hour-old infant, wrapped in a soft flannel blanket, being gently and lovingly held by his dad. His slightly wrinkled brow, placid but apparently engaged expression, plus the hospital-issue soft pointy cap, make him look like a wise gnome.

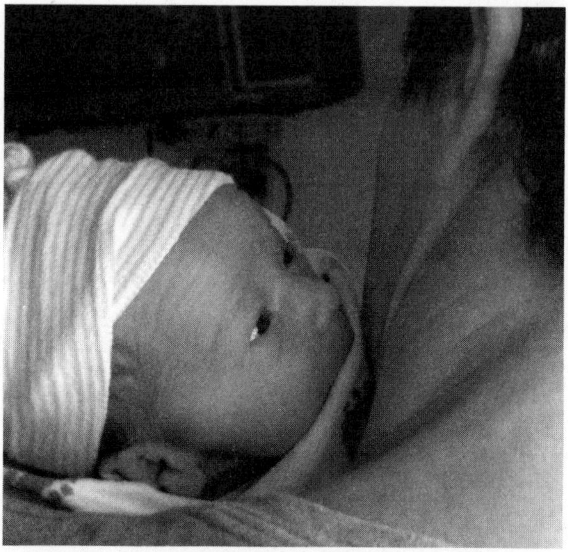

Figure 3.1 Infant's Wordless Experience

He appears to be calmly absorbing the sensations of the new world he has just entered. Imagine the sort of experiences his wordless brain might be registering? Here are some sensory possibilities we envision: *Soft . . . safe . . . gentle . . . close . . . bright . . . warm . . . touch . . . comfort.*

Referring to Piaget's well-known model of development, Varela, Thompson, and Rosch (1991) observe, "The newborn infant has only her own activity, and even the simplest act of recognition of an object can be understood only in terms of her own activity. Out of this, she must construct the entire edifice of the phenomenological world with its laws and logic . . . . The laws of cognitive development, even at the sensorimotor stage, are an assimilation of and an accommodation" to the pregiven world that is, as it has so far been experienced (p. 176).

Metaphor, the Key to Association Though we have represented the infant's experience in words, these are actually sensations that result from signal transmission from one neuron to another. The various environmental stimuli—smell, touch, sight, hearing, taste—have areas of primary input (e.g., the parietal lobe of the cerebral cortex is associated with sensations of touch, the occipital lobe with vision, and the temporal lobe with sound); however, traces of experiences scatter throughout the brain in a chain reaction of overlapping associations. As each small, new person at every moment accumulates additional experiences, these are variously stored in ever-more-complex networks while the brain continues to connect subsequent impressions with earlier ones.

Even so, as these sensations are experienced, categorized, and associated, the (purely sensory, nonverbal) experiences of *gentle* and *soft* and *blanket* and *safe* and so on are likely to be linked in various combinations, perhaps explaining why a "blankie" can become such an important part of a child's self-soothing ritual:

> The early age at which analogies appear suggest that they provide a powerful logical tool for explaining and learning about the world. Analogies also contribute to both the acquisition and the restricting of knowledge, and play an important role in conceptual change. As children's knowledge about the world becomes richer, the structure of the knowledge becomes deeper, and more complex relationships are represented, enabling deeper or more complex analogies. (Goswami, 2001, p. 465)

(See "Further Reading: Analogy and Hemispheric Development.")

Further Reading: Analogy and Hemispheric Development

Genter, D., Holyoak K. J., & Kokinov, B. N. (Eds.) (2001). *The analogical mind: Perspectives from cognitive science* (pp. 199–254). Cambridge, MA: MIT Press.

Varela, F. J., Thompson, E., & Rosch, E. (1991). *The embodied mind: Cognitive science and human experience*. Cambridge, MA: MIT Press.

Chiron C., Jambaque, I., Nabbout, R., Lounes, R., Syrota, A., & Dulac, O. (1997). The right brain hemisphere is dominant in human infants. *Brain, 120*, 1057–1065.

Most relevant to our roles as ALFAS is the realization that everything we come to know and understand throughout our lifetimes, including the most abstract concepts, originated with body-based metaphors and analogies because these are the embodied brain's basic reference point. "A fundamental early mode of thinking that is highly dependent on pattern recognition involves metaphor" (Edelman, 2006, p. 85). Our earliest experiences are constantly being elaborated by further experiences within the psycho-social-cultural surround, thus informing our perception of subsequent experiences.

We acquire concepts through such serial metaphorical scaffolding as a new experience extends the reach of an earlier one, and in so doing, creates a new construct. "Even our deepest and most abiding concepts—time, events, causation, morality, and mind itself—are understood and reasoned about via multiple metaphors . . . which [are] shaped to a significant extent by the common nature of our bodies and the shared ways that we all function in the everyday world" (Lakoff & Johnson, 2003, p. 245).

experiences act as metaphors for later learning?

Metaphor Shapes Experience As a nearly universal example, the terms *close* and *distant*—literal descriptions of the body in relational space—are often used to describe emotional closeness and distance, perhaps even whether we feel loved or not. Such essential metaphors transcend cultural differences. Similarly, associations between *up* (height) and *good* (positive), as in "I'm up for it" and

"This is the high point of the day," occur in languages as removed from one another as Chinese and English. "[In] metaphorical thinking . . . one concept is understood in the context of another. The abstract is understood in the context of the concrete, the metaphysical in the context of the physical, the emotional in the context of the biological. *Through metaphor, body and mind are inextricably intertwined*" (Geary, 2012, p. 93, emphasis added).

Here's what many startled tourists see on the sides of delivery vans in Greece: ΜΕΤΑΦΟΡΑ. Those unschooled in the Greek alphabet may nevertheless recognize Φ as *phi* (often used in the names of fraternities or sororities; pronounced like the letter *f*) and *P* as *rho* (a mathematical symbol, pronounced like the letter *r*). If so, after saying it phonetically, one wonders: what's metaphorical about a truck? Nothing. In the Greek language, the noun *metaphor* simply means a conveyance—something that can transfer stuff from one location to another—hence, a delivery van. This is also a literal description of the use of metaphor in language—the stuff being transferred is the meaning of a word.

As we have seen, ΜΕΤΑΦΟΡΑ is also a literal description for how the brain responds to any new thing, long before that new experience enters conscious awareness (if it ever does). Essentially, whenever the brain is called on to evaluate and begin to make sense of an experience—in other words, every conscious moment—it must begin by finding preexisting locations (associations) to which the new input might be "carried." And since every stimulus is new because every moment in time is new, from the brain's perspective, this metaphorical association/categorization process describes every experience the brain encounters.

> The capacity of organisms to carry out such projections lies at the heart of cognition in its many forms. Far from being confined to problem solving and conscious reasoning, structure mapping [which includes analogy and metaphor] is inherent in all our thought processes, especially in the permanent construction of meaning that

> we engage in effortlessly as we conceive the world around us, act upon it, talk about it, and stray beyond it in wild leaps of imagination, fantasy, and creativity (Fauconnier, 2001, p. 255).

As we go through life, metaphors build on other metaphors; over time, we no longer recognize them unless they are pointed out—and then the people doing the pointing out seem excessively pedantic. (In the previous sentence, "build on" and "pointed out" describe concrete actions, neither of which is occurring in the literal sense. (See "Many Forms of Metaphor.")

> **Many Forms of Metaphor**
>
> *Metonymy* is the term for using part of something to describe the whole of which it is a part. For example, "Come see my new wheels" is an invitation to admire the entire car, not just its tires. *Synecdoche* is also using a part to describe a whole, but in this case the whole being referred to is not directly related to that particular part (as contrasted with wheels and cars). In the often quoted line from *Julius Caesar*, "Friends, Romans, countrymen, lend me your ears," Marc Antony is asking people to listen attentively, not to temporarily hand over the shell-like protuberances on either side of their heads. (See also Geary, 2012.)

Most adults know that a metaphor is a figure of speech—a word or phrase used to suggest a meaning other than the dictionary definition. *He's a big fish in a little pond* has nothing to do with either bodies of water or creatures swimming in them. Assuming sufficient cultural familiarity, we easily and immediately translate such examples into their implicit meaning. We therefore rarely notice how prevalent metaphorical expressions are in everyday language. For example (note the following words in italics), young children are likely to be puzzled about the implications of the fish and the pond until they pass certain developmental milestones (*milestones?*). On the other hand (*other hand?*), children easily create fresh (*fresh?*), compelling

(*compelling?*) metaphors because their minds are unfettered (*unfettered?*) by linguistic convention (*convention?*).

We know that physical experiences may affect psychological states. We may not realize that embodied metaphors do too. Briefly holding a warm or cold object (such as a beverage cup or a heating or cooling pad) has been shown to affect research subjects' interpersonal responses, such as by being more or less generous to others or assessing others as more or less helpful. As noted, the physical experience of warmth is associated with closeness, caring, and other positive emotional states, as cold is with distance and lack of caring.

The inverse is also true. Experimentally induced feelings of minor rejection or isolation (based on how often a presumably neutral computer game allowed participants to take their turn) led to research subjects' perception that the ambient temperature in the room was cooler than it actually was. In effect, the embodied metaphor of *cold and lonely* affected research participants' physical experience. "Metaphors are not just linguistic elements that people use to communicate; metaphors are fundamental vessels through which people understand and experience the world around them" (Zhong & Leonardelli, 2008, p. 840).

Metaphor Shapes Abstract Concepts According to Lakoff and Johnson (2003), "You don't have a choice as to whether to think metaphorically" (p. 257). Even more surprising may be that thinking abstractly is dependent on first thinking metaphorically. Key theories put forth more than thirty years ago have since been verified empirically:

- Metaphors are fundamentally conceptual in nature; metaphorical language is secondary.
- Conceptual metaphors are grounded in everyday experience.

- Abstract thought is largely, though not entirely, metaphorical.
- Metaphorical thought is unavoidable, ubiquitous, and mostly unconscious.
- Abstract concepts have a literal core but are extended by metaphors, often by many mutually inconsistent metaphors.
- Abstract concepts are not complete without metaphors. For example, love is not love without metaphors of magic, attraction, madness, union, nurturance, and so on.
- Our conceptual systems are not consistent overall, since the metaphors used to reason about concepts may be inconsistent.
- We live our lives on the basis of inferences we derive via metaphor. (pp. 272–273)

This points up a distinction between *abstract concepts* and *thinking abstractly. Constructing abstract concepts is based* on understanding something through the serial buildup of metaphorical associations. This, according to Iain McGilchrist (2010), is the work of the right hemisphere (RH), which sees things in context. By contrast, the left hemisphere (LH) approach to abstraction, *thinking abstractly*, requires extracting something *from its context.* "This, and its related capacity to categorize things once they have been abstracted," he wrote, "are the foundations of [the LH's] intellectual power" (p. 50). Although the RH may be the source of the symbolic, metaphorical associations that give rise over time to conceptual abstractions, it does not think abstractly. It is too vested in "the art of *contextual meaning*, and in *using* metaphor" (p. 49, emphasis added). Given this inescapable reality, a largely untapped approach to adult learning would be for ALFAS to explicitly target this RH talent. To better understand this we more deeply explore differences between the hemispheres in the next section. (See "Current Hemispheric Research.")

According to McGilchrist (2010), our primary source on hemispheric difference, the technology available to look inside living brains can see which brain regions are activated during certain tasks by detecting changes in the blood supply to various regions. Results of any neuroimaging studies require complex analyses; a new task will show up differently from the same task repeated at another time. Gender, race, and age account for some, as does "handedness" (left- or right-). "Nonetheless, in aggregate," writes McGilchrist, "we have a mass of information that does suggest consistent [hemispheric] differences" (p. 26).

Current Hemispheric Research

Because much early research on the divided brain involved injured or surgically altered brains, many presumed distinctions between the hemispheres that have become common knowledge are exaggerated or wrong. (A visually stunning example of such assumptions is an award-winning ad for the Mercedes Benz car: http://adsoftheworld.com/media/print/mercedes_benz_left_brain_right_brain_paint.) Although the text is fairly accurate, the ad fails to say the hemispheres always work together, whether on creativity, logic, or language processing. The major difference is how each hemisphere approaches their collaboration.

Left and Right Hemispheric Differences, Updated

According to the clichés, the left brain is analytical and word focused, whereas the right is emotional and sense focused; in essence, so this goes, the left thinks and the right feels. Not so! Even those capacities people tend to ascribe to one hemisphere or the other, such as imagination and rationality—or, more colloquially, poetry and science—require both hemispheres working together. That said, it is true that the LH concentrates on words, logic, and reductive reasoning; limited and defined variables; probabilistic analysis; and objectivity, which distances the knower from the known; it sees the body it belongs to as a compilation of its parts. The RH concentrates on images, feelings, sensations, and inductive reasoning; it is more attuned to the big picture and contextual analysis, is connected to its whole self as embodied, and makes meaning that connects the knower and the known. Unless disease or injury has damaged the brain, neither hemisphere works in isolation; they constantly communicate through a thick bundle of nerve fibers (the *corpus callosum*).

Differing Intentions

Even so, each hemisphere approaches that collaboration with markedly different worldviews in terms of what is most important and how to achieve its purposes. It is not so much about what each hemisphere *does*—meaning the activities it engages in, since both are involved all the time—as what each is most *oriented toward* as it engages.

> The essential difference . . . is that the [RH] pays attention to the Other, whatever it is that exists apart from ourselves, with which it sees itself in profound relation. It is deeply attracted to, and given life by [that] relationship . . . . By contrast, the [LH] pays attention to the virtual world it has created, which is self-consistent, but self-contained, ultimately disconnected from the Other. [It is therefore] ultimately only able to operate on, and to know, itself. (McGilchrist, 2010, p. 93)

The RH's focus is to reach for what is not known: to make new connections, identify heretofore unseen commonalities, and make use of nuance and metaphor and subtlety. The RH also captures everything all at once; thus, it makes sense of seemingly random patterns. Of course, it can also create patterns that may not accurately reflect the results of deeper, more focused (LH) investigation. But by itself, LH will not look beyond what it already has established; instead it will continue to follow essentially the same path, creating ever deeper commitment to it.

LH's internal consistency means it is also very quick and sure of itself. When ALFAS make it a point to engage the adult's RH, we may counterbalance the LH's rush to judgment, which it does to avoid ambiguity or uncertainty. The RH is slower because in taking a broader view, it searches through a wider range of potential but less directly connected associations. For example, the RH's métier includes the more time-consuming decoding of nonverbal input, including images, music, and physical activities imbued with meaning (as in role plays, serious games, and simulations; see chapter 7); it also includes extended linguistic decoding, such as metaphor and analogy (hence poetry, parables, puns, and stories). Unfortunately, when the LH quickly says, "Okay, I've got this," the potential contribution of the RH, which can't immediately speak up for itself, may go unnoticed. (See "Further Reading: Right and Left Hemispheres" for neurology-based RH/LH research studies.)

Further Reading: Right and Left Hemispheres

According to Tompkins, Scharp, Meigh, and Fassbinder (2008), LH interpretations are faster than those that require RH processing because the choices are quickly narrowed, as in our description of the brain's overall desire to be right and fast.

Differences in the kind of analogy being used to process the new experience may also be a factor in how much each hemisphere is involved. According to Schmidt, Cardillo, Kranjec, Lehet, Widick, and Chatterjee (2012, p. 1372), the more "difficult, abstract, and fragile" the connection the analogy represents, the more the RH is involved in processing. Common analogies, the kind that have slipped into everyday language, do not require the RH's deeper attention.

In short, the LH's up-and-at-'em approach to verbal processing focuses on narrow interpretations, direct connections, unambiguous meaning, and often-used metaphors. Clichés are also dealt with in the LH because they are familiar and do not demand the imaginal reach that the RH provides. However, when the connection is indirect or ambiguous, as in the case when interpreting innovative, unfamiliar metaphors, symbolic action, and nonverbal indicators—hence, potentially more complex, contextual meaning—the RH is required.

Triumph of the LH

The notion of *triumph* emerges from McGilchrist's (2010) extensive analysis of how, over the previous four hundred years, what we have come to think of as knowing and thinking has increasingly focused on capacities most identified with the LH:

> In all its major predilections—divorce from the body, detachment from human feeling, the separation of thought from action in the world, concern with clarity and fixity, the triumph of representation over what is present to sensory experience, in its reduction of time to a succession of atomistic moments, and in its tendency to reduce the living to the devitalised and mechanical—*the philosophy of Descartes belongs to the world as construed by the left hemisphere.* (p. 332, emphasis added)

Meanwhile, around the time that Descartes rejected anything other than the mind's way of knowing, the body being particularly suspect since the senses could be so easily deceived (see "No Body?"), Frances Bacon was also developing an inductive approach designed to eliminate subjective impressions and beliefs in favor of objective observation and analysis. Ever since these two great thinkers set the stage for

> **No Body?**
>
> Descartes questioned why his body's sensations of hunger should be connected to his mind's desire to eat, why a feeling of pain should lead to mental distress, or whether he even had a body. McGilchrist (2010) quotes from Descartes' Meditation IV: "I can make probable conjecture that the body exists. But this is only a probability; and despite a careful and comprehensive investigation, I do not yet see how the distinct idea of corporeal nature which I find in my imagination can provide any basis for a necessary inference that some body exists" (p. 333).

what we now call the scientific method, there has been increasing emphasis in science and education on LH approaches.

These differences are also a factor in ongoing discussions of positivist and (or versus) constructivist research methods (see Guba & Lincoln, 2005, p. 201). Only in the past century has a growing chorus of researchers and others who study the philosophical foundations of knowledge itself—how it comes into being—begun to question the premise of "objectivity." As Haskell (1987) wryly noted,

> Despite the positivist claim that they have no premise . . . [their premise is] that the "facts speak for themselves." As can be seen in the literature of the psychology of perception, "facts" are not given but are constructed from inner psychic structures. To perceive, therefore, is to project; it is to "throw" oneself integrally into a fact, to become part of it. (p. 261–262)

Bacon's method effectively externalized the LH's inclinations for a codified, delimited, analytical approach and crowned it the only true method to achieve knowledge. Given the reality of his era—that truth was proclaimed by the clergy (or monarchs whom they anointed, which meant it could shift with the political winds), his *Novum Organum* ("new method") was a much-needed paradigm shift. One result is that Western culture as a whole now believes in logic. That is an intentionally ironic statement. We *believe* in logic. But in fact, in the brain, as we have seen, *metaphor precedes logic.* First the brain uses symbols and images; only then does it begin to construct words and a logical story, which is why, in the case of the Mercedes advertisement noted above, a picture is worth a thousand words.

Recession of the RH

People cannot observe, codify, and articulate RH processes as they can LH processes. Earlier in this chapter, we struggled to create word pictures that might illuminate the brain's approach to its nonverbal, nonvisual process of association and categorization. Compare this with a supposedly value-free classification and linear analysis that can be described with verbal and often mathematical precision; LH is much better at making its case to the world. "By contrast, it is hard for the right hemisphere to be heard at all: what it knows is too complex, hasn't the advantage of having been carved up into pieces that can be neatly strung together, and it hasn't got a voice, anyway" (McGilchrist, 2010, p. 229). Perhaps it is not surprising that intuitive, inductive, and admittedly subjective analyses appear less creditable. The brain's conclusion—that is, its logical, LH conclusion—is that what we can objectively observe and statistically analyze is truer and more trustworthy—essentially, "realer." (See "Working Alone.")

a lot of my feelings around my writing.

Unfortunately, the LH (the brain's "reporter") assumes that the origin of thought is in explicit language. Therefore the LH does not realize that only *after* RH "gets it" can the LH turn it into words. Our embodied brains rely first on processes that are preverbal and precognitive—what McGilchrist (2010) calls RH's global attention precedes and then directs LH's local attention: "We may think that we build up a picture of something by a process of serial

> **Working Alone**
>
> Hemispheric "cooperation" is also based on mutual inhibition. Each hemisphere not only has its preferred orientation, but it works to actively suppress the other. The effects of this suppression become starkly evident when injury, stroke, or surgical intervention disables the other. "Right hemisphere damage disrupts perception of global objects, while left hemisphere damage disrupts percept of local objects" (http://neuroscience.uth.tmc.edu/s4/chapter09.html). With LH totally in charge, detail is king. Only RH can put things in a larger context. Metaphorically speaking, LH is the trees; RH is the forest.

scanning—putting the bits together—because this is the way our conscious, verbal, left hemisphere, when asked to work out how it is done after the fact, accounts for it. But in reality *we see things first whole*" (p. 44, emphasis added).

While LH quickly interprets the experience in language (even, at times, misinterpreting; Baynes & Gazzaniga, 2000), RH seeks to construct more profound interpretations. It attempts to move beyond the LH's self-referential denotative precision—that is, knowing what it already knows, only more so—by searching for more complex, integrative patterns. This kind of learning leads to a higher level of connotative exploration that emphasizes connection: What is the implicit meaning (and for whom)? Why does it matter (and to whom)? Such RH activity can spur the kinds of changes in the brain associated with greater creativity and deeper understanding, as well as with seeing, being, and acting in new, more effective ways.

In a typical learning situation, however, where the disembodied words just keep coming, there may neither be time for the RH to make deeper, more connected meaning nor for the LH to notice what the RH has done. Learning that focuses on content (words) without sufficient attention to context (meaning) ends up being largely about retention and recall. ALFAS who build pauses and reflection time into their facilitation methods give the RH a chance to chime in and make more substantive meaning.

Embodied Brain, Redux

As noted earlier, all learning begins with experience—sensory input to an embodied brain. Experiences—how the brain perceives what is happening within and around the body—are the basis for developing concepts of every kind, and all such concepts emerge as metaphors of primary sensory processes. As Geary (2012) points out, "If our bodies were different, our metaphors would be different.... If crabs could talk, they would undoubtedly describe progress in difficult negotiations as *sidling* toward agreement and express the hope for a better future by saying their best days are still *beside* them. Our bodies prime our metaphors, and our metaphors prime how we think and act" (p. 100).

Figure 3.2 depicts the relationship between experience and analogy. The top arrow attempts to visualize what we have been describing verbally. As we engage in a new experience—and all experiences are new in the sense of the Buddhist saying, "one cannot step twice in the same river"—our brains quickly search through the nonverbal impressions gathered through our lifetime and categorized analogically. The brain finds multiple associations for various aspects of the current experience; similar elements might include times, places, sights, feelings, smells, contexts,

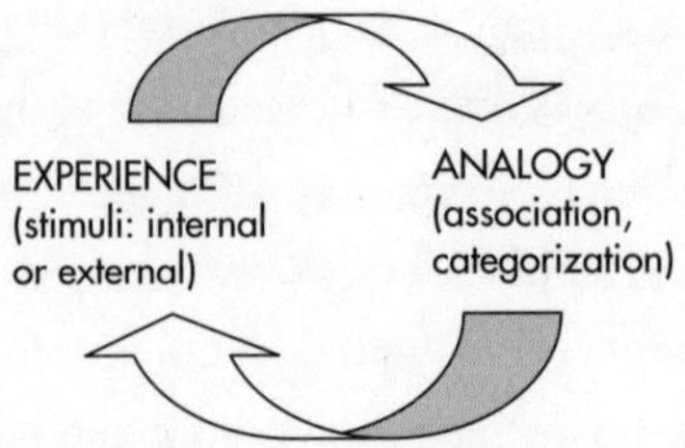

Figure 3.2 Experience/Analogy Cycle

details, and people. Some of these connections are stronger, such as those that were more emotionally intense or happened more recently. "*Since nothing ever occurs in exactly the same way, all so-called 'recurrences' are but analogous (metaphorical) events*" (Haskell, 1987, original italics, p. 262).

Although we may be unaware of the associations the brain has just made, the bottom arrow indicates that they affect how we respond to subsequent experiences, including the current moment. This ongoing process enables us to move through time informed by what has occurred previously rather than having to start each moment as if from scratch. Such changes in our neural networks are what we call learning. However, for reasons already discussed, such as the brain's need to be right and fast, efficient, and to avoid not knowing, we can also become prisoners of long-established analogies. In doing so, we establish and maintain our own Broadways/Grand Canyons—the deeply etched patterns in our neural networks—or as Douglas Hofstedter (2001) calls them, *pet themes:*

> Each person, as life progresses, develops a set of high-level concepts that they tend to favor, and their perception is continually seeking to cast the world in terms of those concepts. The perceptual process is thus far from neutral or random, but rather it seeks, whenever possible, to employ high-level concepts that one is used to, that one believes in, that one is comfortable with, that are one's pet themes. (p. 522)

In the right circumstances, Hofstedter continues, "if the current perception of a situation leads one into a state of cognitive dissonance, then one goes back and searches for a new way to perceive it"—which is to say, adults may become aware of and begin to question such beliefs. ALFAS who understand how thoroughly the embodied brain is steeped in nonverbal analogy and association may have powerful new facilitation approaches available to them. To employ such approaches successfully, however, ALFAS must also consistently attend to the anxiety that goes along with cognitive dissonance. If their anxiety about leaving their pet themes is too great, adults can also refuse to entertain new possibilities. Therefore, we ALFAS must remain mindful to consistently provide support, even as we construct appropriate challenges.

Key Ideas

- We continually update and revise aspects of our own narratives, thus changing how we see ourselves and the world around us. Such changes can enable us to reach beyond our familiar but often limiting ways of thinking toward more complex and creative approaches to the issues we face, individually and collectively.
- Everything we come to know and understand throughout our lifetimes—including the most abstract concepts—originated with body-based metaphors and analogies, because these are the embodied brain's basic reference points.
- Whenever the brain is called on to evaluate and begin to make sense of an experience—in other words, every conscious moment—it must begin by finding preexisting locations (associations) to which the new input might be "carried."
- When ALFAS engage the adult's right hemisphere (RH), we may counterbalance the left hemisphere's (LH) rush to judgment, which it does to avoid ambiguity or uncertainty.
- Over the past four hundred years, what we have come to think of as knowing and thinking has increasingly focused on capacities most identified with the LH.
- In the brain, metaphor precedes logic. First, the brain uses symbols and images; only then does it begin to construct words and a logical story.

- Only *after* RH "gets it" can the LH turn it into words. The embodied brain relies first on processes that are preverbal and precognitive.
- ALFAS who build pauses and reflection time into their facilitation methods give the RH a chance to chime in and make more substantive meaning.
- Experiences—how the brain perceives what is happening within and around the body—are the basis for developing concepts of every kind, and all such concepts emerge as metaphors of primary sensory processes.
- Changes in our neural networks are what we call learning.
- ALFAS who understand how thoroughly the embodied brain is steeped in nonverbal analogy and association may have powerful new facilitation approaches available to them.

? Pause for Reflection

1. What do you recall about your own experiences with embodied learning (though you might not have termed it that way)?
2. What use do you make of metaphors or analogies in your practice? They might be visual and physical, as well as verbal.
3. Where might you be more intentional about listening for metaphors/analogies and using them?
4. In terms of yourself or adults you work with, how do you respond to the distinctions we described between RH and LH?

Part II

Practices That Enhance Adult Learning

WE TURN now to specific approaches to practice and suggest that for adult learning facilitators in any setting (ALFAS), planning to actively engage the embodied brain makes perfect sense. After all, if thinking is so dependent on the body, why not use the body more purposefully as an avenue of thought?

So far, we've used words and familiar analogies (LH orientation) to describe how the embodied brain works and why that understanding is so important to us as ALFAS. Now we adopt a more RH orientation—an extended visual metaphor we introduced in the Preface, the *Theatre of Knowing*. In trying to make visible, linear, and orderly something that is invisible, weblike, and untidy, we present a complex verbal and visual analogy that includes storyboard elements.

Theatre of Knowing

We invite you to reexamine figure II.1 before reading our explanation that follows. Now that you have more information about the brain and how it learns, the drawing may speak to you more directly that it did earlier. In any case, we hope it will ignite further

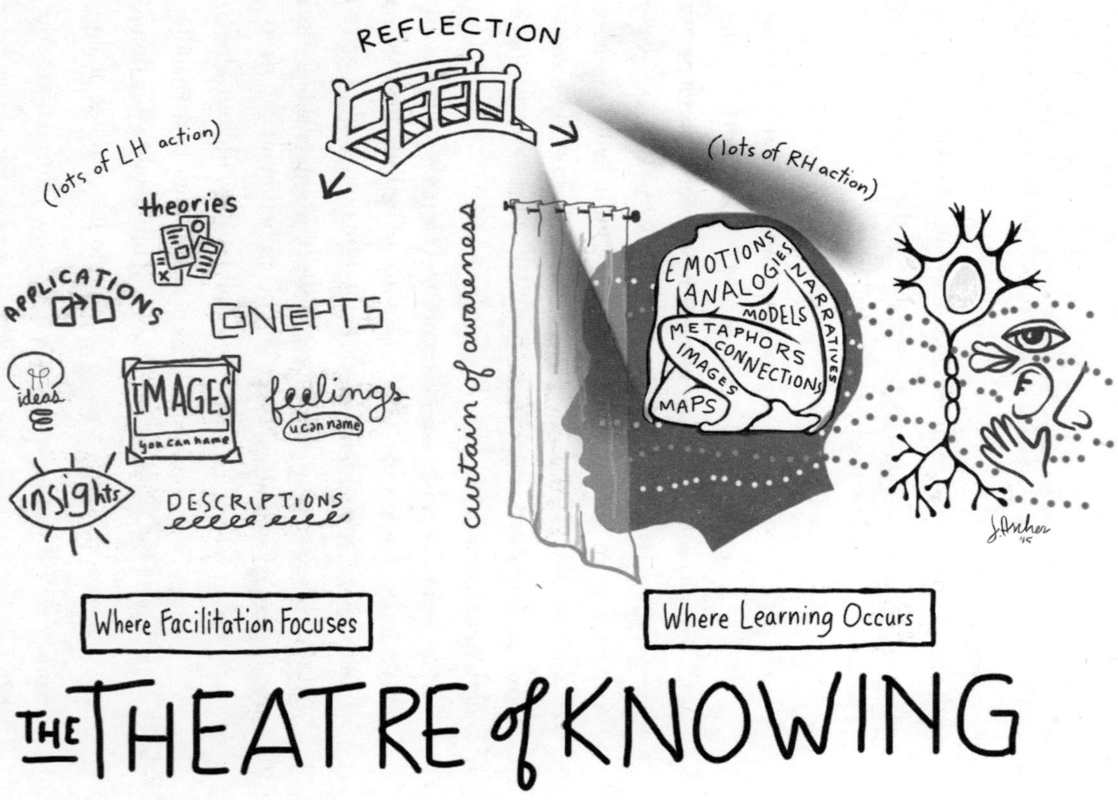

Figure II.1 Theatre of Knowing

metaphorical thinking of your own. Here's a hint: the action starts on the right.

As we said earlier, there are four major areas to the sketch: on the right, indicators of the five senses and a neuron; then the silhouette of a head inside of which rests a body labeled with things that brains do silently and inwardly; in the middle of the page is both a gauzy curtain that separates the images on the right from those on the left and, above it, a bridge connecting them, from which emanates a spotlight; on the left, indicators of things that brains do visibly and verbally.

In terms of embodied learning, the story begins on the right, with experience. Stimuli that originate in the environment—sound, sight, smell, touch, or taste—activate sensory neurons, sending signals to the respective sensory receptors (not pictured). The result may lead to physical movement, thus involving motor neurons (not pictured) and memories being encoded. Memories include traces not only of sensory stimuli but also of associated emotion—that is, the body's biophysical state during the experience.

The headless body inside the head is a visual analogy for the embodied brain (not a homunculus—the little man inside a brain once thought to direct brain function, leading to an "infinite regression" problem: see http://en.wikipedia.org/wiki/Homunculus_argument). The fact of embodiment affects the brain in two ways. First, the only portal to the world outside our skin is through the body's five senses; second, our understanding of what we experience about that world is ultimately a function of how we experience our body in relation to it—through analogy and metaphor.

> Primary metaphors arise spontaneously and automatically without our being aware of them..., most of them learned unconsciously and automatically in childhood simply by functioning in the everyday world

> with a human body and brain.... Such metaphors provide a superstructure for our systems of complex metaphorical thought and language.... [We] think and speak metaphorically whether we want to or not.... Further, since our brains are embodied..., many primary metaphors are universal because everybody has basically the same kinds of bodies and brain and lives in basically the same kinds of environments. (Lakoff & Johnson, 2003, pp. 256–257)

Where Learning Occurs

Over a lifetime, an embodied brain continuously constructs and reconstructs myriad neural networks made of the raw material of memories, emotions, models, maps, images, metaphors, and analogies that comprise what the brain knows. These are indicated in the figure as words scattered inside the outline of the body to signify that they are neither actual entities nor located in any particular place. Bits and pieces, or *traces*, may be accessed through multiple networks and have no inherent meaning.

Each stimulus contributes to established networks through a process of association and categorization facilitated by the activity of white matter, which carries signals throughout the brain (not pictured). The changes that result from continuously elaborating, linking, and reconstructing patterns of connection are what is called *learning*. These changes affect our beliefs and behaviors, but we don't recognize (re-cognize: know again) we are learning unless or until we can verbalize to ourselves or others what we currently think or feel. This happens only on the other side of the Curtain of Awareness in the figure.

Despite this endless whirlwind of activity, it is important to remember that the brain wants to conserve energy. If it isn't urged

Figure II.2 Lazy Brain

to think, it won't. (See figure II.2.) Though it's always ready to leap to attention when danger threatens, in the ordinary course of events, the brain will avoid extra effort by connecting new inputs to well-established patterns.

In addition, activities focused primarily in LH (usually word based) are processed more quickly than those that require more RH input (usually imaginal or body based). Once LH appears to have an answer—that is, an association has been found—the potentially more creative or innovative RH approach may be shunted aside. In other words, though they always work together, the RH may be treated like a junior partner. Because it doesn't speak up for itself, its contributions can easily remain in the background—leading, perhaps, to the feeling of disembodied mind (see "The Body Paradox").

As expressed in our metaphorical sketch of the *Theatre of Knowing*, the LH's primary concerns tend to find expression in front of the Curtain of Awareness, the audience side; the RH's primary activities occur behind it, the stage side. Important to note,

The Body Paradox

Though RH and LH always collaborate in the construction of knowledge, they play very different parts. RH sees things whole, in relational and empathetic context, whereas LH sees separate, impersonal elements that it can manipulate for its own utilitarian purposes (McGilchrist, 2010). Because LH can verbalize its perspective whereas RH communicates far less directly, we are left with the subjective impression that we have a mind that is separate from our body. (Perhaps this is how Descartes could wonder whether he had a body.)

this gauzy curtain does not represent the typical heavy drapery that goes up at the beginning of a theatrical performance and comes down at the end. It is analogous to a special theatre curtain called a scrim—a light, filmy fabric that can be visible or nearly invisible, depending on lighting. When lit from the front by houselights above the audience (in our sketch, the side of verbal expression), everything behind a scrim is invisible. However, if the house lights are dimmed, whatever is behind the scrim (the embodied brain side) is illuminated by spotlights and thus becomes visible, even if somewhat gauzily indistinct. Reflectivity is key to that illumination.

From the perspective of brain function, learning takes place behind the curtain, but we cannot recognize this tacit knowledge until (unless) it is verbalized. As famed philosopher of science Michael Polanyi (1969) noted, "We know more than we can say." Even so, tacit knowledge can help the brain make wise decisions we are unaware of based on experiences we don't remember having had and learning we can't name. Unfortunately, we can also make poor decisions based on associations we are equally unaware of. For example, assumptions about "us" and "them" are often based on early and self-confirming cultural distinctions rather than on currently reevaluated experience.

Where Facilitators Focus

This brings us to the far left side of the image, where we do have conscious awareness. This is typically the focus of most ALFAS' activity, primarily on what can be made explicit: theories, ideas, analyses, concepts, feelings (that can be named) realizations, insights, discoveries, images (that can be named), descriptions, applications, and so on. Even so, to make sense of these activities and experiences—that is, to learn from them—they too must be processed behind the curtain, beginning again with sensory data. Then—unless this is entirely skill-based or performance-based learning—for the new knowledge to be re-cognized, it must be verbalized.

Continuing with our metaphorical storyboard, when ALFAS create body-based experiences—as compared with experiences that focus primarily as a conduit for words, such as a lecture or other static presentation—we effectively dim the house lights. If we then encourage adults to reflect on the body's experience, we attempt to have them illuminate aspects of what is going on behind their curtain. Furthermore, our invitation to create wordless expression through movement or any other art form—to externalize in some way whatever feelings, ideas, questions, experiences, or other aspects of knowing are emergent for adults at that given moment in time—offers another opportunity to peer through the curtain.

Intentionally reflecting on such nonverbal experiences invites the body to speak its mind. Reflection is thus a bridge between tacit and explicit aspects of knowing. What the adult's embodied brain is tacitly learning can rise to awareness through reflection. At the same time, reflection on what is in process of being known—what is at the threshold of being verbalized—may enable the adult to further refine and elaborate the neural networks that constitute this new learning. Furthermore, the process of feedback—support and challenge from ALFAS and others—can encourage that ongoing reciprocal learning activity (feedback is discussed further in chapter 8).

Organization of the Chapters

Building on the premise of the *Theatre of Knowing,* we explore five interwoven brain-aware approaches for ALFAS to consider, adopt, and adapt. Chapter 4 examines approaches that anticipate and alleviate adults' anxieties and also encourage their active participation. Chapter 5 describes approaches that initially emphasize LH orientation and chapter 6 those that initially emphasize RH orientation. Chapter 7 focuses on multifaceted approaches where LH and RH are consistently integrated. Chapter 8 examines the importance of reflection and feedback in continuously engaging both hemispheres. We **bold** contributors' names the first time they appear in the narrative of any chapter and again in association with their own approaches. See Contributor Biographies to learn more about them.

Experienced ALFAS will no doubt recognize many familiar facilitation practices. We trust that you, like us, find it rewarding and illuminating to discover facets of your own practice highlighted here, as well as to see how other ALFAS apply and extend them. We also imagine you will find new approaches to examine and modify with your own settings and practices in mind.

Key Ideas

- The fact of embodiment affects the brain in two ways. First, the only portal to the world outside our skin is through the body's five senses; second, our understanding of what we experience about that world is ultimately a function of how we experience our body in relation to it—through analogy and metaphor.
- The changes that result from continuously elaborating, linking, and reconstructing neural connections are what is called *learning*.
- Reflection is a bridge between tacit and explicit aspects of knowing.

4

Setting the Stage for Learning

For the things we have to learn before we can do them, we learn by doing them.

—ARISTOTLE

EMBARKING on new learning can be exhilarating, but many aspects of adults' prior learning experiences can contribute to anxiety. New situation, new people, new facilitator, new material: *yikes!—tigers may be ahead!* In addition, when adults walk into the classroom, they bring with them echoes of every teacher, counselor, trainer, coach, advisor, or family member they have ever known and carry the embodied burden of long-forgotten experiences of feeling inadequate as learners. (See figure 4.1.) Given the reality of negativity bias, these experiences are more easily aroused than positive experiences are. Many adults are confronted with both ghosts of learning past and the current threat of being seen as not knowing or wrong. Most ALFAS (adult learning facilitators in any setting) realize this intuitively. As **Ron Stadsklev** notes, "Adults tend to come in feeling ill at ease"—but aren't necessarily certain how best to respond.

Figure 4.1 Crowded Brain

Creating and Maintaining the Environment

In keeping with the overarching metaphor of *Theatre of Knowing*, we liken this chapter to the preparations before the performance starts, hence, setting the stage. To create an environment that can reassure an anxious brain and ready it for learning, facilitators need to attend explicitly to the body, where hormone production is increased and traces of prior emotions still linger. This can be simple and direct, as when **Joe Chen** invites adults to name their anxieties, or elaborate and multifaceted, as in **Dean Elias**'s Forming a Learning Circle. Other contributors describe several approaches for how best to welcome adults into the learning space.

In our own practice, we have seen that adults rarely come alone to any learning situation; they bring with them an invisible crowd of many voices and messages, past and present. We find it helpful to acknowledge their veiled presence. For example, shortly after a new session begins, we ask, "How many people are in this room?" After the number is established, we say, "Actually, this room is far more crowded than it appears," and we ask participants to take a couple of minutes to recall messages about themselves as learners that are still with them and the people and situations they associate with those messages.

We provide paper and crayons or colored marker so that everyone can sketch—without writing words—who those people are and what those messages were.

Knowing that many adults seize up at the word *draw* (including renowned adult educators, see Stephen Brookfield's disclosure in chapter 5), we immediately let them know that everyone will use their nondominant hand, to avoid the likelihood of creating art. Plus, once they have recalled the person or occasion they want to highlight, they will have only a minute or so to produce the sketch. We explain that the physical act of moving the pen or crayon on the page to create an image engages a different part of the brain than a verbal description. With that kind of lead-up, especially after we demonstrate on the board some of the scribbles, doodles, stick figures, or smileys and frownys that are the extent of our own artistic capabilities, people good-naturedly do it, though sometimes still mildly protesting.

Even so, debriefing their sketches can evoke powerful feelings most adults are quite willing to share. They often report, whether laughing or misty eyed, that revisiting those experiences lightens their load of negative messages.

Whether the messages were positive or negative, we then invite our participants to take charge of what it means in terms of how they now see themselves. They get to kick some people out of the room and invite others to stay; they may even welcome in someone new. The ensuing discussion about who and why gets at their deeper feelings and suggests ways to take charge of or soften negative messages. Occasionally an adult will hold on to a negative voice, perceiving that it can be motivating. We then move to a discussion of anxious and curious brains, so they understand that both states of mind are expected and that they can continue to seek support and exercise choice.

Joe Chen explicitly acknowledges adults' emotions and lets them know anxiety and uncertainty are normal and to be expected. "Because I realize that unspoken anxiety can become uncontrollable worry," he gently invites discussion of their current state of mind. *Why are you anxious? What are you anxious about?* Joe notes that whereas some cortisol can spur motivation, "too much is paralyzing." Moreover, the emotional centers of the brain are also involved in memory formation, "so attending to their emotions can help learners make more robust connections between and among self, the material, and others." Having their experience validated—and finding out they are far from alone—can be a first step in adults' ability to calm their anxious state of mind. In effect, Joe invites adults to put a new twist on their old stories of who they are as learners.

The extent to which we can tell our brain (or somehow have it tell us) a convincing contradictory or alternative story determines our capacity for reappraisal, that is, regulation of emotions. The other approach is suppression, which means maintaining outward control without changing one's internal experience:

> Suppression and reappraisal differ in nearly every way. Suppression is better at making you look like you aren't distressed, whereas reappraisal is better at making you feel less distressed. Suppression is more mentally distracting, and if you engage in suppression during an interaction with someone, it will actually interfere with your memory of the interaction. Reappraisal doesn't cause the same memory deficit. (Lieberman, 2013, pp. 218)

Adults who stay anxious but don't allow themselves to acknowledge their feelings may learn very little. When ALFAS create situations that support adults in reappraisal rather than suppression, we may be greatly enhancing the outcomes of that learning experience.

A check-in is a useful approach to reappraisal. Everyone is invited to name the issues forefront in their consciousness as a way to set them aside, at least temporarily, thus creating space for learning. Someone who just had a near miss while driving, for example, is in no shape to pay attention to the present moment. Less dramatic provocations (perhaps a sick relative) and even joyful experiences (an upcoming celebration) can also divert adults' brains. Being able to briefly describe the most prominent current distraction goes a long way toward mitigating its effects.

When introducing check-in as a process, ALFAS, sometimes in collaboration with the group, should also establish norms that appropriately limit the time spent on this, with the understanding that major issues, such as a death in the family, may require more attention. As an added benefit, sharing meaningful issues with peers contributes to bonding, which can be especially important in cohort-based settings. Even so, no one is required to check in and anyone can simply pass.

In a similar vein, at the beginning of any first session, **Ann Stanford** asks adults to freewrite for a few minutes about whatever they need to leave behind in order to focus in the here-and-now:

> *Let it rip!* I say. When they've done that, I tell them to ball up the paper and throw it into the middle of the room. There's usually laughter and more than a little determination as they symbolically fling away their distractions and anxieties. Plus, the physical activity gets their bodies into it. The combination of writing and throwing helps them get centered for the rest of the learning period.

Ann's and Joe's intuitive approaches are confirmed by brain research. Lieberman (2013) notes that without our necessarily realizing it, "putting our feelings into words or simply being able to label them can regulate our emotions" (p. 219).

Exaggerating the internal threat or anxiety can be even more effective in attenuating it. For example, when prompting adults to name their concerns, ALFAS can suggest that rather than say something like, "If I am called on, I will be embarrassed," adults may choose to write (or say aloud), instead, "The earth will crack open under my feet and I will disappear, never to be seen again," or something comparable—which is much closer to how the anxious brain really feels. In fact, the group will probably laugh when the facilitator says it. Once the words are written or spoken, the absurdity is obvious and anxiety has a hard time hanging on in the face of laughter.

Ann also creates an anxiety meter by sketching the outline of a large thermometer on the board or a flip chart. "Every so often," she says, "I take their anxiety temperature and we briefly examine what's causing it to go up or down." People can call out their "number" all at once or quickly in sequence, and Ann estimates what the group's average is. Or the group can playfully name the indicators, for example, "freaked out," "confused," "getting it," "making progress," "Nobel Prize." If one or two individuals are noticeably below the mean, Ann can later engage them privately in discussion.

As a corporate trainer whose primary instructional modality is applied improvisation, **Sue Walden** emphasizes movement and metaphor: "I'll also echo the corporation's stated needs when I introduce the workshop outcomes, such as, 'This will be about improving teamwork skills,' or 'We're here to frame the big picture.' Language matching can reduce a group's resistance by answering the concern, 'What is this physical stuff all about?' as it is so different from their expectations."

Sue also scaffolds students' initial experiences with embodied learning, starting with uncomplicated exercises where adults are immediately successful. "Without realizing it, they quickly move into greater receptivity to riskier embodied activities." (For an interesting twist on risk as a platform for understanding learning theory, see **Tony Saddington's** Taking a Risk in chapter 8.) Sue notes:

> I have to design for the potential sense of risk that some people feel—even those who are very willing to be there and contribute. Sometimes even getting them up out of their chairs can seem risky. [Paul Loper notes this in chapter 6.] A guaranteed win can give their curiosity about what happens next a better chance to develop.

Sue starts with verbal games because they are familiar to most people; then she progresses to more challenging activities that often use physical metaphors. As one example, an exercise in team building, participants will have to symbolically create something together that requires their active collaboration. (**Pamela Meyer's** folding a blanket in chapter 6 is a similar activity.)

Though participants sometimes want to stay longer at the more familiar verbal level, Sue tries to build quickly toward the physical and embodied. "More whole body is better," she says. "Multisensory makes learning sticky." She elaborates:

> Of the different ways people learn—visual, auditory, kinesthetic—the last one, doing, is the least used in most learning settings. That's unfortunate, because the body is a storehouse of information, and the more modalities you use, the better. We don't realize how much we rely on what the body already knows.

Tapping into people's tacit or body knowledge can wake them up to new learning of other kinds in other contexts. "When you turn off—relatively speaking—the cognitive, you can access other learning approaches." Sue also emphasizes the importance of play in contributing to body awareness:

> With play you get participation and full engagement—plus you inspire curiosity. That opens the door for exploration, experimentation, and more learning. Having it be playful reduces resistance because people are relaxed. The minute they start to laugh, stress goes down. When you are nondefensive and unguarded, learning of all kinds happens more easily.

During his workshops, classes, and group facilitations, **Donald Proby** works both initially and continuously to prepare the environment—including adults' brains—for interaction, receptivity, and learning. Similar to several other ALFAS' practices, he finds that inviting participants to be attuned to their bodies is a major step toward accomplishing that goal. Having trained years earlier as a massage therapist, Donald is acutely aware of the brain's embodiment: "People have many more nerve cells throughout the body than there are in the brain and spinal column. The gut, for example, is known as the 'second brain.' That's why people experience a feeling of knowing that is so much more than just cerebral."

He usually starts with some movement-oriented exercise and as the day goes on will do regular somatic check-ins, such as, "How are you feeling in your body right now?" to bring participants back to that awareness. Donald also sets up the expectation that they will frequently be invited to move so that it doesn't come as a surprise: "Adults tend to become more engaged, prepared, and excited about the content when I consistently take them back to body awareness, in addition to the usual cerebral activities."

Donald starts out with a brief or guided meditation "to help clear the noise and clutter that is clamoring around" in their brains and nervous systems. He says that this "slows down the mind," making it more receptive to what will follow.

Though at one time meditative practices such as centering or guided imagery were perceived as outside the mainstream, research has increasingly affirmed that these are valuable ways to encourage or enhance the brain's relaxation response. Harvard Medical School professor and neuropsychiatrist John Ratey (2002) writes, "Gradually, the mind becomes quiet and deeper levels of awareness are reached. The body has a physical reaction to this altered state of consciousness . . . [helping to] reduce high blood pressure, relieve chronic pain and migraine headaches, and soothe depression and anxiety" (p. 376).

Derise Tolliver Atta also invites the "whole person" into the learning space at the beginning of each session:

> I bring forward the centrality of the spirit, so we can focus on work and play together while leaving life disruptions behind. To help adults release their life disruptions I create space for *being present.* I turn down the lights and play soothing music, such as Tibetan music or earth/nature sounds, and talk them through a brief guided imagery.

She directs adults to breathe deeply and slowly while she gently prompts them to revisit events of their day up to their arrival at the present moment, "breathing out the tension; breathing in focus and presence." Derise adds that for facilitators unfamiliar with guided imagery, simply directing people to take several deep breaths can also serve to bring them more effectively into the present. Deep breathing alone can trigger the brain's relaxation response. The *guided* part of guided imagery can be a plus, but it is not essential.

Specific Approaches to Embodied Learning

Having offered experienced ALFAS, general observations about preparing and maintaining an environment for embodied learning, we now focus on specific approaches that may be adaptable to various settings.

Body Awareness

Pamela Meyer first creates concrete experiences and interactions that later become a platform for more cognitive activities. She begins with the simple act of *noticing* and what she calls "bringing the body into the room." For example, to get adults up and physically interacting, she may have the group participate in a simple, fun activity—perhaps passing an imaginary object around a circle and inviting each person to transform the object into a new one before passing it on—something designed to be playful, light-hearted, and as risk free as possible:

> Then I'll stop the activity and say, "What are you aware of in your body right now?" I'll have them focus more intently by asking questions such as: "How do your shoes feel on your feet? How does your hair feel on your head? How do your glasses feel on your face? How do your clothes feel on your body as you move? How does the air in the room feel on your skin as you move through it?"

Having heightened participants' attention to what they are experiencing in the moment, Pamela then expands her directions: "Notice your body in space; notice the other people in the room, the space between you and around you."

This kind of activity is designed to alert adults to the fact that they *have* bodies, that they can *notice* their own bodies in relation to the environment, and that their bodies will be very much *present* in whatever other learning transpires. As they go on to encounter other aspects of embodied learning, Pamela's approach also fosters anxiety-reducing playfulness and invites curiosity.

Creating Connection

Caroline Kisiel knows many adult learners have first-day jitters in any new learning setting. She helps shift their perceptions from *we are strangers* to *we are a learning group* through interactive movement activities that introduce participants to each other in non-threatening ways. Their first task is to briefly exchange stories that, she assures them, "don't have to be too personally revealing."

Caroline guides their storytelling according to the InterPlay (see contributor biography) principles of affirmation and looking for the good: "We live in a society that is more about critique than praise." She counteracts this socialization and "the brain's tendency to focus on the negative, on what's wrong, by telling them, 'There is no wrong way to do this.' The movement gets their juices going, gets people used to the physical space, and helps them feel connected with one another."

In this activity, adults tell very brief stories with a series of changing partners. If they are sitting in small clusters, they may simply reposition their chairs. People can also stand and move to a new partner for the few minutes needed to complete the four-round cycle:

> "Find a partner," I tell them for round 1. "You each have thirty seconds to talk about how you got here today." This could be literally or metaphorically. One person talks for thirty seconds; then I tap a small gong as a signal for them to switch roles, for another thirty seconds. We immediately move to round 2. Everyone finds a new partner and plays out the same pattern with a new prompt. This time

> it's, "Talk about something you are excited about in your life right now." In round 3, they switch partners again and the new prompt question is, "Why did you choose this program/class?"

In round 4, there is another partner switch, with the same talking and listening pattern: "What is important to you about [the subject matter or primary objectives of the course, program, or workshop]?" After that, people return to their original places, and Caroline facilitates the group's own sharing rather than leading their discussion in particular directions. "It is important they identify their own knowing about the experience without being led." She says their insights can be affirmed by the facilitator and the group. Then, she says,

> after participants have taken ownership of their experiences, I might ask, "What might you have in common with your peers? What is motivating you and other members of the group to be here now?"

Through this nonthreatening and playful interaction, participants discover they are not alone in their feelings and experiences. "They get off the *afraid island* and start forming community." InterPlay practitioners have found that it takes at least three partner changes to feel connected to the whole group, thus creating safety in the room. Brains that may have arrived on high alert have found like-minded peers with whom to relate, relax, and bond. At the same time, initial threads of content have begun to emerge from people's stories that Caroline may be able to relate to the course or workshop topics that will follow.

Self-Forming Project Teams

Miriam Ben-Yoseph requires teamwork in most of her courses. Yet she understands that some adult learners are apprehensive about working in teams, especially with "strangers" (see "Social

Motivation"). To alleviate their concerns, Miriam offers choice in selecting both teammates and topics. She applies the principle of "get them moving" when she invites adults to form teams during the first session they are together. For example, in her Living and Working in a Global Environment course,

> I post chart papers around the room that are labeled with general topics related to the course, such as Diversity, Home, Customs. Participants walk around the room and stand by the topic that interests them most. As the process unfolds, some adults might also choose a topic because they sense good connection with the others standing there.

> **Social Motivation**
>
> In *Social: Why Our Brains Are Wired to Connect*, Lieberman (2013) points out "the need to avoid social pain and the need to experience social connection are basic needs that can impair learning when unmet" (p. 281).

This process eases the anxiety that many adults might experience when being mandated by an instructor to work together. In return for being able to choose their teammates and topics, Miriam sets the expectation that the team will work in true collaborative fashion. She "will not accept work that suggests tasks were parceled out and then pasted together for their presentation"; rather, she wants to see evidence of the team members investigating and thinking together.

Forming a Learning Circle

In the formal learning environment of a graduate leadership program, **Dean Elias** finds that "receiving people empathically" enables them to "relax into themselves and thus diminish their defensiveness and anxiety." He focuses on inviting people to tell their stories, because "stories are always laden with emotions." It also encourages their intuitive, imaginal, and affective capacities.

Even before that, however, for every class session, he carefully prepares the physical environment to provide a place of welcome and ease. Before people arrive, he reorganizes the chairs into a circle, moves desks to the edge of the room, and plays melodic jazz at background volume. He also provides an urn of hot water, cups, and a selection of teas. As adults enter for the first time, he greets them individually, shakes hands or makes other nonintrusive physical contact, makes eye contact, and engages them in brief self-introductions. Then he takes advantage of the relaxation response:

> When everyone has gathered, I invite them to center. I suggest sitting upright, feet flat on the floor, eyes closed or slightly unfocused. I ask them to take a deep breath that captures distracting thoughts that may be rattling around their brains—and then exhale those thoughts to the universe. Then breathe in a couple more deep, slow, life-giving breaths and, if possible, experience a sense of release. I find this really helps people become more present.

The group then moves to a couple of rounds of checking in. The first is quick and relatively superficial—"name, rank, and serial number"—plus "something about you that characterizes who you are that people in the group may not have experienced yet." This often evokes laughter and playfulness. The second round moves toward greater depth with a more searching question:

> Given that these adults are also practitioners in various fields, I ask them to say something about "what you are doing this for. This program is a big investment of your time and money—what will make this of value to you? What do you fear?" This often leads to more meaningful

> self-disclosure in ways that begin to establish connection and offers an opportunity to address fears in a gentle and sometimes playful matter.

Dean changes pace by going over the agenda for that session, which he finds further dissipates tension. When he hands out copies of the detailed syllabus, he assigns small groups to read a particular section, think about it, frame questions for further discussion, and identify issues for negotiation. He reassures them that his commitment to them is to achieve the purposes described in the syllabus, not necessarily all the specific steps and intermediate learning goals. It represents his current plan of action, and he expects that aspects of it will change in response to learners' interests and needs: "I want them to know I do not expect or want everyone marching in step. We will negotiate changes based on our emergent process. But the changes will always be in terms of moving toward the purpose."

Early in the welcome process, Dean reads a poem; the participants reflect quietly or freewrite for a few minutes on what that experience of hearing the poem was like for them. This usually elicits comments about how they engage differently when responding to a poem than when responding to the linear presentation in the syllabus and how that contributes to their overall learning experience. Almost always, the response is affective and opens different dimensions for sharing. He also invites the learners to bring in poems of their own choosing to be read at the beginning of subsequent sessions.

As do many other contributors to this book, Dean gives foremost attention to creating a climate that is warm and welcoming. He gives adults' brains a chance to quiet distracting "noise" (thus tamping down anxiety) and open up to new possibilities (thus hooking curiosity). Even as he provides the supportive structures of an agenda for the session and syllabus for the course, he also challenges them with the opportunity to shape the course and their learning in ways that are most meaningful to them.

Warming Up to Climate Change

In constructing an annual conference for full-time environmental activists, **Larry Daloz** has to account for the level of anxiety that people dedicated to combating climate change feel about the gravity of the topic. Despite their total commitment to making a difference, the seriousness of the challenge can be overwhelming and debilitating. How, then, to have an effective, informative, and meaningful conference dealing with emotionally charged issues, and still create a safe space where people can protect themselves from overload and possible paralysis?

An added complexity, Larry observes, is that the participants—activists all—"are not drawn to be reflective about or even acknowledge their anxiety. They are inclined to be impatient with a 'touchy-feely' agenda that doesn't seem directly relevant to their most pressing concerns: responding to an increasingly impossible situation." So at the start of the event, conference leaders frame issues in a way that will be most resonant with the expectations of the group. Larry says:

> When dealing with heavy, emotionally charged issues, don't take them head-on. We frame them in terms that people are more willing to explore. Given the emotional quality of what we are working with, it needs to be safe. They need to feel as though they can be honest with one another about feelings they do not often express in words. These folks are struggling with a self-imposed barrier—a form of denial that allows them to go on doing the work they do. Otherwise, you get dragged into a dark hole of despair.

Participants self-select among concurrent conference activities those that feel most appropriate, given their interests and level of comfort or stress about what may be expected of them. Those who want to work at higher levels of intensity around more complicated or difficult feelings are tapped to provide leadership within a given workshop or session.

Once folks are gathered in a session, facilitators invite everyone to share why they are there and what they hope for. Those who are moving in directions that seem most likely to open up the discussion in meaningful ways are acknowledged—tactfully, often nonverbally—thus enabling others to see them as models. Those who are most willing to share their feelings are considered "warmest":

> We then *warm up the room* by using the "temperature" of the people who are the warmest. We set and list expectations for the session—not all of which are discovered initially—and the criteria by which we can evaluate how we did. Now facilitators know where to go and can weave and encourage a set of shared values. That way you start to establish a model that informs the group's activities and intentions.

Larry feels this respectful process establishes an evolving model of experiences and behaviors that other participants might be able to emulate. At the same time, he emphasizes, people must be allowed to be where they are in terms of how far they feel they can go.

This is also a masterful example of creating a holding environment. Robert Kegan, a psychologist and educator whose constructive-developmental model we explore in chapter 9, describes how a holding environment provides the conditions needed for development. All holding environments, he says, consist of *holding on* (confirmation), *letting go* (contradiction), and *sticking around* (continuity). We easily see how this applies to children's developmental needs: a hug when the world is scary; encouragement to venture beyond the safety of the hug; and the secure knowledge that someone is there for them, even if not required in the moment. Less obvious is that these basic elements of a holding environment are also essential for development throughout the life span.

Many ALFAS intuitively offer adults support to quell anxieties and challenge to encourage ongoing progress, as well as a sense of appropriate ongoing connection and commitment. From the standpoint of practice, this may include various kinds of scaffolding and feedback. Other activities that contribute to adults' capacities to engage meaningfully in new learning include reflection and self-assessment (addressed more fully in chapter 8).

Support, Challenge, and Scaffolding

In revisiting the *Theatre of Knowing,* we consider how certain directors encourage improvement in both novice and experienced performers. They support by acknowledging effort and affirming each movement toward accomplishment. They challenge by focusing on what needs to be improved and requiring consistent effort toward greater achievement (table 4.1). Notice that support and challenge are not the inverse of one another. Meaningful learning needs a high level of both.

From the brain's perspective, support may be experienced as tamping down anxiety, but it is also an aspect of alerting curiosity. Similarly, challenge may mean a demand for extra effort, but it can also be experienced as an attractive opportunity. Challenge should not be equated with "negative" or support with "positive." Too much support in the absence of sufficient challenge initially feels good, but before long, the brain gets bored and checks out. Too much challenge in the absence of sufficient support can be

Table 4.1 Support-Challenge Windowpane

	Low Support	**High Support**
High Challenge	High challenge, low support: retreat, perhaps drop out; little or no learning	High challenge, high support: Growth, learning, development
Low Challenge	Low challenge, low support: Boredom, little if any learning	Low challenge, high support: Confirmation, little if any learning

Source: Adapted from Daloz (1999).

overwhelming; the brain freezes or flees. In both cases, adults may still be physically present and going through the motions, but little meaningful or lasting learning is likely.

As our brief visit with Mr. Oog illustrated, the brain was not initially designed for what we now call *thinking* (quick responses? Yes! Thoughtful consideration? No!). Willingham (2009) claims that though we are often curious, "we are not naturally good thinkers; unless the cognitive conditions are right, we will avoid thinking" (p. 3). Without some appealing novel problem to solve (for which the brain will reward itself with dopamine) or likelihood of an external reward (such as social approval that will also lead to dopamine release), the brain will dodge the opportunity, probably by sticking with established patterns.

Fortunately, once adults' brains have developed greater skill and capacity for engaging with increasing complexity, they tend to find such activities intrinsically rewarding and don't require the same level of ongoing external support or challenge to want to keep at it. Many forms of scaffolding offer effective ways for ALFAS to provide both.

If you have ever watched new building construction, you have probably seen scaffolding at work. After a foundation is laid, walls start to go up—mostly skeletal framing that will be filled in as construction progresses. But even before the first level is complete, initial framing begins on the next level. Scaffolding gives workers a secure place to operate from as they extend their reach into the unfinished construction above. It is a temporary add-on that will be removed or repositioned when the newly built areas are solid enough for adults to continue their tasks without it. Given that the brain learns by elaborating new pathways in and between neural networks, the role of scaffolding in fostering deeper understanding and greater complexity makes perfect sense.

Nearly a century ago, Lev Vygotsky (1978) described the Zone of Proximal Development, a major element of which is scaffolding (discussed further in chapter 9). This refers to the space between what someone can do—such as solve a problem or complete a task—entirely on his or her own, without any guidance, and what he or she can't do at all. The zone is where scaffolding can facilitate movement toward what would otherwise be impossible. By providing sufficient structure, including emotional support for the anxious brain, ALFAS encourage adults to venture out to their "growing edges." The scaffold can then shift incrementally as the learner becomes increasingly secure and adept. To counter their sense of not knowing what to do or how to proceed, which would trigger in many adults a brain-stilling anxiety, ALFAS can create for (and with) them a temporary structure within which it is safe to risk the journey into the unknown.

For example, most adults are anxious about having their performance assessed, whether in the workplace or classroom. A reassuring approach uses the idea of scaffolding to frame assessment as a platform for improvement. In the higher education setting, one expression of this is low-stakes or mastery grading. Earlier assignments are weighted such that eventual improvement is what matters most. In some cases, only a final assignment or product counts in terms of being graded. In the workplace, informal, often verbal, reviews are done periodically, leading eventually to a formal performance appraisal.

Instead of being disheartened by a less-than-desirable early performance, the adult remains motivated to improve. In classroom situations, adults' anxiety is compounded by their sense that grades are a measure of their worth, not just an assessment of their accomplishment in a specific assignment. This can be a source of perfectionism—and a vicious cycle where the brain "knows" it can't do well, so it refuses to do much of anything. (Though it is true that "life happens" more often to adult learners, many late assignments are due more to anxiety than circumstances.)

A similar phenomenon goes on in the workplace between employees and their managers. Given the brain's tendency to focus on the negative, informal and occasional feedback, preferably face-to-face or voice-to-voice, that precedes a formal written assessment for the file is more likely to be heard as constructive.

Most adults visibly relax when low-stakes grading or total performance improvement is explained. Especially when adults are treading in unknown waters—perhaps also being asked to learn in unfamiliar ways or perform new tasks—knowing that they will not immediately be expected to perform at top levels gives the curious brain space to explore.

Scaffolding can occur at various levels of involvement and complexity and may focus on different aspects of challenge:

- *Emotional scaffolding* takes into account, in advance, the brain's likely response to new challenges (*Wait! What? Something new? Can I handle this?*) and therefore builds in immediate—even anticipatory—support that is also periodically refreshed. It is also integrated with all the other types of scaffolding.

- *Content* or *structural scaffolding* is familiar as prerequisites. Two- or three-course or workshop sequences that present increasing levels of demand on related topics are also examples of content scaffolding.
- *Process scaffolding* involves iterative small steps that build skills and under standing, such as "draft-redraft."
- *Community scaffolding* addresses the demands of working in groups, whether in a learning environment or the workplace. This work benefits from incrementally moving a group toward greater interdependence and trust.

In the chapters that follow, many kinds of scaffolding are a frequent focus of ALFAS' attention.

Scaffolded Programs

Entire programs—usually cohort-based—may involve many layers of scaffolding, especially if the course sequence is planned such that essential themes are carried forward, becoming incrementally more complex as they are enriched by additional perspectives. Two examples with which we are most familiar:

- http://snl.depaul.edu/academics/graduate/programs/educating-adults-ma/Pages/default.aspx and www.snl.depaul.edu academic sources
- http://www.stmarys-ca.edu/careers/educational-leadership/doctorate-in-educational-leadership-edd/edd-curriculum-research

(?) Pause for Reflection

1. How does your favored way of greeting adults who are about to participate in learning account for the "crowd" that walked in with them?
2. How are you being mindful of the bodies accompanying the brains into the learning space?

3. What aspects of the holding environment are you most adept at providing? Might you need to balance support with more challenge, or vice versa?
4. Are there additional ways you could build in different kinds of scaffolding?

5

Enter Stage Left

We are not what we know but what we are willing to learn.

—MARY CATHERINE BATESON

BARRING disease or injury, the left hemisphere and right hemisphere work together—but not necessarily optimally. Most facilitation focuses on verbal-textual approaches largely identified with LH orientation—theories, concepts, discussion, debate, and so on. Though RH is inescapably also active, as McGilchrist (2010) points out, LH can inhibit more meaningful RH participation. Even minimal attention to RH involvement—movement and metaphor—can begin to redress this imbalance.

Equally important to brain-aware learning is attention to the body. Even highly interactive discussions can be essentially disembodied. As internationally renowned educator Sir Ken Robinson observed in a TED talk, there are people who spend so much time in the space above their necks that they seem to think that their bodies are simply for moving their heads around—he cites professors as a prime example. (https://www.ted.com/talks/ken_robinson_says_schools_kill_creativity?language=en)

Given that the familiar, more typical approach of many ALFAS (adult learning facilitators in any setting) is likely to be LH focused, we start there as well. For ALFAS new to ideas of embodiment who would nevertheless like to put a toe in the water of brain-aware facilitation, movement is the simplest and most direct place to start. **Stephen Brookfield, Urusa Fahim**, and **Gretchen Wilbur** involve movement, sometimes combined with group work.

The positive affects of movement take place on several levels. Just getting adults up and out of their seats starts their blood pumping a little harder, slightly increases their respiration rate (other than glucose, oxygen is the real "brain food"), flexes and stretches muscles (which affects oxygen uptake), and refocuses vision. In short, it generally wakes people up and disrupts what otherwise easily becomes a checked-out, daydream state.

Another potentially positive effect occurs when people are grouped and regrouped. Moving in and out of different spaces and relationships leads to greater alertness. Their brief venture into the unknown will trigger mildly increased adrenaline or cortisol production, which can enhance learning.

Even more substantive embodied approaches might include symbol- or metaphor-based movement activities that speak more directly to RH, as does creating and viewing art in all its forms: plastic arts (sculpting/collage), movement and other performing arts (acting, dancing, improvisation), visual arts (film, painting/drawing), and musical and verbal arts (poems, stories, songs).

Alexis Kokkos, Arieahn Matamonasa-Bennett, and **Derise Tolliver Atta**'s contributions include elements associated with an RH orientation, such as symbolism, art (creating or interpreting), and intentionally evoking emotions or feelings. Brookfield, who also evokes emotions and feelings through discussion, uses technology to create an environment where adults can feel safe to express those feelings. **Miriam Ben-Yoseph**'s approach to case study emphasizes stories that engage both head and heart.

Such approaches may augment more traditional, predominantly LH, learning modalities; we examine approaches in which such elements predominate in chapters 6 and 7. For now, we enter stage left and view typical ALFAS activities through a brain-aware lens. For facilitators who wish to proceed cautiously, these may suggest ways to incorporate minimal changes in current practice.

Rotating Stations

Stephen Brookfield's first approach exemplifies a tentative move in that direction (pun intended). He admits to having only recently considered what he calls the "kinetic element" as something he might wish to employ.

With his graduate students, in professional development sessions, and in conference workshops, Stephen emphasizes issues related to critical thinking and social justice. He carefully organizes discussion and dialogue, a typical LH emphasis, to ensure that all voices are heard. He also strives to engage participants playfully and physically as part of the discussion process:

> I'll have small groups work for a few minutes on a question or respond to a reading that lends itself to being summarized. Each group posts its idea or summary on chart papers I've posted all around the room, then stands next to its chart. At that point, I go around and post another blank piece of chart paper next to the one they've written on.

At his signal, each group, as a unit, moves to the next post around the room, talks about what their colleagues have written, and then writes their responses to both posts. After a few minutes, this is repeated until every group has gone full circle and responded to every other group's multiple posts. In orchestrating this process, Stephen says:

> My "go" signal is often musical. I'll "dance" them to the next post. Depending on the size of the large group, the whole activity may take twenty to thirty minutes, during which everyone has interacted with every other small group's post and response. The approach is much more effective than doing the typical, group-by-group verbal debriefing. The movement also keeps energy and interaction high.

Stephen (2013) is unusually—and delightfully—self-disclosing about his reaction to just the idea of embodied or imaginal knowing. We highlight his admission as possibly echoing what many ALFAS feel but may not wish to acknowledge quite so publicly. (Please note in chapter 4 what we have found to be an effective way of handling fear of drawing.)

> If I'm in a workshop and the facilitator tells me I'm going to create a drawing or graphic representation of my ideas, I'm struck with panic and usually retreat to hiding in the shadows of any small group I can find! What is even worse for me is being told that I'm going to have to use my body as a site for learning.... I would probably feign a fainting fit and be taken to the emergency room! (Brookfield, 2013, p. 185)

At the same time, Stephen recognizes that engagement with the aesthetic dimension can mobilize political struggle and revolutionary potential. He approvingly cites critical theorist Herbert Marcuse's (1964) argument in *The One Dimensional Man*, about art's subversive potential—"that any kind of art, even non-political art . . . was inherently revolutionary" (Brookfield, 2013, pp. 188–189).

Stephen acknowledges that it took him "a long time to realize the importance of the kinetic element." Now, when he includes physical movement as an adjunct to his primary focus on discussion method, "a few people think it's hokey or rushed. Most give it a solid thumbs up."

Anonymous Online Persona

Given the importance of honoring RH sensitivity with regard to social connection (see "Social Motivation" in chapter 4), **Stephen Brookfield** pays close attention to safety in a course on racism. Knowing how socially and emotionally threatening such topics can be, he is intentional about creating an environment that while requiring engagement and self-disclosure, does not stretch adults too far too fast lest they "snap—leave the class or clam up and overtly or covertly refuse to participate." The course as a whole adopts a critical theory perspective:

> We grow up soaking in ideology. We can't choose it or help it. I want to get across this is not about confessing or revealing what a shameful person you are. No guilt necessary, just acknowledgment of the reality that none of us can escape. This is not about your deep, dark, dirty shame, it's about acknowledging how you have been socialized, ideologically manipulated.

Part of his providing safety in a productively unsettling environment is being the first to disclose his own missteps including, if the example presents itself, a microaggression he may have just committed in the class.

Microaggressions are the "daily examples of racism, sexism, homophobia and other forms of exclusions that are embedded in tone of voice, body language, and gestures, as well as direct speech" (Brookfield, 2013, p. 209). They are felt as exclusionary by those on the receiving end even if the perpetrator had no intention toward exclusion. In fact, when it's pointed out to the perpetrator, he or she usually denies any responsibility because that was not the intent (see also Sue, 2010).

Given how difficult or daunting it might be to carry on face-to-face discussions on certain topics, Stephen has developed a way for the class to engage anonymously in real time. He creates a web page (e.g., on todaysmeet.com) that he can project on a screen at the front of the room and asks everyone to quickly create a fictional persona on that site. Stephen then posts a question or item for discussion and gives people a minute or so to think and answer; he does so also, anonymously. When all have responded, he brings up the screen and everyone can see what everyone else has said without knowing specifically who said it:

> This becomes a platform for further on-screen discussion. People can respond and comment more freely than if what they say is directed at a known person. The screen can be left open for further comments and people can continue to respond online, or even during the class. Or I can turn it on and off. Creating the anonymous persona is another way to depersonalize and democratize the environment.

Though he pushes the adults to deal with contentious issues, Stephen also instructs them, "It's up to you what you wish to disclose." If it is too anxiety provoking to discuss their own experiences, he says, "Try to find an example you have seen in someone else that may parallel your own experience. For example, 'I had a colleague who . . .'" By providing safety about issues that ordinarily limit frank conversation, Stephen enables the brain to stay with what might otherwise be a reason to freeze or flee.

Critical analysis and discussion, Stephen's primary approach, which he elaborates in *Discussion as a Way of Teaching* (1999), are typical LH activities. However, given the deep emotionality of the topic of racism, it can be difficult for people to engage openly. When exposure is problematic, as in, say, a televised interview that could lead to dangerous repercussions, technicians pixilate the speaker's face and alter the speaker's voice to make them unrecognizable. Stephen has done this metaphorically within the confines of his classroom. Though he might not couch it in these terms, as we see it, he has used technology to address the RH's concerns with empathy and the need for connection.

Shifting Perspectives

Having for many months at a time alternated living in two cultures, the United States and Pakistan, over the past several years, **Urusa Fahim** experiences her own embodiment acutely. "I feel different in my body in each place. I move and sound and gesture differently, not just because I wear traditional clothes or speak another language in Pakistan, but because in each place my body has a distinct cultural memory of 'how to be.' That is a vivid reminder to me of how we are formed by our cultural perspectives." With this in mind, she uses movement in an unusual way:

> When people choose the same seat, often with the same small group, they may feel more comfortable with the familiarity, but be unconsciously avoiding novel experiences. There is an understandable desire for the feeling of safety that comes with familiar surroundings and with known people or peers. However, this avoidance of the "unknown" carries over to learning new things, especially with adult learners, and can spill over to how they engage with the content of the learning experience. In programs where personal development is part of the learning objectives, such as counseling, their unconscious concern could be about being unable to predict what that change might lead to.

Urusa describes what she calls a "pull-and-push" effect—the pull of curiosity toward new learning and the push of anxiety away from what new learning may entail: "For instance, moving from either/or thinking to multiple perspectives may lead one to question the familiar beliefs and attitudes one is comfortable with or grew up with—a particularly challenging undertaking in Pakistani culture."

Shifting one's place in a classroom could also be a metaphor for looking at the world differently and adjusting the lens through which one typically sees the world. And so shifting one's location physically can be a somatic invitation to shift perspective.

Especially if learners are limited to fixed, theatre-style seating, Urusa will at some point ask everyone to pick up their belongings and move to a new spot:

> It usually begins with laughter—perhaps even some disbelief—and a little apprehension, but often the process of getting up, gathering their things, moving two chairs to the left or a row down, has helped them "shift things," and they sit down again more energized, more ready to focus. If they always sit in the same place, they always have the same *perspective*. I want them to try to *see things differently*, perhaps starting with their literal perspective. Some have told me that their curiosity about what would happen next piques their interest and raises their anticipation.

Urusa also finds that in doing her own work, if she feels blocked in what she is thinking and writing, picking up her laptop and moving to a different work space often gives her a fresh view. It may be relevant that the RH takes in a broad, contextual view, whereas the LH focuses on a narrow, reductive picture.

Both Jigsaw and Case Study are widely practiced approaches to facilitation. We include them here to highlight implicit RH involvement in Jigsaw and to show how **Miriam Ben-Yoseph**'s adaptations to case method create more explicit RH involvement.

Changing Spaces, Changing Minds

Gretchen Wilbur uses Jigsaw, a cooperative learning activity, where complex material is involved, such as in her advanced undergraduate course, Collaborative Inquiry for Social Change. Gretchen chooses this approach because it gets adults moving from one space and group to another. (See "Setting Up the Jigsaw.") "Such movement," she notes, "encourages intellectual movement as well and possibly [as Urusa also noted] changing perspectives."

Setting Up the Jigsaw

Just as each piece is essential to forming the whole picture in a jigsaw puzzle, each person's contribution is essential to forming the whole understanding in a learning situation. In this process, different groups take responsibility for particular aspects of the new learning and then selected members of each group form new groups within which they share their own knowledge and connect it to others'. (See http://serc.carleton.edu/NAGTWorkshops/coursedesign/tutorial/jigsaw.html for a diagram of how jigsaw groups are formed and re-formed.)

For her Jigsaw activity, Gretchen assigns sections of complex or lengthy material to small groups to be read in advance. Members of each small group are expected to immerse themselves in the topic and become as informed as possible about their assigned section. When they next come together in class, each small group meets for about ten minutes to discuss their section and share their knowledge. "Then," says Gretchen,

> I regroup the class. Each new group has a representative from each of the previous groups so that the new group

> has expertise from all sections of the reading and discusses the complete reading for about twenty minutes. Each new group then synthesizes its collective expertise to form generalizations about the whole article for another fifteen minutes or so. Finally, each group shares its insights and generalizations about the whole article with the entire class, to seed further discussion and, with my input, to clarify misconceptions, about twenty to thirty minutes more.

Gretchen finds that this activity is worth the time it takes. Engaging adults in coconstructing knowledge can lead to deep, thorough analysis that generates multiple perspectives. In this case, the collaborative activity also fits well with the subject matter of the course. Adults benefit from seeing how others analyzed the material and thus learn more about the process of analysis itself.

The activity underscores the fact that multiple perspectives are invaluable when dealing with complex material. The structure also makes evident that although not every adult "gets it" immediately, that is no reason to feel inadequate or give up. The brain's sense of social responsibility to the small group also encourages everyone to make more effort than they otherwise might in terms of their engagement with the initial material so that they are ready to contribute as meaningfully as possible to the discovery and discussion process.

The primary embodiment is the movement from group to group as the essentially LH discussion-analysis-synthesis process unfolds. The secondary RH contribution is the hoped-for empathetic connection involved in establishing new and expanded groups and in working through the material together.

Analyzing Case Stories

Case Study is another widely known approach and one that is seen as honing analytical—presumably LH—skills. However, in the social sciences, where it originated, Case Study must be grounded in multiple contexts, an RH orientation.

Miriam Ben-Yoseph adapted the Harvard Business School case approach to subjects ranging from "living and working in a global environment" to "life and career transitions" in both face-to-face and online environments. Even more RH-ish, stories feature prominently in her adaptation, as she sees a good case as a "form of story that engages the head and the heart—both cognitive and affective." She also uses visual stories, such as film clips, "because they carry multisensory messages" and makes use of personal stories from her own and the learners' experiences. For example, to coach adults on how to use a personal story effectively, Miriam shares brief, relevant stories of her own:

> In my global course, we might talk about forced migration—I will share a bit of my story about being forced, for political reasons, to leave my home in Romania as a young teen. In a course on transitions, I might describe having transitioned from being a bank manager to becoming a university faculty member.

Miriam also uses critical incidents, another form of story, to convey, for example, two cultures colliding. The process of analyzing a case involves several tightly scaffolded steps, and, Miriam notes, "It typically takes a couple of cases for adults to get the rhythm." After they have submitted their final analyses, Miriam describes how their processing of the case has affected her own thinking, thus inviting RH connection and empathy. She models openness to being influenced by the alternatives and analyses they offered and, if relevant, what changed her mind from her own initial analysis of the case. This intentional modeling of considering various opinions and, at times, changing her mind is especially meaningful to adults who tend to wrestle with their need to be right. Miriam gives them permission to change their minds. In fact, she says she expects them to, "in some way, about some thing—this is my bottom line."

In addition to the contextualization inherent in the Case Study method, Miriam's approach is built on embodiment. Stories, verbal and visual, can illuminate connections emerging behind the Curtain of Awareness.

ARTiT Methodology

Alexis Kokkos uses aesthetic experience as a spark to transformative learning. The essence of the ARTiT process, a methodology used in various graduate and undergraduate courses in Greece, is to engage adults in critical thinking using artwork as an imaginal prod to generate creative ideas and discussions. *Critical* in this context (and in Brookfield, 2009) refers to its meaning within the Frankfurt School of social and political philosophy (Ozman & Craver, 2003).

> ARTiT methodology is an integrated approach to learning. Through art, we use not only the cognitive dimension but also the emotional and intuitive. Using art emphasizes all these elements working together. We focus on what are considered "good" works of art, as they work best to stimulate thinking. We also use reasonably accessible works to help us reflect, so they tend to be more representational than abstract.

The initial course sessions include readings, discussion, and reflection papers on a focus question that lends itself to social and political critique, the hallmark of criticality. For example, in a course that explores the conditions of modern working life, the focus question might explore worker alienation. The discussions and short reflection papers include the adults' personal experiences and existing knowledge, along with critical analysis of the formal readings. These predominantly LH activities establish a foundation for the introduction of the "artworks," which might be drawn from figurative or abstract art (drawing, painting, sculpture) or the expressive arts (literature, film, dance).

The facilitator usually proposes relevant works of art, although the adults also may make suggestions. For example, for worker alienation, the facilitator suggested Charlie Chaplin's silent film, *Modern Times*, and the participants identified John Lennon's song, "Working Class Hero." "When using a film," Alexis notes,

> we first we ask people to describe what they saw. What visual elements stayed with them—not necessarily just the plot incidents, but perhaps the camera angle or the lighting. Then their emotional responses: How did they feel at various points? Then we move to analysis. How do these images and feelings connect to the focus question? How do they connect to the earlier readings, discussion, and short reflective papers? What new questions or perspective have arisen as a result of the film? Their formal paper explores these links.

Alexis explains that the introduction of the film appears to catalyze more creative analysis and deeper insights. For example, in several scenes of *Modern Times*, the workers' endlessly repetitive task is to use two huge wrenches to adjust two large square locknuts as they advance on a conveyor belt. (There is no discernable purpose for the adjustment, only that it has to be done quickly and repeatedly.) Later in the film, when the factory worker, Chaplin, walks down the street and sees a woman whose dress buttons look like the locknuts, he uses his wrenches to try to "adjust" them also. In the subsequent group discussion, that scene elicited an insight about how dehumanization and depersonalization cannot be contained at the workplace because they affect every aspect of workers' lives. Alexis notes:

> One can feel a shift in the atmosphere when dealing with the work of art. People become more open and expressive of emotions, not just ideas. This tends to promote substantive reconstruction of their initial perspectives. We know this because near the beginning of the first class, adults write a short initial paper about their knowledge, beliefs, and attitudes about the focus question. They do the same at the end of the last class, in response to the same questions. They can see and we can see how their ideas have changed. When they reflect on these changes, they sometimes specifically say that the vivid artistic representations contributed to their coming to see things differently.

These art-related experiences appear to stimulate associations other than the default patterns linked to a lifetime of socioculturally validated beliefs. What began as a fairly typical critical thinking analysis of a social issue opened up to more insightful, empathetic perceptions when the visual images were interpreted with regard to feelings as well. Alexis sees this as a "disorienting dilemma" that enables adults to move in the direction of Mezirow's (1991) description of transformative learning, thus provoking greater self-awareness and complexity of mind (see chapter 9). Note that the four steps in the process of analyzing the work of art echo **Wozniak's** Metacognitive Cycle, **Williams and Kelly's** Guided Conversation Method, and Reed's Journaling Learning, which appear along with further discussion of the analytical process, in chapter 7.

Artifacts of Inspiration

Arieahn Matamonasa-Bennett uses Artifacts of Inspiration in one of two ways: as an assigned project to be completed outside the session or as an impromptu activity during a session. To know when to suggest that adults work on the artifacts, Arieahn listens and looks for verbal and nonverbal cues that something is bubbling up and wanting to be expressed or that some participants "seem stuck in trying to grasp an abstract concept." In either case, "Artifacts of Inspiration are best suited to a situation that emphasizes experiential learning and deep reflection so that learners have a rich source for exploring the deeper symbolic part of themselves."

Arieahn has participants create a physical representation of their symbolic (metaphorical) understandings related to the processes and content. Artifacts can be a drawing, song, poem, photo collage, or any other form of aesthetic expression. The materials available and the learners' imaginations are the only limitations as to what the artifacts will be. Inspiration for these creative works is likely to be drawn from generally LH course activities, such as discussions, their own reflective journals, assigned readings, and in-the-field experiences.

This can happen, for example, when teaching a course in which adult learners who are nearing the end of their undergraduate programs experiment with new modes of learning or new subject matter. One of the course deliverables due at the last session is an artifact of inspiration that represents that adult's key learnings throughout the course. Participants choose their own medium and message.

Because Arieahn wants learners to have "the fun and joy" of mining meaningful learning from their experiences "without fear of judgment," she does not formally grade this piece of work, though she considers it significant. Rather, in the last class session, she invites participants, in either round-robin or poster-gallery fashion, to "share their highly personal symbol(s) of what they have learned—and to articulate the learning that stands out for them." In the discussion that follows these presentations, adults often ask questions and exchange insights and observations.

As another example, Arieahn prepares for participants to engage with an impromptu artifact of inspiration by providing pipe cleaners, moldable clay, markers, colored paper, sticky notes, and other supplies. As with the assigned project, Arieahn tends to use this activity as an active form of reflection. She waits until later in the term to suggest this, when "adults feel safe with each other and with me." She notes that "many adults feel quite vulnerable when asked to 'create something'—shadows emerge from past school experiences during which they learned 'I am not creative.'" (Doug Paxton and Ken Otter describe in chapter 7 hearing similar anxieties from adults they have worked with. And Stephen Brookfield describes himself as being one of those adults.)

By that point in the course, Arieahn has introduced participants to ideas of symbol, metaphor, and theme, and the students have practiced locating these in the readings and during discussions. She explains that in contrast to the end-of-course project, the impromptu activity

> engages adults in creating something right away without having time to be worried about being creative. [Urusa Fahim concurs about the potential advantage of giving adults less time to worry.] Most are happily surprised that they can quickly produce something symbolic. If they are struggling to understand an abstract concept, they are more likely to have a breakthrough by creating something in the moment and also seeing what other people do.

Typically Arieahn allows about twenty minutes for impromptu creation. Some learners prefer to work alone in a nearby space, assuming that one is available. Each participant then has a couple of minutes to explain how her or his artifact connects with the course material and what new learning, if any, the artifacts themselves represent.

Similar to **Ken Otter's** Comfort Me with Crayons activity in chapter 7, spontaneous symbolic (that is, RH) constructions can tap into tacit knowledge with which the explicitly verbal LH doesn't readily connect. Or perhaps it is in the act of construction that the new perspective emerges. In either case, such integrative activities can have surprisingly meaningful outcomes that may not be immediately evident but emerge over time.

Four Corners Perspective Change

Gretchen Wilbur intends this activity to lead adults to "consider complex social issues" by shifting from the perspectives they initially hold to alternative perspectives they must subsequently try on and defend. The concepts she deals with are often "dense and thorny," such as marginalization, inequity, and social change:

does NWCDC address this?

> I start by posing different points of view around a concept—or various viewpoints that may have emerged from class discussion. Then I assign four different points of view to four corners of the room. By physically moving, students literally *take a stand*, as they stand in front of the point of view that is closest to their own.

In this way, the embodied brain activates its preferred *I already know this* perspective. Then Gretchen has them shift—again, literally. Each group moves to a different corner she directs them to (e.g., "Everyone move across the room" or "Move one position around the square"). The groups now revisit the issue discussed earlier, but this time from the perspective assigned to the corner they now inhabit. Following that, one person from each corner—a volunteer or chosen by Gretchen—together comprise a panel that then engages in a four-corner debate. Not only are the panel members no longer in their comfortable default mode, but they also have to debate with their original preferred perspective.

Gretchen reports that "they find the experience powerful and challenging. This exercise pushes them to consider other points of view, ones they often have not been open to because they feel they must defend their own." In this carefully orchestrated activity, adults are prompted to revise the neural networks that comprise their "Broadways."

In their final written reflections, adults' descriptions of being required to shift perspectives suggested that their brains relished the challenge. "Sometimes I walked out with a massive headache. But in a good way," one woman said. Another observed, "Different perspectives give whole new meanings to how you think about a topic. Sometimes what *you* think is a problem is truly a blessing for someone else." And, "It helped me open up to other ideas and possibly see if there is another way to think about a problem that I think I already know about."

Reframing African Diaspora Classics

When **Derise Tolliver Atta** created her Classics from the African Diaspora course, she was concerned that typical readings would not speak directly enough to the adult learners who would be taking the course, mostly African American women. She decided to "turn the traditional notion of classics on its head." The classical material she introduced was authored or performed by people of African American descent. For example, "Our explorations of social justice and human rights included Nina Simone's music." Derise also assigned readings by African American essayists and historians as context for the issues that Nina Simone framed in her music and tackled in her social change efforts.

Derise then constructed an embodied and symbolic activity centered around one of Simone's prominent pieces. "We had listened in class to Simone's 'Four Women,' which represents experiences of diverse women of African descent spanning the 1800s to the 1960s. I formed the class into four groups, representing the four women in the song." Initially the learners discussed connections between the historical perspectives in the readings and the experiences and perspectives that each of Simone's four women represented. However, Derise wanted to engage learners more fully and creatively with issues that speak to them:

> The surprise element was that I asked the groups to create something in the moment, right there in class. For example, they could create a skit, a responsive monologue, a movement piece—something to help their peers appreciate the meaning and depth of the historical perspectives as each group experienced it. I also warmly invited them to embrace the surprise of needing to create something together, on the spot. My intent was to spark their creativity and not give them time to be scared. I find that too much warning can generate too much worry.

Prompted by Simone's song, learners were galvanized to creatively improvise: among the imaginal product that emerged were a story in Greek chorus form, a skit, and a dance. Derise noted that this impromptu activity sparked learners' further curiosity about historical and current issues that confront those of African descent far more than only by reading and discussing them. As an added benefit, these activities connected adults of African descent with their historical past and offered vivid imaginal impressions of meaningful events that they themselves may not have experienced firsthand. Derise adds, "The course also serves an important purpose for students of other cultural backgrounds: exposure to other authors who might be excluded from the lists of conventional classics. I intend that course not be perceived as primarily for students of African descent." For all participants, the various forms of embodied expression, sandwiched between more traditional LH approaches, enlivened and deepened learning.

Learning is embodied. Many approaches in this chapter incorporate various kinds of movement that experienced ALFAS in diverse settings use to foster the potential for change in adult learners. Though serious about learning, they do not approach learning as serious business. They intentionally rattle adults' synapses by incorporating RH-inspired activities. These facilitators appear to enact Mary Catherine Bateson's (1994) perspective that openness to learning and changing is more important than what one knows at any given point.

? Pause for Reflection

1. When engaging adult learners in analyzing and interpreting complex topics, how might you employ their LH ability to dissect elements along with their RH capacity to contextualize and connect the parts?
2. Which approaches in this chapter piqued your interest or suggested connections to your own setting or practice?
3. What might encourage you to try a new approach (or adapt part of one)? What might be a barrier to doing so?
4. How could you find support for doing so and address whatever seems to be the obstacle?

6

Enter Stage Right

Imagination is more important than knowledge. For knowledge is limited, whereas imagination embraces the entire world.

—ALBERT EINSTEIN

AS COMPARED with the previous chapter, which emphasized starting with LH-oriented approaches, contributors to this chapter tend to lead with various forms of embodiment and analogy—hence we now "Enter Stage Right."

Several of these ALFAS (adult learning facilitators in any setting) use physical metaphor—that is, they engage adults in embodied activities that are analogs for the topic being illuminated. For example, **Pamela Meyer**'s imaginary blanket folding raises issues of communication and teamwork. **Tony Saddington** asks people to examine their reactions to taking a risk, which turns out to illustrate the learning cycle, itself. **Urusa Fahim** uses engagement with unfamiliar objects to stand in for the research process. We two use an actual jigsaw puzzle to represent organizing a dissertation-level literature review. **Russ Rogers** focuses intently on verbal metaphor, sometimes with a physical overlay. **Ken White** used participants' embodied experiences to design an impromptu intervention to a workshop that had been briefly underway.

Rather than analogues, **Donald Proby** engages adults in role-playing and embodiment-focused experiences that demonstrate aspects of cultural expressiveness. He also has them experience a kind of listening that contrasts with how most listen. **Pamela Meyer**'s role play enables adults to back into theory, a recurring theme. **Melanie Booth** describes an activity that elicited somatic identification with the topic of the informational workshop that followed. **Akilah Martin**'s scientific explorations engage adults' experiential connections to their actual neighborhoods and contexts. As a result, people who initially see science as a subject totally foreign to them come to recognize themselves as capable of doing science. Similarly, **Jim Iler**'s evocative approach to math transforms adult math-phobics into people who love math.

Each of these approaches also includes elements of traditional facilitation familiar to many ALFAS. Here we emphasize those aspects that are more in tune with what we consider brain-aware facilitation. **Paul Loper**'s approach is last because it is entirely about embodiment. Even so, the content can be applied to various groups and settings, from workshops on creativity, leadership, and communication to formal graduate classrooms.

Folding an Imaginary Blanket

Pamela Meyer's improvisational activity requires both self-reflection and awareness of oneself in relationship to others. It thus alerts participants to their tacit assumptions about collaboration or other kind of group work.

The immediate objective is for groups of four people to silently fold an imaginary blanket. If the group does not easily divide by four, some participants may be assigned as observers. Once the groups are formed, Pamela gives them two to three minutes to work on the task, during which time they may gesture (and almost certainly will laugh) but are not to talk. Then she instructs everyone to pause and asks them what has been going on:

> I want them to start reflecting on their embodied experience during the activity, such as, "What, if anything, did you notice or feel about the physical space and the other groups. How did you negotiate the task? What emotions showed up? How?" I also want them to stay focused on their individual experiences rather than the operational aspects—not, "When he did X, I did Z." The point is to become aware of their own experience rather than jump too quickly on what they or others were doing.

These few minutes of reflection on how each person is experiencing this activity so far, with its emphasis on the individual, sets the stage for the next step of the activity, which adds the element of communicating with one another. Some participants find that this reflection makes the folding task easier; for others, it becomes more complex. Pamela has the same groups repeat the task for about three minutes, but this time they are to reach agreement, still silently, about their next step before they perform it.

When Pamela next instructs the groups to stop and reflect, she repeats the focus on the individuals' experiences. What did you notice this time? Did anything change for you from the first round? As before, she steers participants away from operational aspects, such as, "When I stepped closer, you moved to the side," or, "When we nodded our heads, we accomplished one more fold." After about three minutes of volunteer sharing, Pamela shifts to questions that concern transfer of learning—for example:

> If things went more smoothly this time, what did you do differently—specifically—that helped? If it didn't go

> more smoothly, what did you notice was going on? What assumptions did you make, for example, about how to work together without words? What different approaches did you see being tried or offered? What cues did you take from each other to know whether you were in agreement about what to do and what to do next?

Up to this point, the activity illustrates how Pamela focuses first on the individual experience within a group context. She then shifts participants' attention to the relational learning aspect of the experience and moves the conversation toward connecting the specific experience with the larger objective of the activity. The blanket becomes a metaphor for collaboration. Pamela asks the group probe questions such as these: When was the last time you tried to fold a blanket with your team? What happened when you or someone else tried to move a project along without checking on buy-in of the others involved?

Pamela intentionally positions the "transferability questions at the end of the activity, after participants have had a chance to become aware of what they were experiencing." She advocates using ways of processing activities with participants that can be repeated over time. She advises against "the hummingbird approach—flitting from exercise to exercise, from idea to idea." Rather, her intent is for participants to "explore and heighten"—be in and deepen—the experience they are having: "I want to help learners become more attuned to their embodied experience and develop the habit of checking in with themselves. The more access we have to what we are experiencing, the greater body—pun intended—of knowledge we have to draw from."

From Pamela's illustration, we see how a playful somatic metaphor can be used to seed the conversation about the subject matter at hand while also giving participants an invitation to deeper knowledge of themselves and others. (See "Playspace.")

Playspace

In her book *Playspace* (2010), Pamela Meyer explains the importance of improvisation as an embodied approach:

> Playspace reclaims the very word *play* to open up more room for new ways of thinking and being. Playspace is the space for more play in the system, the play of new possibilities and perspectives, for people to play new roles and develop new capacities, as well as space for improvised play. When we reconceive innovating, learning, and changing as play, we breathe new life into these processes and create the very space needed to ensure that they thrive. (p. xviii)

Taking a Risk

Much of **Tony Saddington**'s recent facilitation efforts have been in programs designed for adults who were denied access to education during South Africa's apartheid regime. Many of them are training to become adult educators, thus magnifying opportunities for the large segment of the population in need of further educational and professional qualifications. Having seen how adults' anxieties can plague them in new learning situations, Tony uses this activity with every new group. He begins by saying, "The upcoming exercise involves some risk. I'd like three volunteers." Everyone wants to know what the risk is, but he says, "Please just volunteer by standing up," and then he waits. One person tentatively stands up, then another, and another. Tony says, "Thank you. That was the risk. Please be seated." "Then," he says,

> we look at what happened. We deconstruct the experience they just had a few moments earlier as well as the larger reality: "Were there any risks in coming here today?" Clearly there are, even if it's only the fact of driving. If we're processing the whole group at once, I compile a list of the risks. It takes about twenty minutes to work

> from there to generalizations about what constitutes risk and how we respond to it. Or I might break them into smaller groups to do the listing and generalizing; then we all come together again to see what we've discovered.

Following this, Tony begins to unpack Kolb's (1984) theory of experiential learning (explored in chapter 9), a major theoretical framework of the course on adult learning. He illustrates his explanation of the learning cycle—from experience through reflection, abstraction, and application—by drawing on the Taking a Risk activity as a common experience. Instead of these adults feeling immediately overwhelmed by trying to grapple with an unknown and abstract theory, "words like *reflection* and *experience* and *making sense*" now feel familiar and can be interpreted in terms of concrete, embodied meaning.

Feeling One's Way into Research

Although in an entirely different setting and culture from Tony Saddington's, many of **Urusa Fahim's** graduate students are daunted by the idea of research. Introductory reading assignments in her Research Methods course rarely alleviate their concerns. Urusa developed two embodied activities that enabled adults in the first instance to back into a fundamental understanding of the task that research represents, and in the second, to deal with a block or impasse affecting their progress.

Backing into Research

Early in the course, Urusa prepares a small paper bag for each adult in which she has placed one of several common items she finds around her house, such as an oddly shaped piece of jewelry, unusual kitchen tool, small sculpture or knick-knack, and so forth—something that is not immediately discernable by touch.

> I tell them not to look inside, but to put one hand in the bag to feel what it is. They can do that once or several times. Then I put a stack of blank paper and a pile of crayons or markers on a table and let them choose whatever they want. Their task is to draw the object still in the bag. When they have done that, I ask them to write a story about the object. Not long—just a few sentences—any kind of story, as long as it focuses primarily on the object.

Once they have written the story, Urusa invites everyone to look at their object, then to participate in show-and-tell. Learners display their object and their drawing, and then they tell the story—usually to general amusement. The participants also describe how the drawing emerged from what they felt in the bag, and, now that the object is revealed, in what way their stories relate to the object (if at all), what surprised them, what worked well for them, and so forth. "And now," she says, "comes the interesting part":

> I connect this activity to the research process, talking about "trying to *get a feel* for their research or their question," which is something that they probably have some inkling or clues about but can't yet fully discern. I point out the assumptions people made based on the shapes and textures of the felt object and how that limited perspective nevertheless led them to certain decisions or conclusions. We discuss how the brain strives to make up stories that seem to fit. After we examine those issues as analogs to the research process, I start with a more formal introduction to research methods.

Urusa noted that participants told her this activity reminded them how often they fill in blanks with assumptions and underscored that what they take for reality is really their interpretation, often based on insufficient information or knowledge. She also pointed out to them that the activity helped make the case for validity or verification criteria.

Overcoming an Impasse

Later in the course, when students are overwhelmed with reading and thinking about the variety and complexity of possible methods they need to consider, Urusa returns to an explicitly embodied approach. In order to get them "out of their heads" and without warning them in advance, Urusa brings in a box of crayons and a stack of papers—"my favorite classroom tools: easy to carry and always available." Sometimes she provides other supplies: markers, scissors, tape or glue sticks, piles of old magazines, calendar photos, pipe cleaners, stickers, and other simple art supplies. Urusa explains:

> I ask them to draw—or make a collage—of their method. Or of their intentions for their research. Or of the feelings they would like to have while they are doing their research: something that stands in for the current impasse. But I ask them not to use any words in the drawing. I'm trying to connect them to places they cannot verbalize. At first they look surprised, but before long, they are happily snipping and gluing and drawing.

As the adults get more into their process of creation, the room becomes silent with only occasional conversations. "This to me is a sign that they are going inward." When they are finished—this takes only twenty minutes or so—all the products are taped up on the walls around the room. Each person in turn describes the inspiration behind her or his construction and any other feelings, thoughts, or questions that have arisen:

> Students often report that while they are creating their art, or soon after, they have had some realization about

> why their research study is so important to them or how they want to go about it. A few mention that accessing and creatively demonstrating their feelings about the task ahead of them helped them deal with anxieties and stress about succeeding and their ability to complete the research project.

As Arieahn Matamonasa-Bennett also noted, in Artifacts of Inspiration in chapter 5, externalizing, in imaginal form, emotions and feelings that adults may not yet be able to verbalize can give the brain a way to say things it cannot yet say in any other way.

Lit Review Puzzle

Similar to Urusa Fahim's approach to graduate students concerned about research methods, our approach with students about to embark on their dissertation literature review also focuses on how to help them work with what they cannot yet know. At the first session, we bring in a medium-sized jigsaw picture puzzle and randomly divide the puzzle pieces among small groups of four to five people.

Their task is to figure out how best to organize the pieces they have (kidnapping another group's pieces is not an option!). They are free to manipulate the pieces in whatever way they wish. As each group works on its plan for categorizing and organizing, a note taker within the group captures the flow of their ideas, discussion, and ultimate agreements.

As we float among the groups, we provide additional guidance in the form of probe questions if they seem stuck:

- Where [or how] do you want to start this task? Why?
- What next steps seem likely?
- What are advantages and disadvantages of the various strategies you are considering?

- Does manipulating the pieces help in your process? If so, how?
- What are you feeling about the task? What does that suggest?

After twenty minutes or so, we elicit from each group a description of its process. By now, most participants have made explicit links to the demands of writing a literature review. For example, they may note:

> "We don't have all the pieces or a defined boundary to fill in."
>
> "We have to figure out how the pieces we have available might connect."
>
> "A few pieces can sometimes be brought together, but connecting piece-by-piece, one at a time, is not a workable strategy for the entire task."
>
> "Making piles according to apparent similarity (that is, color or pictorial theme) is a good starting point."
>
> "What seem at first to be similar identifiers—colors or shapes—may turn out not to be."
>
> "It may take several tries to get a clearer sense of the existing relationships and what's still missing."

A fruitful discussion can then center on how the picture-puzzle analogy differs from the real-world task of the dissertation lit review. The puzzle box originally contained everything needed to complete the total picture; that is not the case with a lit review. Nor do graduate students recreate something by piecing it together again; they create something they design and must also construct their own criteria to guide that design.

Though we had often described "we make the road by walking" (Horton & Freire, 1990) as a mantra for the dissertation process, participants said they now got it in a new and visceral—that is, embodied—way.

Though originally designed for graduate students about to tackle their dissertation literature reviews, the incomplete puzzle metaphor appears adaptable for any group about to launch a creative endeavor that will require building on available information in new ways.

Organizing Metaphors

Embodiment is not related only to movement of the body-brain in present time. As we noted in chapter 3, all metaphor is ultimately embodied. In his role as an organizational development consultant, **Russ Rogers** listens to language as a key to understanding the speaker and helping him or her peer through the Curtain of Awareness. Russ listens "intently, not only to the words spoken, but to the meaning behind the words." Then, he says,

> when I am invited inside an organization, I no longer listen to the story of the problem or current state as the most significant part of the communication. I see the *organization* as a conversation, the *team* as a conversation, and the *person* as a conversation. So I listen for the ways in which the story is told—usually more than once and by various people—as being most revealing of the issues at hand.

Beyond the "what"—the content of the story—Russ listens closely to the "how" of the description—the way it is told. This necessitates that he listen respectfully while actively taking note of the language—the metaphors—that people are using, which may or may not be in their conscious awareness. Later, he will use these metaphors to engage their brains as part of the change process. Russ gives the following example:

> If someone says, "We seem to be going in circles," I might say, "Tell me more about the circles. Would you say that they're the same circles as, say, five years ago? Big circles? Small circles? Fast circles? Slow circles? Anything about their direction? Can you give me an example?" Sometimes, when the metaphor they've used is incidental—a bit like sloppy language—probing will cause it to falter. However, when the metaphor is telling and we explore it a bit, a level of rapport emerges—like creating a sandbox in which we are all able to play. I try to pick up on their words, intentionally using their metaphors or similar ones, and then use these metaphors to help them notice what they are saying.

Once Russ becomes familiar with their metaphors, he becomes more intentional in using compatible metaphors to interrupt participants' existing habits or patterns of thinking. He is not being intentionally disorienting, but rather expanding their capacity for thinking differently—that is, learning:

> Even if I am initially somewhat clumsy in trying to join their metaphorical framework—and perhaps when I attempt to link it to another trial metaphor—I am eventually better able to approach them in a way that aligns with how they see, feel, and/or hear an issue. The trick is to approach their metaphors tactfully so that my using these metaphors isn't perceived as mocking. Once I have found the correct metaphors, we are in a common space for learning and change.

Russ also recognizes that adult brains seek safety in what is familiar and when possible will default to existing patterns.

Metaphor is an effective strategy to help adults broaden their perspectives:

> The adult brain tends to be too black and white—it needs color. We are schooled to think that the environment (place, space) doesn't matter to getting the task done or the learning done. We seduce ourselves into thinking it's just about the content. Use of metaphor can spark the brain to bring color, nuance, and texture back into the world.

For Russ, another power of metaphorical language is that it aligns with how adult brains work (see "Further Reading: Language and Change"):

> The overall strategy with metaphor is playfulness, which usually gets left behind in adult life. We need to limber up our brains to be playful. As Einstein so eloquently put it, "Playfulness is the essential feature in productive thought." I've also come believe that all change is linguistic in nature. Eventually, and frequently initially as well, the way we talk about things—to others and to ourselves—needs to shift in order to open up the possibility of change.

Further Reading: Language and Change

For a constructive-developmental view of connections between language and change, see Kegan and Lahey's *How the Way We Talk Can Change the Way We Work* (2001). (Chapter 9 examines constructive-developmental theories.)

Killing Weeds or Growing Corn

After listening attentively to how executive leadership development clients describe their most pressing issues in terms of the language and images they use, **Russ Rogers** approaches their concerns by joining their metaphorical frameworks. By using their symbolic language or images, he avoids offering concrete suggestions that originate with him. Instead, he evokes intuitive responses that originate with the clients themselves.

In one case, executive leaders seemed stuck on how to prioritize the actions they deemed essential to the economic health of their organization. One option was to focus on growth as the first step to improving the organization's bottom line. The other option was to focus on eliminating unnecessary expenses as the first step. "Ultimately, of course, they have to do both," Russ noted, "but what seemed to be getting them stuck, or keeping them stuck, was an embedded linear premise or assumption—an either/or viewpoint rather than a both/and approach." He needed to break through the impasse of the perspective that froze them in place and didn't allow them to prioritize their options.

Having earlier heard enthusiastic banter among the participants around their experiences of gardening and growing up on farms, Russ used this as a basis for a visual metaphor. He projected a color photo of a young corn stalk growing in a field with weeds crowding its base:

> I then posed a question for discussion: "Do we feed the corn or kill the weeds?" My intent was to lead them to think this issue through analogically instead of immediately defaulting back to their usual position taking. It also introduced the possibility of additional metaphors. What, in their tacit system, might be the analogue of *weedkiller* and *fertilizer*? What about planting hardier varieties of corn or finding a targeted, more ecological way to get rid of weeds?

The ensuing discussion capitalized on the gardening and farming experience in the room and soon evolved into a both/and perspective. The participants saw that focusing solely on the weeds was probably shortsighted, and ignoring the weeds completely was probably naive. Russ knew he could have simply reported to them at the outset his observation about needing to integrate a both/and perspective and then tried to get them to adopt it. However, the visual metaphor spoke to them at a more basic feeling level that didn't trigger their typical cognitive responses.

Later in the day, the phrase *corn/weed thinking* emerged numerous times in the discussion as participants referred back to this earlier metaphor as a way to identify their unhelpful, more rigid thinking. "They had externalized their earlier limitation by identifying it with the photo of a goofy cornstalk and a bunch of weeds—images that they were now beginning to move beyond." At one point, an executive asked Russ to put the picture of the cornstalk/weeds back up as a reminder of the way of thinking that they were shifting.

Pocket Swatch

As an executive coach, **Russ Rogers** also uses explicitly embodied analogies, not only those spoken. In one example, he worked with an executive whose staff complained that he was too gruff or harsh. Although the executive told Russ he understood and agreed with their feedback, he struggled when asked to explain specifically what his staff meant and to articulate what he would need to do differently in response. Russ noticed:

> As he strained to describe what he thought their feedback meant or how he might behave differently if, or when, a desired state were to be achieved, he kept rubbing his fingers together as if trying to describe a texture of some sort. He also used words and phrases like *sandpaper* and *sharp edges*.

Given these kinesthetic cues, Russ tried a tactile experiment. He brought into the next meeting fabric swatches of different weights and textures and asked the executive to choose the texture that best represented "gruff" and another that represented more of what he would like to be. The man had no difficulty selecting the gruff fabric—a thick, nubby tweed—but had trouble making up his mind about an alternative. Finally he chose a soft flannel piece—not silky but much softer and smoother than the nubby tweed:

> I found that as he massaged the swatches in his fingers while talking about and comparing them, he was much more articulate about the topics that had been so difficult for him to describe at the previous meeting—i.e., his gruffness and a possible shift from that way of being. We agreed to an experiment.

Russ suggested that the executive keep the preferred swatch—soft, smooth flannel—in his pants pocket every day for the next two weeks and use it as a tactile reminder of his preferred state each time he reached for his keys or pocket change.

> When we met again, he was animated in his description of how he wanted to be and reported noticing more quickly when he was "not being like this," referring to the swatch in his pocket, he was able to make different choices accordingly.

Russ's strategy demonstrates how directly the body can interpret a physical metaphor even when the mind has difficulty with the concept it represents. This situation was enhanced by Russ's ability to determine the modality—in this case, kinesthetic—to which the executive was most receptive. For a client whose metaphorical language focused on "seeing" and "looking," a photograph or other visual representation of "gruff" might have been more effective.

In the Driver's Seat

Russ Rogers also employs his gift for using metaphor and embodied knowledge in his role as graduate program faculty mentor and instructor. The adult learners are midcareer professionals in the process of trying to design their individualized degree plans based on their interests, aspirations, and experience. Despite their wealth of experience, many are anxious about their skills, capacities, and resilience. Even adults who have been highly effective and successful in the world of work often find the requirement for self-direction—not only in constructing the degree plan but executing it—a daunting proposition.

Russ brings to the first session a model of an automobile dashboard that he constructed from materials available in toy stores. The dashboard is small and light, but it includes a steering wheel and various gauges (or sketches of gauges added by Russ) including fuel, speedometer/odometer, temperature, tire pressure—enough to create a playful image of a dashboard.

> I put the dashboard on a table and invite the adults to brainstorm the purpose of a car dashboard—reminding them that in the history of the automobile, dashboards themselves evolved. Eventually the discussion surfaces something about "providing data to the driver in support of the driver's intention to get somewhere." At this point, I bridge the discussion from a mock dashboard to a graduate learning plan with the graduate student as the driver.

After asking for a volunteer to sit behind the dashboard, in the "driver's seat," Russ interviews the adult along the lines of: Where do you want to go with your graduate study? What fuels your interest? What indicators do you want to monitor along the way to ensure that you're roadworthy? Russ writes each answer on a sticky note and places it on the dashboard. Soon, he says,

> the dashboard is customized to the driver and we are discussing what constitutes a worthy program of graduate study and what it will take to successfully "drive" it. All of these points, which I could have lectured about, are also made in program materials. However, something powerful happens in this playful, symbolic context as the conversation usually continues with extended metaphors.

The ensuing discussion is likely to examine a number of topics:

- What is it is like to be "behind the wheel" of your own program?
- Which of the indicators on the dashboard are likely to be important, when, and why?
- What are the implications of a "check engine" light or "running on empty" warning with respect to one's graduate study?
- What role might "service stations" play while matriculating?

Using the dashboard as a visual metaphor, students interpret and describe the meaning of the various symbols and their applicability to their individualized degree plans. Russ finds that

> the driver's seat/dashboard becomes a physical analogue for self-directed learning. It may also remind some graduate students of the toy dashboards they had as kids, and thus evoke a distant memory of pleasure and safety. It also builds on their ability to read dashboards in real cars and drive themselves where they want to go—just as we are now asking them to do with their graduate learning. Finally, it clearly underscores that I, as professor, am not driving. I'm standing to the side.

write about how these can be used for co-ops

By inviting these adults' brains to see something difficult and challenging (the degree plan and a self-directed graduate program) in terms of something familiar and unthreatening, this approach gives them an opportunity to imagine and feel, at a body level, that they are in charge of this process, rather than at the mercy of it.

Anything to Declare?

Ken White's work with nonprofits and nongovernmental organizations has focused on transformation at various scales, from the group and organizational up to the global. Participants might include organizational members at several levels, as well as faculty and graduate students in both traditional and nontraditional educational settings, often of various nationalities. In such circumstances, Ken notes, "cultural assumptions, which are always present but often largely invisible, can make collaboration—or even just discussion—challenging."

In one case, his organizational group had been invited as participants-observers–*agents provocateur* for an event in which two groups with strong intracultural identities had been brought together to embark on conversations toward collaboration. He found that

> at one early session, it was clear the conversation was not going well. There appeared to be a lack of understanding about the worldviews and work styles of the respective parties. The groups were from two different educational systems, and each group included people of various nationalities. Several misalignments seemed to be creating a sense of confusion and mistrust.

During the break, Ken's group brainstormed an intervention building on the international character of the participants. The metaphor of crossing borders seemed a potentially useful way to build on familiar (i.e., embodied) experiences.

In an area just outside the meeting room, Ken and his colleagues arranged tables and chairs and posted signs (handmade in the moment) announcing that this was the Customs point, the crossing point into a place of trust building and collaboration. Setting up their official domain and roles, they tricked themselves out with name tags and amusing bureaucratic "titles," brandished notepads or clipboards, buttoned up their shirts, and tried to look semiofficial. They also maintained a playful stance, laughing and joking as they moved the participants through the activity. "First," Ken said,

> we herded them out into the courtyard and announced that before they could again enter the meeting, each person had to go through Customs—our little table and chair gauntlet. They would be asked if they had "anything to declare." By "anything," we meant any assumptions they were carrying about other people or organizations, or the nature of the work they might try to do together, or just something they had on their minds. They could get that out now and not have to bring it with them into the larger work session.

Ken's group explained that each participant would be questioned by a "customs officer," who would give them the chance to explicitly articulate whatever feelings or ideas about other individuals or groups might get in the way of careful listening and open attention. Participants easily joined in the role play and queued up in a way that provided privacy for those currently being interviewed.

> In the interview, the simple question, "Do you have anything to declare?" was surprisingly effective. If someone too breezily said, "No, I'm fine," we good-humoredly sent him or her to a second customs officer. That officer might

> remind them, "This is a great place to park baggage you don't need to take into the room," and let them know that if they wanted to pick up that baggage later, it would still be there, waiting for them. That usually got a laugh and a response. There were about forty or so participants, and a half-dozen of us, so the whole activity took about twenty minutes. Participants from both groups called the activity a positive experience of having been heard, and the tone of the ensuing discussion had noticeably shifted toward more open engagement.

Bringing to awareness and verbalizing ideas and feelings that otherwise remain unrecognized can also often attenuate them. Like some prehistoric photophobic organism, anxiety often loses its grip when exposed to the light. Some version of this activity could be adapted to many situations where groups of "outsiders" need to join and collaborate with the "home team."

Multicultural Awareness

In his workshops on topics ranging from community mediation training to diversity training, **Donald Proby** emphasizes the importance of multicultural awareness:

> Although the brain is wired to establish who is "like us" and "not like us," the categories we use to make that distinction are culturally learned. So after we have created a safe environment for this kind of exploration, I provide some context—such as an identity wheel—that describes core identities. [These are available on many websites.] It helps us locate some of the many ways in which we organize ourselves into categories, often without realizing it.

Then Donald uses imaginal activities that involve body-based memories. After inviting people to pair off, he starts by naming a specific real-world experience that he invites participants to bring back into consciousness—for example, cooking a meal, meeting a friend on the street, or going shopping. (Each pair agrees on one topic.)

Participants have a minute or so to revisit the memory of a specific—perhaps recent—occasion. Then he asks them to pantomime the experience: "Sounds are okay, but not words":

> I'll say, "Now pretend you are cooking—pantomime your actions in the kitchen," or, "You are walking down the street: greet someone you haven't seen in a long time," or, in a group that has not yet reached a sufficient level of freedom about body movement, I might ask them instead to briefly journal about their experience—a couple of minutes is usually sufficient once they have agreed on the topic beforehand.

After they act out the experience, Donald asks them to explain to their partner what they were doing (this often leads to laughter: "Oh, *that's* what was happening"), or to explain what they journaled about. In both cases, Donald prompts to help them elaborate the context as they tell the story: Why was this experience happening in this time and in this way? What makes this occasion pleasant or unpleasant? As you were enacting or writing, what associations came up that you might not yet have expressed about experiences in the same category?

When the partners have had a couple of minutes each to share or enact their stories, Donald asks them to briefly validate themselves and one another: What did you most enjoy about sharing/telling your story? What did you enjoy most about your partner's story? Following that, the pairs look for contrasts: What was most noticeably different about your stories/enactments? What was your initial reaction to that difference? "These experiences," he says,

> begin to highlight our invisible assumptions about how we move through life on a daily basis. Do we greet friends with a handshake, a slap on the back, a hug, or a fist bump? Is cooking an elaborate activity that brings us close to family and friends, or are we more likely to open a can or zap a frozen dinner? Is a department store a fun place to go and look around, or a place where we are sometimes followed around by a security guard?

Finally, Donald asks the whole group to highlight any part of what they discovered in their pair interactions, underscoring the fact that each person needs to pay attention to the tendency to conflate difference and judgment. "Ideally, there is no right or wrong way, yet we often assume our own way is better."

Donald sees this exercise as a step in building trust and the capacity to talk about sameness and difference and about some of the life experiences that may contribute to these perceptions. Part of the sensitization toward improving mediators' capacities—or those of anyone else operating in any diverse environment—is to recognize some of the many ways the brain has already assimilated and prioritized cultural assumptions and associations.

Listen with Intention: Empathic Listening

Donald Proby trains community mediators in the skills essential for dispute resolution, conflict transformation, peacemaking, and community building. To be effective, mediators must first develop high-level skills in active listening and communicating empathically. This requires learning with and through the body.

In order to put participants at ease and thus set the stage for the activities that follow, Donald immediately establishes a sense of familiarity by modeling empathetic presence—mirroring that individual's own presence—as each person initially walks into the room.

> For example, I note their comfort level around body ease or tightness. If someone is being formal, I meet that with a similar level of embodied energy and formality. This is not mimicking, but meeting individuals where they are. By matching their energetic approach, I seek to evoke in them a more relaxed, engaged way of feeling and being as we move on to the specific activities that are the focus of the workshop. Through kinesthetic intelligence, I am better able to contextualize the interpersonal experience and perhaps, better understand where people are "coming from."

Donald finds that becoming better communicators depends on participants' first becoming more intentional listeners. "For many people," he says, "*listening* is what they call thinking about what they want to say next. So we start by working on this typical cultural habit."

Before explaining the theory behind active listening and why it is important, Donald has adults engage in a three-part embodied activity. (With twenty people, it might take forty-five minutes to an hour.) For the first round, they are invited to pair off and take turns telling one another the story of recent conflict in their own lives—one they are comfortable sharing. For the activity,

> each person has three or four minutes. I ask them to *just listen* to their partner, which means no body language, no facial expression, no verbal or audible responses. This isn't about being a robot or a stone; it's an invitation to just be present without the usual outward demonstration

> of being present. Essentially, listeners are asked to be empathic at their core, in whatever way that shows up for them that does not include facial or body movements, or sound.

Donald debriefs the experience with the whole group by asking, "How did it feel to listen and not use your body or words at all?" He then shares with them "some of the things I noticed in the room."

> Even though they are trying to just be present, people engage in all kinds of nervous listening habits: smiling, nodding, looking away. Others are being stiff and rigid. I don't identify any specific individuals, but when I name and even exaggerate these ingrained habits, people start laughing—which is usually a sign of their releasing tension they are holding in their bodies. I explain that while a mediator may choose to use certain communication habits to create connection, it has to be done with intention and awareness, not because they can't help themselves.

For the next part of the activity, one person in each pair moves around the circle, establishing new pairs. Then everyone tells their story again, to their new partner.

> This time the listener may use body language, but use it *with* awareness. I ask them to be mindful: "Notice what you are doing with your body and why." After that I again ask them how it felt to listen or to be listened to in this way.

Donald says another thing that often emerges during the debriefing process is that the storytellers start to notice rehearsal patterns in their repetition. These tend to reveal how they have positioned themselves within the conflict. By habit, people reinforce their patterns. However, the opportunity to be heard and validated from someone outside the conflict—an empathic listener—may enable them to let go. It is important that a mediator learn—and, even better, experience—that aspect of the multiple dimensions of conflict.

For the third round, half the group again moves to create new pairs and retells their conflict story. This time the listener may use body language and verbal acknowledgments, again in a mindful way. "I remind them," he explains,

> "Don't interrupt just to say something or just to prove your attentiveness. Be aware and intentional in your actions." Afterward, I first have them debrief within their final pair, sharing their discoveries and getting feedback from one another. Then I ask people to share with the group as a whole: What did they experience as listeners in each phase? What did they experience as speakers in each phase? What was going on in their bodies? I also speak to patterns I have observed as the process has unfolded.

By the time participants have gone through three rounds, they have identified areas in their typical response patterns—some physical, some emotional—"where they may need to make new decisions." Making these observations out loud and finding empathy and support in the group is an important step toward embodying change. Donald uses this experiential activity as a springboard to a discussion of the theory of active listening and its importance not only in mediation but also with a spouse, in the workplace, or within a community. Days and weeks later, learners in the training frequently report that the active listening alone had immediate application and impact in their personal and professional lives. They find that by listening deeply and empathetically, they are able to more effectively support others in transforming stress, alleviating strain, and overcoming difficulties.

Generating Hunches

Pamela Meyer teaches practitioners, some of whom are—or will be—adult educators, as well as in other fields. "A big challenge for practice-focused adults, Pamela said, "is having to focus on theory and understand how their experiences can be a basis for theory generation." Having once directed improvisational theatre, Pamela knows that adults can learn by doing and cocreating first, then reflecting and conceptualizing or generalizing afterward, so she begins with a playful, no-stress-attached scenario:

> I might say, "Frank's cell phone rings in the middle of our class session. He answers, listens briefly, and then jumps up and runs out of the room. What's going on with Frank?" They start to generate possibilities, some serious, some humorous: *there's a medical emergency; he won the lottery; a pipe burst in his business and the place is flooding*, and so on. I point out that generating these possibilities is actually a rudimentary form of theorizing. Then I work with them to continue building on this awareness.

Working with the whole group, Pamela continues to ask questions that encourage further conscious hunch generating or theorizing: "If X is your theory about what's happening with Frank, what might you need to do to find out?" Pamela helps them notice that it is important to try to verify their hunches or theories in order to use them effectively in planning subsequent actions because

> for many adults, the idea of theory seems out of reach to them. They don't easily see that many of the choices they make in their everyday life and work are based on their active, if unconscious, engagement in theorizing.

Pamela's approach—to focus first on adults' theories in use—is in line with what many experienced adult educators have found through practice, and runs counter to the more traditional assumption that a formal introduction to theory should precede application. In general, beginning with what the body already knows can often be more effective than trying to introduce something the adult's brain does not recognize as familiar.

Rather than being confronted with an unfamiliar theory, which is likely to be anxiety provoking, adults are invited to rediscover and build on what they already know and can do (nonthreatening and, in the case of a scenario such as that above, also fun and laughter provoking). At that point, being asked to reframe something familiar in a new (theoretical) way is simply elaborating a connection to an existing (embodied) pathway. The understanding that "I have been theorizing all my life" is an important shift of perception from theory as an unknown and slightly scary new idea to becoming a theory generator and user.

Poverty at a Distance

Melanie Booth participated in a powerful and evocative embodied activity that remains etched in her memory. In a brief introduction at the start of the workshop, the facilitator, Donna Beegle, (http://www.combarriers.com/), described her personal and professional experience with the topic of generational poverty. She then asked everyone—over one hundred people—to step outside and line up shoulder to shoulder. Melanie notes it was a lovely day and there was a wide, flat lawn available:

> Then she read out a list of questions and you either stepped one pace forward or one pace back, according to your answer. For example, if you own your own home, step forward. If you rent, step back one pace. If someone in the family owns a vehicle that is used primarily for

> recreation, like a boat, RV, or classic car, step forward. If you have a BA degree or higher, step forward. If your parents did not complete college, step back. Advance a step if your parents paid for your education. Step back if you have ever been unemployed for more than a year when you didn't want to be. And so forth. Based on your answers, sometimes you advance, sometimes you lose ground.

It took only a few minutes to run through the twenty or so questions, and by that time, people were spread all over the lawn. Donna then said, "Would the people nearest the front please turn around." "It was suddenly very clear to everyone," said Melanie,

> that the people in front, who had the most advantages, would not see the people behind them unless they turned around, whereas the people nearest the back could see everyone ahead of them. Then we all returned to our small table groups in the hall to debrief.

Melanie noted that people who had chosen to observe rather than participate in the activity (the facilitator had offered that option) were still able to contribute from that perspective.

> After we debriefed the activity, Donna went into the rest of the workshop, which was a much more typical PowerPoint-focused presentation infused with a few opportunities for small and large group conversations. But that physical experience really hooked and grounded all of us. We could feel and see how generational poverty tends to move people back over and over, and that it's really hard, when you keep moving back, to ever move forward or get much closer to the front.

Discovering Science toward Social Action

Akilah Martin teaches a course on what she calls "urban dirt"—a soil course—to undergraduate adult learners. She notes that many of them are "scared to take a course that has anything to do with science, yet are curious about the 'dirt' part." In the first class session, Akilah tells them, "We are going to get into discovery mode," and emphatically encourages adults to forget about any negative past experiences with science.

To introduce the discovery process, Akilah has adults bring to class three different types of soils they have collected in their own neighborhoods. She then engages them in discovery mode by setting up in-class, hands-on activities that "help them relax their minds and be open to learning." She establishes a no-risk environment within which they can learn to identify the soils they brought in and then seek information about what might grow in these different soils. Her goal is to "get them involved in doing science while I am with them during the discovery process, so I can point out aspects of the scientific method in action." She notes that "learners are not likely to link concepts with experience on their own at home, so I want to be there to catch things they don't understand and underscore major concepts."

By focusing these adults on something meaningful and familiar (their "own" soil) and providing reassurance and guidance as they reach toward unfamiliar concepts using unfamiliar tools, Akilah is scaffolding their engagement with a formerly anxiety-provoking topic. It isn't long before many say delightedly, "Hey, we're doing science."

Akilah's larger aim, however, is to connect to adults' emotional responses as they learn more about conditions of the environment they and their community share, a largely RH connection—in this case, through learning about soil in their own urban settings. Her hope is

> that at least some of the adults will feel concern, even outrage, when they reflect on how badly we are treating our environment—that we are leaving a terribly damaged home for our children and grandchildren. I'd like this to spark some advocacy on their part. I'm encouraged when some tell me that they do go on to teach their kids or others in the community about ways to take care of the environment.

As an environmental educator, Akilah believes that "the need to recognize and interact with one's social context is essential because our contexts are not neutral. Recognition of factors that impact our behavior provides fodder for self-reflection and social action."

In every class discussion and in every reflective journal entry, Akilah prompts adult learners to surface their feelings about environmental issues and "to reflect on why they feel a certain way or why they behave in a certain way." Within the supportive climate of the class, she encourages them to focus their new understandings, both content and emotion based, toward forward-looking curiosities and larger implications.

As **Larry Daloz**'s activity, Warming Up to Climate Change in chapter 4, also illustrated, issues with implications for societal survival can arouse emotional responses that are more paralyzing than energizing. Rather than act, many adults seem to retreat into denial behavior and a defeatist attitude as they think, "I can't make any difference anyway." Through her carefully orchestrated balance of support, challenge, and ongoing hemisphere-bridging reflection, Akilah helps adults contextualize and connect (RH strengths) with their potential role in trying to be part of the solution. We return to issues of complexity and commitment in chapter 10.

Backward Math

Jim Iler knows that for many adults, math is the biggest bogeyman of all—even bigger than science—so he immediately offers reassurance because, he says, "They have to feel safe. If they don't, they shut down." He is also careful "not to teach over their heads, or I'll lose them immediately." Rather than start by explaining and working through an abstract formula, he begins college-level algebra with a concrete answer and works backward, calling on adults' intuitions to figure out what it took to get there. This leads to transparency about why the formula works, not just mechanically walking through the steps of the solution. As an example, he uses the addition principle:

> I do it backward: I *start* with an identity statement such as 2 = 2. I write it on the board and ask, "Is that true?" and wait until they answer. Then I add something to one side and ask them what I have to do to protect the equality. They say I need to add the same amount to the other side. Then I do something else to one side, and they tell me what I need to do to the other side. Adults tell me this makes sense to them. No one ever explained it to them this way before; they were just told to memorize the steps and the formula.

Jim also creates carefully scaffolded worksheets, "so they can look at the problems they've solved for hints on how to do the more complex problems." When an adult finishes a problem correctly, he has that student go to the board and share how she or he did it: "Being able to put it in their own words reinforces the learning." He also acts as a cheerleader, encouraging and praising their courage and persistence in going to the board. "We not only have to work on the subject matter," Jim said. "We have to work on their emotional reaction to the subject matter."

Jim creates groups, making sure each group has at least one strong participant, and encourages adults to check with and explain things to each other, "so they are essentially tutoring each other. This is a very different approach from 'do your own work.' I also encourage them to stop me and ask for clarification." He walks around, checking what they're doing, talking them through the work when necessary, "so there's no way they're going to do it wrong." He recognizes that "repetition is important, but repetition of doing it *right*. Then their confidence goes up and they stop being afraid."

> For the advanced courses, I have students make their own textbook. For each topic we're working on, they write down in their own words how to do that kind of problem. That creates ownership. And they can have their personal textbook for the final exam, which is the only time they can't work together. It's open book, using their own notes. I tell them that I believe the purpose of exams is to test concepts, not to fail people.

Jim finds that for many adults, finally succeeding at math is a major victory—one that seems to have positive spillover in terms of how they feel about themselves in other learning situations. This is an entirely plausible scenario, given the dopamine rushes that tend to accompany feelings of achievement and puzzle solving.

Aside from the excellent scaffolding and the deeply caring personal attention, by starting with an analogical approach rather than an abstract formula, Jim's initial backward framing seems to appeal to RH intuition, which creates the basis for eventual LH engagement with abstraction.

Embodying Communication, Creativity, Leadership

Many of our ALFAS contributors found their way to embodied learning as an outgrowth of experiential learning and, over time, elaborated on practices they found especially effective. Given **Paul Loper**'s early background in dance and drama, and later in the study of transformative learning, his practice began with embodiment, and he developed a foundational theory about how movement and analogical experiences contribute to meaningful adult learning. (Pamela Meyer and Sue Walden also began with theatre improvisation and later made the influence of embodiment a topic of their academic research.)

Paul sees embodied learning as fundamental to "dislodge the embeddedness" of adults' socioculturally reconfirmed ways of knowing. As an example, he finds that the invitation to move out of the cognitive and into the embodied is for some adults an immediate anxiety trigger:

> Sometimes if I say to a group, "All right, everybody, let's move the chairs to the edge of the room, stand up and come into the center of the room, and now we'll . . ." They don't even hear the next thing I say because they're, "*Whaaaat*? I don't get to sit safely behind a table holding my notebook or laptop in front of me?" The lizard part of their nervous system fires right up, and they get ready to fight or flee.

Paul attends to creating a place of safety, "so that we can progress through the next hour without people freaking out, mostly because their relationship to their body is so under the thumb of cultural norms." As a performer, Paul is very aware of how self-conscious people are about how they appear to others.

He points out how they can feel trapped by this, without their realizing the source of their anxiety:

> I'm not going to upload a photograph of myself unless it's a good angle. I'm not going to upload a video of me dancing if I'm looking like a fool. So don't ask me to look like a fool, because I don't realize that the layers through which I judge how I'm experiencing this are so thoroughly mediated by society's stories about what looks good or isn't looking good. People have been taught that the body has to be this kind of pretty, this kind of sexy, this kind of good at moving. It's a very objectifying and transactional use of the body—and very affected by twenty-first-century consumer-oriented cultural assumptions.

This cultural overlay exacerbates the fact that the brain fears not only being exposed and vulnerable, but also having others witness that vulnerability, so Paul focuses on a number of ways to creating what he calls a "safe-ish" environment:

> I want to bring people's uniqueness into the room right away. It can be as simple as asking everyone to briefly introduce themselves by describing "one small thing that happened so far today that pleasantly surprised you." In other words, I want their first connection to the group to feel positive rather than negative. Having contributed right at the outset in some way, they are no longer strangers in a strange land.

Furthermore, by bringing in everyone's voice immediately, Paul also helps establish that the participants are valued cocontributors to the activity, not just passive recipients waiting to be judged by others. Working from these basic understandings, Paul creates unique experiences that illuminate the topic of the particular workshop or course.

This approach engages adults at all levels of comfort or discomfort with body expression, largely because there are no right answers and no wrong moves and everyone is on an equal footing with everyone else. Paul has used this activity with widely varied groups, such as a master's degree program in leadership, a Silicon Valley-inspired workshop for designers of apps, and an internship training program for an inner-city community center. He begins in this way:

> At the start of a new session or group, I have three big flip charts on the wall. On one are words like *nose, elbow, right leg*; on another are words like *light, friendly, dramatic, thick*; on the third are *on a diagonal, moving slowly from right to left*, and so forth. Then, as people come into the room, I say, "Please go to each one of these charts and write one additional word or two, based on whatever you think it's a list 'of,'" since I don't put the name of the category on the top.

Then, after everyone is in the room and has added something to each of the three flip charts, Paul asks them to choose one item from each list—not necessarily the words they added—and jot them down. After everyone has done that, he describes what will happen next:

> Each of you, in turn, is going to do whatever you can with your body that enacts the things described in the three phrases you selected. Embody them, be them, play with them—however it works for you. And *we're all going to follow you*. However you integrate, mash up, activate these three dimensions in your body, we're going to do it too.

> We will do our best to join you, mirror you, and engage with you in your own exploration. And that's what it's about: your exploration, not your idea about what this might look like, but what it looks like, right now, as you create it.

Paul says that this contradicts two expectations most adults have: that the expert at the front of the room knows what to do and that there is a right way to do any of this. He reassures them that "everyone engaged in this activity is at some point a co-leader—a co-creator—and all choices, responses, and reactions are simply what they are. There can be no judgment attached." Also, having adults jump in and participate in the experience before having time to reflect on it—and perhaps judge it or themselves in relation to it—reduces the likelihood that people will stay in their accustomed mental, habitual, and psychic "grooves." (Note: we call these "Broadways/Grand Canyons.")

> They are engaging in an activity that has clear rules, but there's no way to do it "righter" than someone else. Plus, as each person forms the action described on his or her selected words from the three charts, the whole group mirrors him or her at the same time, so everyone shares all the silliness. The inevitable laughter helps too. The full participation of the group, including me, also reduces the social anxiety. No one is audience; everyone participates. This runs counter to the cultural, consumerist norms that contribute to making performance so anxiety provoking.

Paul finds this activity is a particularly effective warm-up activity with groups where the focus of the learning is communication, creativity, or leadership:

> In addition to the freedom that comes with the suspension of judgment, the fact that we all follow each

> other, even though we don't know what we're doing, adds another layer to the experience. During those moments of somatic mirroring, we feel and reflect the feeling of being joined, being met, being seen. And I see this as related to how leadership happens in learning and in creative processes. With this activity, I'm hoping to establish a visceral awareness of the experience of collaboration and being in a place where people's voices will be welcome just as they are—and everyone can show up differently. So, in essence, we are priming the pump of how we are in the room—together and with ourselves.

Occasionally people have such a high level of negative activation at the outset that they simply cannot participate. Paul honors this decision. "Take care of yourselves," he urges; however he also asks that they not leave the room. "Please stay and be with us in the spirit of being part of the group." He explains:

> Even if they are participating in a way that does not look like the actions of others in the group, it is important that they not be disconnected. But I do ask them to "check in with yourself. What does 'too scary' mean in this moment? If it's mostly, 'Well, it feels uncomfortable and different,' then you might be restricting yourself from an opportunity to learn, which is what we are here to do."

Paul tells the nonparticipants he will be open for feedback later and hopes that as the activity progresses, they may be able to challenge themselves about the degree to which they are willing to stretch their capacity. "That said, if it isn't the right moment or the right activity and they think it is better to not, then don't."

Paul does not necessarily debrief the activity as soon as it's over. He notes that it can be more effective and powerful if the experience is allowed to gel. Immediate interpretation—the brain's shift from embodied and tacit to verbal and explicit—also is immediate limitation and delimitation.

Pause for Reflection

1. How does the prospect of adapting or creating embodied activities strike you? Freeing? Silly? Enticing? Anxiety provoking? Creative/imaginative?
2. Which of the approaches in this chapter has potential for adaptation to some aspect of your practice? Try to identify three possibilities you might work with.
3. Can you make a tentative plan—perhaps jot it down right now—for what that might look like and what you would need to carry it out?

7

Center Stage

> *The thesis of the* embodied mind *is more accurately rendered the thesis of* embodied mental procedures.
>
> — MARK ROWLANDS

WITHOUT necessarily identifying them as such, many experienced facilitators use embodied, analogical activities in their workshops, classes, or coaching and consulting settings because they have found them to greatly enhance adults' grasp of key concepts as well as their own practice. Other ALFAS (adult learning facilitators in any setting) have been following the expanding literature on brain and learning and have discovered additional justification for using brain-aware approaches with intention.

This chapter focuses on multifaceted and often multilayered approaches where embodied, imaginal (RH), as well as verbal and analytical (LH) aspects are explicitly interwoven, hence "center stage" in the Theatre of Knowing metaphor. In comparison to most approaches described in previous chapters, which tended to focus on a specific assignment or activity, many here are comprehensive. They involve more than one session, whether consulting with clients, presenting professional development workshops, or teaching in academic settings. Even so, aspects of the approaches are usually applicable in smaller doses. Though the details described are generally presented in terms of a particular instance or group, most contain elements that may be used in various settings.

For example, **Ken Otter** integrates similar embodied and imaginal activities with both corporate clients and graduate students. The biggest difference may be the kind and amount of reading involved. **Bruce Williams** and **Jim Kelly** offer virtually the same Guided Conversation Method and Multiple Intelligences seminars for graduate students and professional development participants. Several pieces of their multipart multiple intelligences workshop can be adapted as stand-alone activities, as well. **Doug Paxton**'s description of engaging a group of engineers in a multi-session collaborative inquiry in order to address organization-wide communication problems is not limited to engineers or communication problems. With minor modifications, **Kathryn Wozniack**'s course in writing, a vehicle for fostering metacognitive skills, has been offered to graduate students, corporate clients, and even faculty. **Barry Sheckley**'s concept maps, used here with graduate students in adult education, have been used with many other groups, such as professional development for math teachers and employees of a call center, to improve their bottom line. The underlying approach of **Susan Reed**'s learning journal is applicable to many situations where adults need to make the most of concurrent in-the-field learning experiences.

The section on serious games takes a different perspective. Rather than describe in detail how to construct games and simulations, **Ron Stadsklev** and **Dennis Glenn** explain how and why such approaches enhance learning in accord with brain-aware practice.

Comfort Me with Crayons

As an international consultant and also as a faculty member in an executive master's in business administration program, **Ken Otter** often engages participants in imaginative experiences. His approach, which he refers to as story mapping (we might say imaginal mapping), is used for professional development in corporate and other institutional settings and with graduate students. Ken explains his overall intent:

> Adults work at many levels—kinesthetic, somatic, imaginative, affective, social, relational—so I want to engage them in multiple ways. I want to tap into parts of the brain that are more open, and sort of peel away the overlay of the social, cultural, and individual filters that get in the way of new thinking.

Ken designs activities that require creativity and imagination. For example, when consulting a group interested in developing their organization in a new way, Ken offers this prompt: "If the future could speak, what would it say?" or "What would it look like?" He forms small teams of three or four members each to create their story about the future. Their story needs also to include a map or visual of some kind—representing past, present, and future—that illustrates their future vision. Ken acknowledges to the participants at the outset that they might find this kind of activity a little unexpected or unusual. He explains:

> This isn't about their usual biography, professional success, and achievements. They're doing something they aren't necessarily good at—telling stories about what they imagine this organization or team might be doing. So they're a little off-balance, but in a positive way. I want them stretching but not straining.

Ken's clients come to him because they "realize they don't need to do more of what they're already doing. They are not looking merely for skill development, but for growth: they want to go where they have not gone before." His approach takes participants at their word when he invites them to participate in these unaccustomed ways:

> I find it often shifts their whole way of being together in a professional context. Perhaps engaging their brain in a different way allows for something unexpected in themselves—not their usual patterns of thinking—which also evokes that creativity in others. It gets at something that is there, but may be just beyond their current awareness.

Since his embodied and imaginal approaches are unfamiliar to most adult learners, Ken pays close attention when a workshop participant appears to be showing evidence of discomfort—for example, "someone who engages in the activity for about fifteen seconds and then starts chatting with their partner about other things." Ken usually addresses the adult directly and gently, "How are things going for you?" and then affirms and validates whatever experience the person is having. "If someone is resisting, I'll engage the person and try to create a pathway to a new perspective, to see the activity in a new way." He may also use mild humor to help adults distance themselves from one of their familiar and comfortable habits.

For example, a high-ranking police officer was uncomfortable with the idea of drawing something imaginal. "So," Ken said playfully, "you have no problem being on a SWAT raid in full protective gear, never knowing what is waiting for you inside the building, but the idea of using a crayon gets your heart thumping?" He sometimes finds it necessary to modify the task. If it seems that identifying and drawing a metaphor or analogy is beyond someone's reach, Ken allows that person to use a more concrete, storyboard approach but asks that it still be done in colored pens or crayons:

> The point of the activity is not to engage with color, but if coloring inside the lines, so to speak, is all that person can manage at the moment, that's better than not coloring at all. I want to rebalance the brain so that the person can be more open—as a child is—to the way the world is coming to them, without getting too caught up in their filters. Or at least, I encourage them to hold that interference more lightly, so they are more open to direct experience and surprise.

Given that Ken is likely to be working at people's growing edge, he has to remain cognizant to avoid "tripping the anxiety button." At other times in the workshop or class, the group may discuss professional materials or other content-focused texts. Ken find that these conversations are richer after people have relinquished their certainties, which is typically an outgrowth of intentionally engaging their more symbolic and analogic thinking processes. If those conversations stall or seem to regress to role and position taking, Ken will again introduce an imaginal activity. Inviting more explicit embodied and RH engagement can revitalize openness to creativity.

Penny Game

Many of **Ken Otter**'s training sessions and consultations focus on relational aspects of leadership. In Penny Game, pairs of adults put a penny between their index fingers. Then, without talking the pairs move around the room for about a minute, trying to keep the penny from dropping. They have to negotiate a space that contains chairs and tables as well as all the other moving pairs. Ken refers to it as

> a somatic metaphor. Those holding the penny experience a constant switching back and forth in terms of who is leading and who is following—and also how they negotiate that reality between them as they silently deal with the challenge of moving through the space and around the other participants.

The ensuing discussion looks at how they initially approached the task, how they implicitly agreed (or not) on their strategy, what they noticed about how they handled a dropped penny, and whatever other observations they have about how they or other pairs performed. "It easily applies to many aspects of the workplace and can be broken down into intention, decision, and execution or enactment."

Sometimes Ken introduces a more structured debriefing that makes use of the Kolb cycle (see chapter 9): experience, reflection, generalization, application. After that, he also has participants reflect as a group or individually on the experience as a whole, including the process by which they arrived at whatever they have so far discovered. Then he asks them to write brief individual reflections on what they see as overall implications for leadership—their own and that of others—in various settings.

> I then instruct them to circle key words in their written reflections, such as those with emotional charge or that were unexpected. Next, I suggest they use these key words in some other creative way—for example, by making up a story or poem. I ask them to reflect on what they created to see if that contributes a new perspective. Although this is largely verbal expression, it also backtracks to tap

into further imaginal expression, perhaps surfacing ideas that were at the edge of awareness, but not immediately available at first.

Penny Game lends itself to other imaginal applications that may lead to deeper and more unexpected discoveries. Many adults experience moments of creativity or insight when engaged in physical activities that allow the brain to flip between automatic (background) and in-the-moment (foreground) focus, like walking the dog, taking a shower, or driving a car. The specific embodied metaphor at the center of this activity can then become the springboard to bringing such tacit knowledge to awareness.

Guided Conversation Method

This method can be used to facilitate group discussion about myriad topics, particularly, say **Bruce Williams** and **Jim Kelly**, when a goal is "to occasion participants' critical thinking and to encourage insightful contributions within groups." The guided conversation method (GCM) can be used in graduate or undergraduate courses, training workshops, one-to-one conversations, or even to reflect on an important meeting just completed. The time frame for the GCM can be adapted to various audiences and contexts. This description is drawn from a graduate course, Facilitating Adult Learning.

This three-hour-long segment is designed to show, through modeling and engagement, how to facilitate a guided conversation by applying it to relevant course content. In this case, the group's shared experience (the content focus), is a twenty-minute training video, *The Pygmalion Effect,* about the power of expectations. Following the video, Bruce and Jim lead a guided conversation about the content and significance of the video. The example that follows explains the method by generalizing from the case of how to guide a conversation on that particular training video.

A guided conversation begins by identifying two types of objectives, rational and experiential, that determine and shape how the conversation questions are crafted. Bruce and Jim articulate the objectives in advance (later, when participants use the GCM, they also craft objectives in advance). With regard to the video activity, the Statement of Rational Objective is "to learn or relearn the power of expectations." The Statement of Experiential Objective describes the desired attitude, feelings, and motivation that will ensue. In this demonstration, they say, "participants will be motivated to communicate positive expectations in their words and behavior." The combination of the two types of objectives allows participants to process the experience both cognitively and emotionally.

After the group watches the video, Bruce and Jim begin the guided conversation with a brief opening statement: "Let's talk about the video to see what we all got out of watching it." This is the segue to the ORID process (observe, react, interpret, and decide), the sequence that guides the conversation. The first set of questions in each group that follows is specific to the shared experience of the video—in this instance, expectations (the content of the *Pygmalion Effect*). The second set consists of generic guiding questions to be adapted by ALFAS for their own content.

In Observe, the first step in the process, participants are asked to recall the factual information and the sensory data in order to recreate the shared experience of watching the video:

Observe

Questions specific to content (the particular shared experience)

- What scenes do you recall?
- What characters do you remember?
- What lines stick with you?

- What are the components of the expectation cycle?
- What are the factors in communicating expectations?

Generic questions to adapt to particular GC content or experience

- What facts do we know about this?
- What did you hear the speaker saying?
- What did you see?
- What do you remember from the presentation?
- What pictures or images, words or phrases, or sounds do you recall?

In the React step, participants are called on to access emotions and feelings, including those associated with past experiences, to acknowledge the importance of the affective domain in learning:

React

Questions specific to content

- What surprised you?
- What made you curious?
- Where did you find yourself getting upset? Feeling empathic?
- What have you personally experienced related to the expectation cycle?

Generic questions to adapt

- What emotions did you observe in others?
- What are your own feelings?
- What was your first response?
- What has this reminded you of?

At this Interpret stage, critical thinking starts to occur, and valuing and meaning making come into play. Participants analyze and consider values, meaning, significance, and purpose:

Interpret

Questions specific to content

- What is the relevance of *The Pygmalion Effect* for us as facilitators of adult learning?
- If you had to tell someone in a sentence what this video is about, what would you say?
- Which are the most important ideas that came out in this presentation and experience?

Generic questions to adapt

- What are the most critical implications from what we have just heard?
- What are the crucial points we need to discuss in order to be able to make a decision on this?
- Where do we already agree?
- Where do we have the most disagreement?

In the final step, Decide, the conversation turns to resolutions, options, and next steps:

Decide

Questions specific to content

- What situations come to mind that you would like to influence with your expectations?
- After watching this video, what do you want to incorporate into your development as a facilitator?

Generic questions to adapt

- What are our next steps?
- What is the first thing you are going to do tomorrow?
- Who needs to be the first to hear about this?
- What change is needed in how we are operating now?

Following the ORID conversation, brief closing prompts mark the end of the guided conversation experience: Where do we go from here? When do we meet again? What did you notice about how we have done in this meeting [or session]?

ORID is a powerful brain-aware approach. It requires the brain to retrace its learning process. First, in Observe, the brain takes in sensory data. Next, in React, it recognizes affective reactions to the sensory data and revisits what may be fleeting or significant emotional connections from past experiences. The brain always makes those associations, though we are aware of them only when they become feelings. Then, capitalizing on the first two steps, the process of critical thinking and categorization engages the brain as Interpret. Finally, the process solidifies with Decide, which will guide its decisional responses. Most adults usually operate in terms of Interpret and Decide, thus potentially missing information that Observe and React can contribute, if invited to do so.

With this possibility in mind, and depending on the size of the group, some facilitators initially ask everyone to contribute one brief item to Observe, without repeating what someone else said. Doing so alerts everyone's brain to be present; it also fills in the shared experience with additional data.

In the context of the Facilitating Adult Learning course in which the GCM is also content, there are four additional scaffolded steps:

1. Following the GC activity focused on the topic of the Pygmalion video, Bruce and Jim give an interactive presentation that reveals the structure and rationale of the GCM, itself.
2. Bruce and Jim give participants an opportunity to create and lead their own guided conversation in class.

3. They give a homework assignment for each student to create and lead a guided conversation outside class on a topic and in a place of their own choosing.
4. Bruce and Jim continue modeling the GCM by leading guided conversations throughout the remainder of the course.

The origins of the ORID process point to its wide applicability beyond classrooms. It was initially created by the Institute of Cultural Affairs (ICA) and has been used for decades as a focus for community development discussion and action. See Stanfield's *The Art of Focused Conversation* (2000). Workshops in this facilitation method are offered by ICA-US.

Engaging Multiple Intelligences

As cofacilitators, **Bruce Williams** and **Jim Kelly** typically plan a tightly scaffolded, multilayered process that can be adapted to graduate courses or professional development workshops. They find that Gardner's theory of multiple intelligences (MI) offers them a primary framework for working effectively with adults' brains. "The crucial question about any learner is not how smart are you," they explain, "but in what ways are you smart?" (See chapter 9 for more about Gardner and about Bruce's publications and work with multiple intelligences.)

Though the following description is based on how Bruce and Jim introduce MI to graduate students in their Facilitating Adult Learning course, it can also be adapted to a professional development workshop for ALFAS. This design again uses theory to inform content in two ways: MI is the theory being presented and the highly interactive process reinforces the theory using six carefully scaffolded embodied and imaginal learning activities.

To introduce the session, Bruce and Jim begin with a quick overview of Gardner's eight intelligences: verbal/linguistic, logical/mathematical, intrapersonal, interpersonal, visual/spatial, musical/rhythmic, bodily/kinesthetic, naturalist (see figure 9.7, Multiple Intelligences Wheel), tying the model to the real-life example of someone who demonstrates strong abilities in certain areas and is notably lacking in others. As an example, Bruce tells the story of his son, Daniel. If ALFAS evoke the image of a specific person, the experience of hearing it will be more meaningful, as it will activate adults' RH sense of empathy and connection.

Step 1: Business Card Activity: Seeing Ideas in Pictures, Not Words

Each participant is given a blank five- by eight-inch notecard (figure 7.1). They are instructed:

- Write your name in the center of the card.
- In the upper-left corner, draw an image of a place you've always wanted to see. (1 minute)
- In the upper-right corner, draw an image of a skill you have. (1 minute)

An image of a place you've always wanted to see	An image of a skill you have
An image of a something you enjoy doing for fun	An image of an instrument you play or always wanted to play

Figure 7.1 Business Card Activity

- In the lower-right corner, draw an image of an instrument you play or always wanted to play. (1 minute)
- In the lower-left corner, draw an image of something you enjoy doing for fun. (1 minute)

Next, the participants engage in partner sharing:

1. Find a partner. Share your images and a brief explanation of them. (2 minutes for each pair)
2. Move to pair up with someone else. Repeat one or more times, depending on the time available and size of group, before returning to your own seats. (2 minutes for each additional pair)

If the activity is being used to model facilitation of multiple intelligences, participants engage in reflection on the shared experience from that perspective. They use an abbreviated guided conversation method with guiding questions such as these:

Observe: What did you see going on? What did you hear?

React: How were you feeling while drawing on your cards? What feelings did you experience while sharing and listening?

Interpret: What might be the intent of conducting an activity like this? What would be some of the unspoken messages you would be communicating to the participants by using such an activity?

Decide: How could you adapt this activity for use in your own practice setting beyond as an ice breaker? What multiple intelligences came into play in this activity?

This activity serially engages different parts of the brain and helps participants feel more comfortable around personal disclosure. Asking first about a place someone desires to visit activates a positive, future-oriented response. Disclosing a skill contributes to understanding the richness of experience embodied in the learning community. Revealing an instrument to play or desire to play sets the stage for introducing musical/rhythmic intelligence. Declaring a favorite thing to do for fun reinforces the "play" chapter from one of the course textbooks, Daniel Pink's *A Whole New Mind* (2005). Although this approach is designed around brain-focused intentions, Bruce and Jim do not yet explicitly disclose this aspect of their planning.

Step 2: Table Talk Activity: Translating Complex Concepts into Lay Language

As segue, Bruce and Jim revisit the personal, introductory story, asking what intelligences Daniel, whom they used as an example at the start of the activities, might display. They then have the groups collaboratively generate ideas about the topic at hand—that is, intelligence. Note that the facilitators have not yet described multiple intelligence theory in detail. As **Pamela Meyer** (Generating Hunches) and **Tony Saddington** (Taking a Risk) also demonstrated, backing into theory is often an effective and more meaningful approach. At tables of four or five participants, one of whom is a volunteer recorder, Bruce and Jim ask each group to discuss two questions, each for about five minutes.

The first question is, "What is intelligence?" After they discuss, each table reports out one or two working definitions or characteristics of intelligence. ALFAS record key phrases or terms on chart paper—for example, intelligence is the ability "to be effective," "to absorb and use information," "to be reflective, and "to allow for failure.

The second question is, "How does one become (more) intelligent?" The process is the same as for the first question. Typical responses might include "invite curiosity" and "reduce fear or anxiety."

Step 3: Theoretical Background Activity: Connecting Participants' Ideas to Gardner's Theory

Bruce or Jim presents a brief PowerPoint overview about Gardner, the multiple intelligences wheel, and explanations of each intelligence. (See chapter 9 for further discussion of MI theory and example of the multiple intelligences wheel.)

The meaning that each participant has so far made is anchored in the next piece of the scaffold, which engages them in exploring their sense of their own intelligences.

Step 4: Jagged Profile Multiple Intelligence Self-Assessment

Each participant makes eight vertical folds, accordion style, in a sheet of plain paper eight and a half by eleven inches. Participants write one type of intelligence at the bottom of each fold: verbal/linguistic; logical/mathematical; visual/spatial; musical/rhythmic; bodily/kinesthetic; interpersonal/social; intrapersonal/introspective; naturalist.

Bruce orally describes the characteristics of verbal/linguistic intelligence and then asks participants to provide examples of people in whom this intelligence is strong. He supplements those answers with additional examples. Participants then tear off the upper part of the first fold to create a bar that represents how much of that intelligence they feel they have. Then they write on the remainder of the bar a phrase or sentence that summarizes how they manifest that intelligence—for example, "I have a good vocabulary and write well", or, in the case of another, less strong, intelligence, "I love hearing music, but I'm tone deaf when I sing." They then repeat this for each of the remaining seven intelligences. Finally, everyone briefly holds up their jagged bar graph profiles and looks around. This dramatically illustrates the breadth of differences in stronger and weaker intelligences.

Bruce and Jim briefly revisit the importance of MI theory to facilitators designing learning activities for adults and explore ways to work with differences. They say to participants, "Show your paper bar graph to your tablemates. Discuss among you the strong intelligences and then decide what you might do in six months to become more comfortable in one of your weaker intelligences."

Bruce and Jim then rehearse some key points of Gardner's theory:

- Everyone has all eight intelligences.
- Some are stronger and some weaker.
- An individual's mixture of intelligences is as unique as a fingerprint, yet can be modified.

Step 5: States of Matter Activity

To demonstrate how to apply MI theory to other kinds of content, Bruce and Jim use the topic of teaching the states of matter. First, they elicit from the group relevant points in a unit on states of matter, such as the number of states of matter, the characteristics of each state, the movement from one state to another, and so forth.

The whole group is divided into three smaller ones, one representing gas, another liquid, and another solid. Each group stands in a different part of the room. Each is now asked to come up with a body movement or gesture that represents their assigned state of matter. Once the groups have done so, Bruce and Jim ask each group to model their movement for the others by calling out liquid, gas, liquid, solid, liquid, gas several times. (The element of surprise is part of the fun, as well as anchoring the movement for everyone.) After the participants return to their seats, they look at the various aspects of states of matter they wanted to convey to see how many got covered in this simple, lively activity.

Step 6: Remembering the Eight Intelligences

To wrap up this ninety-minute session, Bruce and Jim lead the group in an exercise with body motions for each of the eight intelligences. This embodied activity anchors their memories of the eight intelligences.

Step 7: Final Large Group Processing

The final group processing session addresses discussion questions regarding getting and staying engaged with the concept—for example:

- What intelligences did you see the facilitator using or modeling during this segment on MI?
- What were the highlights of these learning activities for you?
- When were you especially involved?
- How would you characterize the mood of the group right now?
- What would you like to incorporate from this session into your own practice setting?

During this multitiered segment, Bruce and Jim engage participants in learning activities that have both kinesthetic and reflective aspects, create a space for social learning, and stimulate both the right and left brain hemispheres. These brain-aware activities introduce MI in a creative way that makes the theory come alive for participants. This entire session models scaffolded, embodied facilitation practices.

Teaching People to Fish

In his work with corporate groups, **Doug Paxton** intends that participants develop understandings that will enable them to carry

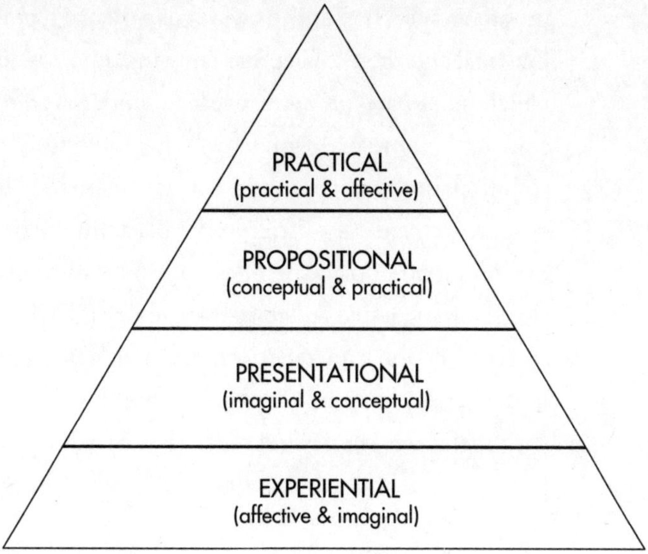

Figure 7.2 Stages of Inquiry/Facilitation (Ways of Knowing)
Source: Heron (1999).

on creative, meaningful change processes after he is no longer there to facilitate: "Changing our minds often requires changing our practices." He uses Heron's four-step learning model, experiential, presentational, propositional, practical, because it explicitly includes an imaginal or symbolic phase, called *presentational* (figure 7.2). "You're not doing deep, path-breaking work if you are interested only in doing propositional [cognitive] and practical [application] knowing."

In one application of this approach, Doug, working with a cofacilitator, consulted with a dozen engineers who worked as an intact team and were themselves part of a consulting firm working on environmental issues. Though some members of the workshop were newly hired and others were directors, they came together as equals to explore team building, leadership, and ways to create a culture of innovation and creativity. Working with his colleague, he began by sketching out Heron's extended epistemology pyramid and briefly explained the logic of the up-hierarchy: Beginning with experience, building through imaginal and then conceptual knowing, it yields affective learning which culminates in a creative new understanding. "The typical analytical approach works well for finding the answer to a technical problem, but not one where the solution has to be created—to emerge—from other places in the brain, and within the group, other places besides positional authority."

Doug suggested collaborative inquiry (CI), because it involves cycles of action and reflection and requires using the full pyramid. The first step in CI requires that the participants come up with their own inquiry question, thereby taking ownership of the process. He described how this worked with the group:

> After an hour or so of brainstorming, dialogue, and multiple iterations centering on "what's the most important thing we can change about ourselves that will contribute to creating a culture of innovation?" their final question was: "How can we increase our capacity to provide honest, caring, effective feedback that fosters excellence and growth?" They saw that without meaningful feedback within their team, they wouldn't be able to learn from what was happening around them, so they might miss opportunities or follow dead ends.

Once the group had established their own inquiry, they were ready to embark on the hierarchy of Heron's model, which begins with direct, relevant experience. Doug again explained how this worked:

> For the next twenty minutes, they paired off and took turns giving and receiving feedback. When they came back as a whole group and before they started verbalizing

> about the experience—a left-brain focus—they had to do something from the presentational or symbolic realm—a right-brain focus.

Doug therefore asked each person to draw an image: "It is not meant to be 'artistic,' but people get caught up in that trap, so we suggest that they use their opposite hand, thus ensuring no one is going to create art." Then each person presents his or her image of that experience (in this case, of giving and receiving feedback) to the group, explaining only what the image is, without drawing analytical LH conclusions about it. "This can be tougher than you might think," he said and then continued:

> People are taught to go straight to explanations. We don't yet want, "This part is meant to represent *x* and this image is meant to represent *y*." Highly analytical people—engineers are a great example—are really fast to jump to making meaning. So part of this symbolic expression is to slow down that process and give them time to engage both sides of the brain. People often say, "It's faster to do just the top two levels": propositional and practical. We explain, "Yes, but only if you are dealing with a problem where there is a known answer out there, somewhere—in other words, a technical problem—and all you have to do is find it. When people present their images without already having characterized them, they sometimes see things that surprise them. This means they are beginning to tap into those unexpected places. It also allows others in the group a chance to make their own interpretations and connections, without someone else first telling them how they are supposed to see it.

Doug emphasizes the differences between technical problems and adaptive challenges. A technical problem, according to Ron Heifetz of Harvard's Kennedy School of Government, is one for which a solution exists or can be found because the know-how to solve it exists; it just has to be searched out and applied (Heifetz, Linsky, and Grashow, 2009). An adaptive challenge, by contrast, does not have a solution waiting to be found. The know-how does not exist, usually because these are multifaceted issues for which there are no answers. Approaching an adaptive challenge often involves taking what Heifetz and his colleagues call the balcony view—looking at the issue from a comprehensive, systemic perspective. It may also require that the people who are looking for or likely to be affected by the proposed solution actively participate in developing possible strategies and then take responsibility for acting in accord with what they have found:

> With an adaptive problem, which is most of the big problems we all face, everyone's thinking is essential, not just the "smart" ones who usually speak up immediately. This is when people need to bring out the best in the whole team, in order to create, innovate, and adapt.

Doug describes the experiential and presentational parts of the hierarchy as "rightish" and the propositional and practical parts as "leftish"—referring to the brain's right and left hemispheres, though he adds that he doesn't mean that literally.

After the group members reflect on and talk about their individual and collective experiences of creating the images, Doug asks: "If these are our images of feedback, what does this say about how we think and feel about feedback and therefore what should constitute the next step of the cycle?" He finds their ideas now come "from a completely different place. They are no longer a typical, analytical description of what constitutes good feedback skills." At this point, participants are ready to embark on the next step of the cycle:

> They were due to meet with us again in three weeks for another half-day. So they laid out a plan—now they could use all their fabulous engineering and organizational skills—about how many times they would give and receive feedback, both within their team and in the larger organization. They also knew that when we all came together again, they would once again first represent their new experiences symbolically and find out what else they could discern from the nonanalytical parts of their brains. And they did.

After that, the facilitators' role was over. The engineers could go it alone because what they had adaptively created—in terms of being able to give and receive effective feedback—could now be refined and expanded as they worked on the technical problems that are their company's bread and butter. Having also empowered themselves to set up an ongoing inquiry into changing their team's culture of communication, they saw implications for changing the larger organization. It's about "teaching people to fish," Doug said, "rather than giving them fish." It's also about giving voice to the slower and more innovative RH, before the quicker and less creative LH jumps to conclusions and ends their discussion.

Metacognitive Cycle

Kathryn Wozniak, a full-time writing instructor who sees her primary role as "a coach or guide," has a keen interest in helping adults develop their metacognitive abilities because "it is a tool for lifelong learning." (See "Further Reading: Metacognition.")

Further Reading: Metacognition

Metacognition is a learner's ability to monitor, reflect on, and improve on his or her learning activities and strategies, a key factor in successful transfer of knowledge and skills to new learning situations (Flavell, 1987; Bransford, Brown, & Cocking, 2000; Akyol & Garrison, 2011). For more on metacognitive frameworks, see Flavel (1979), Veenman and others (2006), and Mayer (2011).

She uses a learner-centered metacognitive process to guide participants in their reflective practice—whether on ground or online—that can be used in various settings, from college students in project-based learning to corporate employees doing team projects. As an ALFAS, Kathryn believes that

> it's important that we try to determine ways to leverage the adult brain's reaction and means of dealing with their experiences. For example, when an adult has a concrete work experience, how can I help them reflect on whether and how that experience succeeded or failed, on lessons learned, on skills gained? How can I directly encourage adult learners to be mindful of the most meaningful ways of doing something?

The metacognition framework Kathryn has adapted has four main parts (figure 7.3). Though only the last part specifically names reflection, it is the primary focus of all four: (1) plan and organize, (2) track and monitor their own work, (3) direct their own learning, and (4) self-reflect. She adjusts the following questions, clustered into the four quadrants of the framework, to fit particulars of a specific assignment, or of a course as whole.

Kathryn also provides ongoing scaffolding for the course writing projects, from preassignment through final submission. Before she gives an assignment, she will have introduced adults to the

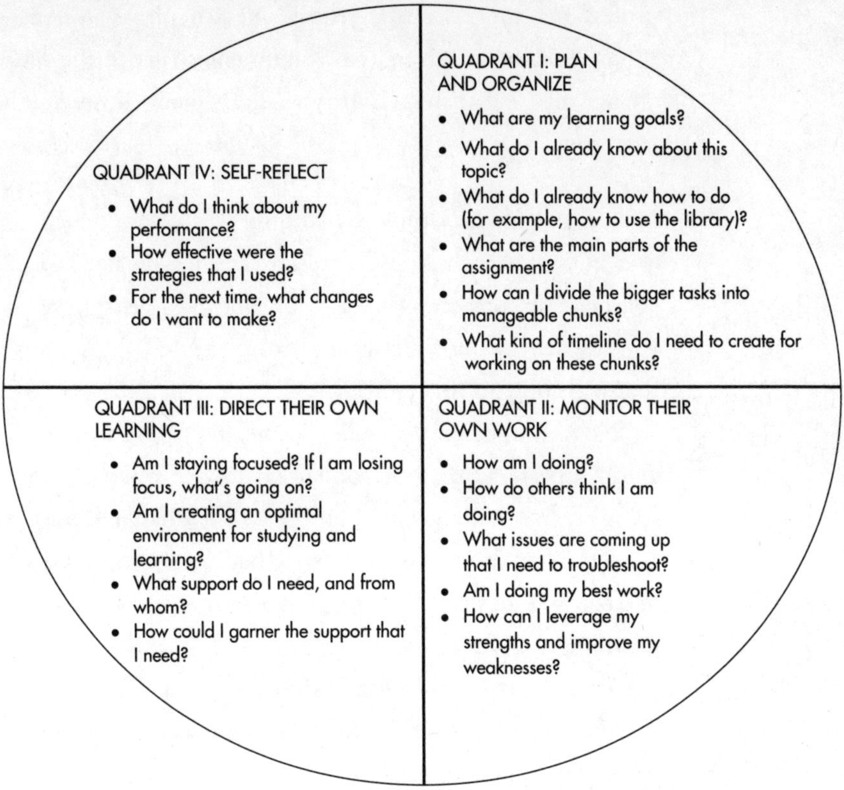

Figure 7.3 Metacognitive Cycle, adapted from Ambrose, S. A., Bridges, M. W., DiPietro, M., Lovett, M. C., & Norman, M. K. (2010)

components of professional writing genres and how to organize text in a logical fashion for a specific audience and purpose.

In the following example of an online professional writing course for adult undergraduates, Kathryn asks learners to play the role of a manager of a resort. The writing task is framed in terms of responding to a community leader who has asked for free use of the resort. The resort manager must decline the request and still try to make a sale without upsetting or offending the community leader. This gives adults practice with rhetorical appeals (such as *logos, ethos*, and *pathos*) and in applying genre conventions in the professions, processes that require metacognitive awareness. Once participants are given the assignment to write the letter conveying the bad news, Kathryn takes them through the metacognitive cycle:

> First, I give them a project planning worksheet, which asks questions such as: What resources will you need to complete this project? What is your time line? What have you learned in the readings and from previous projects that will apply to this project?
>
> Next, I ask them to talk, in the discussion board, about a personal or professional experience where they had to deliver bad news and to discuss what happened as a result. Now they draft the letter. They are also required to answer and submit to me self-assessment questions including, What are the strengths and weaknesses in this draft? What was easy and difficult about this draft? What questions for feedback do you have for your peers and instructor?

Kathryn then directs them to do peer reviews, in pairs, of each other's drafts. After that, she gives adults individual feedback, making sure that questions posed by the writer or the peer have been answered. Learners take all the feedback into account, as well as ideas they may have gleaned from the peer review they conducted, and revise their own draft for final submission.

> As a summative self-assessment of the project, I ask them to write another letter that serves two audiences: both me, the facilitator, and learners who will take this course in the future. In this second letter, I ask adults to reflect on their role in completing the "bad letter" project, what they

gained from going through the process, and what they would do differently next time. Each person posts her or his letter in a discussion board so that all members of the class can compare their thoughts and evaluations.

For this one project, learners have cycled through the metacognitive prompts multiple times (discussion, planning activity, postdraft self-evaluations, peer review and instructor feedback, summative evaluation of themselves and the project). In doing so, they have not only stretched their metacognitive abilities with regard to writing assignment but have also begun to internalize a process of reflection that can be extended beyond the boundaries of any particular course.

Several brain-aware nuances are invisibly integrated in this approach to the writing assignments, as well as in the entire metacognitive cycle. Asking developing writers to role-play the letter-writing assignments combines an LH-oriented approach (apply organizational rules and genre conventions) with an RH-oriented approach (communicate emotion-laden meaning). The project planning worksheets and other reflective activities require ongoing self-assessment as well as giving and integrating feedback. (We discuss these two important aspects of brain-aware facilitation in greater detail in chapter 8.)

Concept Maps

Barry Sheckley uses concept maps in both formal educational settings and when consulting to private industry. Concept maps enable adults to integrate experience-based tacit knowledge with explicit understanding of events and ideas. They also allow learners to think in terms of complex relationships and interactions as they address problem situations. (See "Defining Concept Maps.")

Defining Concept Maps

Most often, especially as used in primary and secondary classrooms, the term *concept map* refers to advance organizers of upcoming lessons or graphic descriptions of already-established connections, such as a "tree of mammalian evolution." As Barry uses it, however, it is a tool adults can use to construct increasingly complex, reciprocal, and interactive relationships among concepts as their learning process unfolds. Once the map (or multiple maps by individuals working on a common issue) has been sketched out, it serves as a focus of discussion and possible action, based on the relationships depicted in it.

Barry described a specific application involving graduate students in a doctoral program in education, where adults usually take three to five years of classes before they get to their dissertation research. Typically graduate students go through a series of classes, each focused on a specific topic. The classes tend to be loosely coupled with each other. Connections with an eventual dissertation topic are infrequent. They therefore struggle when they complete their course of study and have to anchor a dissertation research project within an integrated theoretical frame:

> To address this problem, we introduced students to concept mapping in their very first course. Instead of asking them to study for a midterm and final exam or write a term paper, we asked them to integrate the information they covered during the course into a concept map that showed the relationships between the ideas and concepts they studied.
>
> In each course, as they read research articles and conduct pilot research projects, they formulate their own propositions about the topic and then construct concept maps that illustrate the key aspects of their propositions. Then in their next course, they use the new

> ideas and concepts to build on, refine, and expand their initial concept map. This process of building a concept map and using it as the framework for a conceptual paper continued throughout their entire program of study.

In other words, instead of shelving the previous course when going on to the next, the learners had to keep making connections between ideas in current and prior courses. "Everyone's concept map ends up being different," Barry points out, "because people emphasize different ideas depending on their own interests." Through this iterative process, learners' concept maps grow with them throughout their program. They also write a paper for each course that provides a rationale for the interactions outlined in their map. "Eventually," Barry says,

> their course-based propositions and maps form the conceptual framework for their dissertation proposal. Then they test out and refine their propositions (concept map) through their dissertation research. In the last chapter of their dissertation, they present their final, research-based version of their concept map. They don't have to seek out a separate theoretical framework from the literature; they can use the theoretical framework they have constructed in their concept map because this map integrates key ideas from all their course work. Most important for the learners, the map isn't something "out there." It's *theirs*. It's a framework they can use as a springboard to their dissertation research.

Barry, who has long been interested in brain research, highlighted the fact that the ultimate purpose of the mapping activity was to facilitate and enhance the mind's ability to make connections through analogical reasoning.

Journaling Learning

"In a service-learning context," **Susan Reed** says, "reflection is *the* key to learning from experience." She continues:

> Adult students often bring prior experience, but in order to be in sync with the fieldwork, they need to integrate new learning with what they already know and can do. Adults have an advantage in many service-learning situations—they may be able to offer skills in project management, or do excel spreadsheets, or organize teams. However, they also have the disadvantage of being unaware of how much they still need to learn.

Susan sees experiential learning acquired in the context of service-learning as "involving the whole brain." Adults have current embodied situated field experience; they read abstract theories; they engage in challenging, occasionally emotional, discussions with peers (and sometimes with clients); and they draw on memories of prior experience. Susan's multilayered approach helps them connect and interpret these disparate experiences as they construct new knowledge.

1. *Identifying prior knowledge.* Susan uses Melissa Peet's generative knowledge interview technique (2013) to help participants identify their prior knowledge about doing service and about the subject areas connected to this particular setting and course.

> First, I interview one adult in a fishbowl, asking her to tell me three stories about any prior experiences of civic engagement. I listen for themes and patterns about what she knows, as well as attitudes and assumptions. Then the group as a whole processes what this learner might bring to—or what obstacles she might encounter in—the upcoming service-learning placement. Using

that interview as a model, pairs of students interview one another with the same intentions. The insights that emerge are shared with the large group to help everyone get primed for their service-learning ventures.

2. *Structured-learning journal.* Once adults are in the field site, Susan requires them to keep a journal to reflect on their service experiences, connect those experiences to issues raised by the course material, and also examine their own process of experiential learning. She gives these instructions:

- It is important that you journal as soon as possible after you do your service work so that your impressions and reflections will be fresh.
- Each journal entry you turn in should relate to one service visit, although reflection is likely to refer to other visits or past experiences.
- The length of each entry in your journal will vary, but it should be about three pages or 750 words.

3. *Structured analysis.* "This is essential because I can't assume that adults will reflect effectively on their own. I need to teach them and help them with how to reflect for learning—not just reportage. They also need help on how to analyze what they've described." She uses Kolb's learning cycle (see chapter 9) as the framework for their analysis in the journal:

- *Doing (concrete experience).* Write an account of the events of the day. Don't evaluate; just write the facts. Describe what you did. This should be the shortest section of your journal entry, no more than a half-page (150–200 words).
- *Reflecting (reflective observation).* Describe your feelings and perceptions about what happened during the day. This is your subjective account. What catches your attention? What gets you angry, upset? What piques your curiosity? Write about your impressions, ideas, feelings. What makes you feel

satisfied, disappointed, hopeful? What do you notice about how you approach learning, and what methods of learning seem to work best for you?

- *Thinking (abstract conceptualization).* Analyze what you are learning from experience. Draw connections between your experiences, personal reactions, and issues raised by the course. This is where you generalize from your service experience and draw conclusions about the social meanings of what you have learned. Consider the following questions to get you thinking:
  - How does your service experience resonate with class topics and readings?
  - Where might your previous assumptions regarding service or the issues raised in the course been shortsighted or faulty?
  - Given your experiences, do you have any critiques of the theories/issues in the readings/class discussions?
- *Applying (active experimentation).* Looking back on your reflections and conclusions, what choices will you make in the future about your work in the community? About your professional life? How will you apply what you have learned as you continue your service-learning project?
  - How has learning from service affected your understanding of the issues we study in class?
  - How might what you have observed about your learning style affect how you learn experientially in the future?

  (Note that the structured learning journal contains elements similar to **Willams and Kelly's** Guided Conversation Template and also contains aspects of **Wozniak's** Metacognitive Cycle, especially in steps 3 and 4.)

4. *Assessment rubric.* Susan provides adults with an assessment rubric (table 7.1) concerning levels of reflection in their journals. Three levels of performance, with 1 being the highest, are articulated with regard to each of the four components of the Kolb learning cycle.

Table 7.1 Service-Learning Journal Rubric

	1	2	3
Experiencing (description of the service experience)	The journal entry describes, in detail, the events the student experienced while doing community service. The entry identifies events that are significant for learning.	The journal entry describes, in detail, the events the student experienced while doing community service. The entry may spend a disproportionate amount of time and space summarizing events without selecting them according to their significance.	The journal entry inadequately describes the events of the service-learning experience. The entry may be incomplete or unclear.
a. Reflecting (personal reactions to the service experience)	The journal entry explores how service work has stimulated the student's feelings and personal growth, exploring the implications of his or her personal reactions by considering the people she or he has encountered, the social issues she or he is confronting, the possible impact of the service work, etc.	The journal entry alludes to the student's feelings about the service work, mentioning that the service work has affected her or him, without exploring more deeply the roots of her or his personal reactions or neglecting to consider the social issue or people she or he encountered.	The journal entry does not describe or explore the student's personal reactions to the service experience.
b. Thinking (analyzing the service experience by drawing connections with course readings/ themes)	The journal entry identifies a main argument or issue presented by an author and takes a position on whether the argument resonates with the service experience, providing specific examples. The journal has a speculative tone that hypothesizes as to causes and connections, reflects on questions and dilemmas, and/or draws general conclusions about the issues raised by the course and the service experience.	The journal entry identifies a main argument or issue presented by an author that relates to the service experience, without providing specific examples. The journal draws general conclusions about the issues raised by the course and the service experience.	The journal entry does not refer to the readings or draw connections between course issues and the service experience.

(*continued*)

Table 7.1 (*Continued*)

		1	2	3
c.	Applying (implications for action/change)	The journal entry applies what the student has learned at the service site and from course readings/discussions by speculating on problems or issues that are raised by the service experience and exploring ways to address these problems. The entry also examines the student's attempts to change her or his own behavior or interactions with those at the service site, exploring the impact of her or his actions on others as well as the impact of the experience on the student.	The journal entry explores what the student has learned from her or his service work by pointing to problems or issues raised by the service experience and may explore what actions the student can take to address these problems.	The journal entry does not discuss how the student is applying learning to her or his service work.

Susan is committed to helping adults connect past learning experiences to their current service-learning work in order to integrate new experiential learning with interactions in the community. She recognizes that their prior experience can be either a help or hindrance to learning in the new context depending on the quality of student reflection. Given that some will be curious about the new setting and others will assume they already know what's going on, Susan uses reflection prompts to help them recognize either possibility and identify additional ways that they may act in order to more fully realize their goals in the community.

Serious Games

Ron Stadsklev and Dennis Glenn are long-time experts in using formally structured games and simulations to facilitate learning. Given the resurgence of interest in technology-based games and simulations, we draw from their extensive history and experience to highlight the brain-aware aspects of this facilitation approach. We do not, however, include directions for any specific games, as reams of published resources are already available.

The overarching educational purpose of serious games is creating a learning environment with built in feedback loops that inform the player of progress toward a specified goal or learning objective. Gamification creates a fun and engaging experience; serious games promote task or concept mastery.

Simulations and Games

Ron Stadsklev began using simulations and games nearly forty years ago as teaching tools in the social sciences. In the intervening years he has worked extensively in training other facilitators in various professional development contexts, some of whom were startled by his embodied approaches. "They were preparing to teach or train in experience-based ways," he wryly noted, "but they weren't ready to learn that way."

Ron also clarified the difference between simulations and games: "A simulation creates an environment—a model of 'reality'—that will help learners feel and experience situations that are comparable to, or symbolic of, real-world situations. A game introduces the element of winning, whereas a simulation does not." Both, however, are embodied and imaginal. Simply reading and listening rarely involve participants to the degree that simulations do. Simulations and games tap into tacit knowing by "creating a vicarious experience. Done well, a simulation can be a safe way to look at serious issues, especially about which people are likely to have vested opinions."

With open-model simulations, "The outcomes can vary depending on how it is played and who is in the room. People respond based on the attitudes, beliefs, and prior experiences they bring with them." They are also affected by their interactions with others who bring different attitudes, beliefs, and experiences.

In a closed-model simulation, the outcomes are predetermined and the activities or messages are stacked toward achieving that outcome. "In the Ghetto Game—written decades ago by a social worker, Dove Toll, when she was a graduate student—it becomes painfully clear that there is little likelihood of making it out, staying out of jail, finding a job, or keeping your family together."

> **The Ghetto Game**
>
> Details of the updated *Ghetto Game* are available on Amazon.com (http://www.amazon.com/Ghetto-Ron-Stadsklev/dp/149289527X/). Additional information is available at http://diygames.us/. It includes an Android app that avoids the need to print and cut chance cards used in the game.

A well-designed, well-facilitated simulation for adults can challenge existing assumptions while also providing safety when they don't know the right answer or when the outcomes contradict their assumptions. As one example, Ron described a simulation game used to better understand the challenges of growing old in our society, End of the Line. Participants take on roles of either seniors trying to deal with economic, physical, or social limitations or as members of helping agencies. Game elements include messages typical of an older adult's situation: "Go back to Social Security to fill out another form," or "Your hearing aid battery goes dead, and you miss a phone call from your doctor." Participants soon experience how frustrated seniors might feel when trying to negotiate everyday aspects of their lives and also begin to develop possibilities for interventions that can make a difference.

Simulations are especially effective for exploring social systems through the activity of role playing, which can be a surprisingly intense and affecting imaginal experience. The powerful outcomes of simulations and similar role plays have sometimes gained notoriety, such as the Stanford Prison Experiment.

Further Reading: Role-Play Experiments in the Media

See Stanford Prison Experiment http://www.prisonexp.org/ and PBS's Frontline feature on Jane Elliott's classroom role play on racism, later repeated with adults in corporate settings: http://www.pbs.org/wgbh/pages/frontline/shows/divided/etc/view.html.

In comparison to simulations, games are more focused on rules and winning. To be an effective learning tool, luck should not be the primary determinant of who wins, though most games necessarily include elements of chance, Ron says. He continues:

> Games should be designed so that those who win are those who best understand the underlying message that the game is trying to teach. For example, in an ecology game, one of the game cards might read: *You threw a bottle out of the window: lose 3 points*. Without anyone saying so explicitly, that player's brain has been alerted to negative outcomes associated with an unecological act. By itself, that tacit awareness may not make much difference in what people think or do. To accomplish any substantive or lasting change, the facilitator needs to follow that up in other ways.

Most people are attracted to playing games, and the element of fun helps to attenuate what in other circumstances might be perceived as threatening. For example, in a group where some people tend to dominate and others hang back, it can even out their participation without making a point of doing so. Games and simulations can be one-time events, they can be carried on over several sessions, or they can be a starting place for more conventional learning to follow. It is also possible to organize the game so that more traditional course work, such as outside reading or seeking additional sources of information, can be worked into subsequent sessions. "The game is a great hook to maintain a high level of activity and interest," Ron says. Games also provide a shared group experience that people can continue to refer back to as a common touchstone.

Though Ron sees great potential for technology-based games, he believes people-to-people interactions are more effective:

> You really need to include the affective realm. That gives people opportunities to understand more about someone else's perspective. A good facilitator needs to create a culture and practice where people are supported in effective communication that enables them to get at these multiple perspectives with a more open-minded stance.

Because games or simulations may bring up viewpoints very different from how adults know or believe things "really are," the facilitator's role in debriefing, especially open-ended simulations, is important. This realization led Ron to pioneer an approach to simulation debriefing that has become standard in the field. It is known as the EIAG model:

What was the Experience?

Identify the facts and what was happening for you.

Analyze those facts, providing evidence.

Generalize in terms of what lessons can be learned.

Stadsklev (2012) offers a detailed description of how the EIAG approach to simulation debriefing is used to foster meaning making (pp. 47–58).

Dealing vicariously with potentially provocative topics is likely to feel safer than an intellectual discussion in which people tend to want to prove their own point. "In the long run," Ron says, "experiences like simulations and games are more likely to affect someone's existing perspective."

Games for Problem-Solving

For **Dennis Glenn**, creator of games and simulations for professionals in medicine and law as well as for college courses, having fun while learning is serious business. He regrets that for many people, "learning stopped being fun by about third grade," yet adults' brains gravitate to "learning experiences that are fun and playful." While it seems obvious why children like to play games for learning, Dennis observes that there are compelling reasons that games also appeal to adults—prominent among them, permission to fail without major penalty.

Adults seldom have that luxury and most do everything they can to avoid it, because few learning environments encourage exploration or trial and error. Games, however, depend on players making mistakes, so they accommodate failure with second chances and alternative methods of success. Once adults get comfortable with that notion, some will choose to fail just to see what happens and to get a sense of the game space they are playing in. Failure is not just allowed; it is acceptable and assumed.

For Dennis, gamification is a powerful method to support adults' learning in both school and work. When serious learning is the goal, gamification strategies focus on the learner's engagement with solving problems with immediate feedback rather than testing the content of what they know. He underscores that games rarely value remembering information for its own sake; the goal is to use information to solve problems while working with others. He also echoes Ron's observation about dealing with potentially provocative topics in a nonthreatening way.

Learners get to engage in learning that is both personalized and collaborative. Social learning is value-added: through serious games, we are helping to improve social interactions that can be transferred from the game to real-world settings.

Given Dennis's insights, it appears that serious games afford learners the opportunity to experiment with rules, emotions, and social roles. They get to make mistakes, get immediate feedback, and try alternatives. They get to collaborate with others in ways that satisfy social needs. The playful aspect of games seduces and rewards the curious brain while permission to make mistakes quiets the anxious brain.

Each of the approaches in this chapter involves carefully integrated and scaffolded RH and LH activities. We envision them as center stage based on this continual interaction. Though some approaches may call for experienced facilitators, reading through them may spark ideas for others who appreciate the rich learning potential and have the confidence to try them out.

Pause for Reflection

1. Which of the multifaceted approaches might have relevance in your practice setting?
2. Consider trying a selected approach. How would you scaffold your own experiment? Which parts might you try out first? How might you build your experience bank?
3. What approaches do you already use that you might build on—perhaps using some aspect of what you have just read—to create a more multilayered, hemisphere-integrated learning experience for participants?

8

Spotlight on Meaning Making

Learning is mostly a matter of reconstituting the already constituted world.

— FERENCE MARTON AND SHIRLEY BOOTH

IN CHAPTER 3, we described the brain's internal process of categorizing and associating new experiences with previous experiences, which is key to our ability to eventually make conscious meaning. First, the brain organizes prior experiences in ways that enable an individual to revisit and reconsider them, thus gaining the benefit of hindsight when engaging in further learning. This embodied learning is how people can know things they don't know they know. To bring such knowing to awareness, so that we can know what we know, we must reflect on experience. That means discovering and making visible associations the brain has tucked away in various networks; reflection can provide the necessary illumination.

Reflection: Making the Tacit Explicit

Since the brain cannot determine which of the potential links in its neural networks will turn out to be most appropriate for interpreting and making new meaning of an event, it tends to default to a well-traveled path, which, from the perspective of saving energy, is the most appropriate link. Such familiarity is likely to give rise to the feeling of understanding, even when it is inaccurate or partial. However, when adults intentionally attempt to reflect on what they think they (are coming to) know, and in this way bring to awareness some of the tacit connections their brains made during the association process, they can use additional, perhaps more thoughtful criteria to evaluate what has now become explicit. We therefore think of reflection as "a process of inquiry into one's experience" (Fiddler & Marienau, 2008, p. 76).

As depicted in *Theatre of Knowing* (see introduction to part 2), reflection is the bridge between metaphorical associations that precede articulable thought and logical, analytical awareness that we recognize as reason. In fact, as Haskell (1987) notes, "Reason requires both logic and metaphor" (p. 260). Reflection is thus essential to the kind of learning that is meaning making. By reexamining what is already known in light of new experience, the brain can construct a new understanding, perhaps leading to more inclusive and complex perceptions and ways of seeing and knowing. The spotlight of reflectivity enhances the brain's capacity to revise existing patterns as it constructs new awareness.

As was evident in previous chapters, most ALFAS (adult learning facilitators in any setting) use a variety of reflective approaches, often without realizing it. In this chapter, along with **Tony Saddington** and **David Boud**, we describe directed self-reflective activities that can change how people understand themselves and each other, as well as the content of a course or workshop. **Janise Hurtig** describes an approach to teaching self-assessment. Also related to reflection, **Melanie Booth** explains how different kinds of feedback can accomplish assorted purposes and provides a guide for helping adults learn to give and get effective peer feedback. **Michelle Navarre Cleary** describes an iterative writing feedback loop that involves the facilitator, peers, and the adults, themselves. And **Roberta Liebler** demonstrates how ethical meaning making can be enhanced with a tightly scaffolded approach using multiple rubrics—yet another vehicle for reflection.

Self-Reflection Fosters Self-Responsibility

Tony Saddington observes ironically, "Adults are lifelong learners who need to learn how to learn." Early in his courses and workshops, having emphasized the importance of experiential learning and the power of learning from one's experience, he startles participants with: "You don't actually learn from experience."

> And they look at me and say, "What?!" And I say, "No, you learn from reflection on experience. You can go through life having experiences and learn nothing. Something may stick, but it's incidental learning."

Tony was introduced to the following approach many years ago when he attended a workshop that David Boud facilitated. It is now a standard part of Tony's repertoire.

> Dave started out introducing a subject area. After about fifteen minutes, he said, "Take a piece of paper and write down what you are aware of right now with regards to yourself." Then after a minute he said, "Now write down what you are aware of right now about the other people in this room." Then he said, "What are you aware of right now about this learning environment?" And finally, "Please put that paper aside."
>
> We then broke up into small groups to discuss the topic. Ten to fifteen minutes later, he again asked us to

> write our answer to the same questions: "Answer just for yourself, and honestly. No one will see it." He repeated this process three or four times in a period of less than an hour. Finally, he asked us to look at all of what we had written. "Is there a pattern? Is there something you need to do with what you've written down?" and "What do you want to do about it?"
>
> I had been sitting back most of the time, even through the experiential activity. My written comments were along the lines of, "This is boring. These people in my group are boring. Maybe I should go get a beer." By the third or fourth time, I noticed, "Who is being bored?" I moved my chair in, got involved, and saw that these were interesting colleagues having a worthwhile conversation.
>
> I can no longer remember the content of the rest of the activity, but this was a huge aha! that underlined my participation (or lack thereof) and put the responsibility squarely on me to shift that.

Tony now uses this self-reflective approach with his workshops and classes to encourage adults to take more responsibility for their own learning, to be more "present," and to make the learning experience their own.

Managing Self-Reflection

David Boud is also a strong voice for reflection as a crucial aspect of learning. Because adults have spent a lifetime constructing and living out their sociocultural assumptions, they cannot see that those filters affect how they make meaning, especially with regard to psychosocial issues. Without adults' explicit self-reflection, they can remain profoundly unaware of how these external and internal influences limit their perspectives. At the same time, the process of attempting to uncover such assumptions, especially if they seem to run counter to current learning or skill development objectives, can also be deeply discomforting. And when grading is involved, adults' vulnerability is heightened; they will almost certainly deliberately construct "self-reflections" they think the ALFAS wants to hear.

Another area of Dave's professional attention is to create learning contexts wherein adults are encouraged to take responsibility for their own learning. Especially when working with graduate students and practitioners, who bring considerable experience and expertise, Dave structures course work to give adults leeway in terms of their learning goals and activities. At the same time, the requirements of institutional assessment tend to run counter to fostering such objectives.

With these factors in mind, Dave developed a structure that requires intense self-reflection but strictly limits learners' self-exposure—and though the reflections themselves are neither shared nor assessed, they inform the content of what is graded. First, Dave establishes a context for reflection by introducing his reflective learning model (see figure 9.6) He explains that developing these skills will enable adults to take greater responsibility for their learning in various contexts:

> There's not one way to take responsibility—most especially, I can't thrust it on them. So I give them tools that enable them to manage their own learning. Reflection is one such tool. It's not useful with traditional "content"; technical knowledge is not what it's cut out for. But it's excellent for practitioners working with the human dimension.

The heart of his approach is a learning portfolio (LP) that adults are strongly advised (but not, strictly speaking, required) to keep. He explains that it is a record of their learning, not "the objective—that is, content-focused—stuff."

> A trigger for their LP reflection is where something doesn't feel right—feelings tell us where the learning is to be had.

> I assure them, "I will not read this or ask you for it. You will know your LP is going well if you include things in it you would be deeply embarrassed for me to read."

When they wonder, "What are we going to be assessed on, then?" Dave describes two products: a traditional assignment—the usual academic paper on a relevant topic—and a self-assessment schedule (see Boud, 1992). In that schedule, which is handed in, they plot their learning path through the entire learning experience:

> They identify their learning goals, what they did, what evidence they have for their achievements, and their subsequent activities or plans based on the learning.
>
> However, the source document for that schedule is the learning portfolio. If they didn't engage with the LP, they can't produce the assignment. But I explicitly tell them not to reproduce raw material from the LP. They are to use it only as a platform for the kind of reflections that are suitable to be on the schedule. Even then, they are not to include more than brief excerpts, if any.

There are other structured opportunities for reflection, such as one-on-one discussions between learners. They may, if they choose, bring up for examination in that context—which Dave also is not privy to—aspects of their raw material. However, any subsequent discussion of that dialogue in the larger group is guided to focus on the process, not the content of anyone's personal reflections. The group may choose to facilitate further reflection by drawing someone out with open-ended questions, but not to satisfy their curiosity about personal details. Having been shielded from public exposure, these adults are much more likely to deeply explore feelings, ideas, and experiences linking their existing knowledge to course-based information—in other words, to make the most of the learning opportunity.

Reflecting on Practice

Reflection is one of three metacapacities (along with agency and flexibility) adult learners continuously self-assess throughout a graduate program in adult learning that includes participation in periodic group reflection seminars facilitated by a faculty mentor.

The three-part assignment described is first completed as an individual written piece, then debriefed in a group setting with peers. The process is repeated every quarter so that learners (and their mentors) can discern changes in their perceptions, understandings, feelings, and behaviors as reflective practitioners. (See chapter 9, Kolb's Dimensions of Complexity.)

Part 1: What WAS . . . Identify/describe an incident or situation that occurred within the last three months that you considered challenging/frustrating/irritating/bothersome. What transpired? Who were the key players? What was your role? What were you trying to accomplish? Focus your description primarily on what YOU said, did, thought, felt and observed.

Part 2: What MIGHT HAVE BEEN . . . Now, assume that your description in part 1 (that is, how you showed up in the situation) was and is assessed by you and others to be a 5 (on a scale of 1 to 10). Based on this understanding, develop a rich description of what a 7 might have looked like. How might you have shown up in that situation if you had been able to bump your reflective capacities up a few notches?

Part 3: Enhancing WHAT COULD BE . . . Given your detailed description in part 2 (description of you-up-two-notches in terms of your capacity for reflection), what specific skills do you need to work on to increase the likelihood of attaining that level of functioning more consistently, going forward?

In this scaffolded reflection process, adults are led through a sequence that engages their brains in recall, interpretation, and evaluation of their own performance; it is essentially a reflective *self-assessment*. They then project a mental image of themselves as being capable of a more satisfying performance. Envisioning such a possibility is a first step toward achieving the necessary skills to accomplish it. (This approach was devised by a small group of colleagues who have contributed individually to this book.)

We are not conscious of most things until we ask ourselves questions about them.

— DAVID EAGLEMAN

Self-Assessment

From the preceding approach it is clear that another way to think about aspects of reflection is through the lens of self-assessment. Self-assessment has a long and respected history in the field of adult education. (See "Further Reading: Self-Assessment Resources.") It is both a process and a product—an act of self-reflection as well as a written exercise in doing just that. However, the focus of self-assessment is less on the content or material being learned and more on the adult's own activity and experience of being a learner in that context.

Although educators typically associate *assess* with tests and grades, the derivation of the word is "to sit beside"; self-assessment thus implies *to sit beside oneself*. This requires metaphorically being in two places at once—as both an actor and an observer and evaluator of those actions: How did I approach this task? What might I have done differently? What do I now understand about both the content or material and myself as a learner that might inform future practices and decisions in my personal or professional life?

Adults who can develop this capacity are likely to enhance their learning from experience in a variety of settings. Such questions prompt the brain to look for deeper, more meaningful connections and applications. In this way, self-assessment can be a spur to metacognition and to explicitly internalizing new standards of performance. When adults are practiced at self-assessment, **Melanie Booth** notes, "they tell me they can hear my voice in their heads, but I know that means it has become their own voice, and they can start asking themselves the kind of questions I formerly had to ask."

Further Reading: Self-Assessment Resources

Candy, P. C. (1991). *Self-direction for lifelong learning: A comprehensive guide to theory and practice*. San Francisco, CA: Jossey-Bass.

Loacker, G., & Alverno College Faculty (Eds.). (2000). *Self assessment at Alverno College*. Milwaukee, WI: Alverno College Press.

Marienau, C. (1999). Self-assessment at work: Outcomes of adult learners' reflections on practice. *Adult Education Quarterly, 49*(3), 135–146.

Taylor, K. (1995). Sitting beside herself: Self-assessment and women's adult development. *New Directions for Adult and Continuing Education, 1995*(65), 21–28.

Taylor, K., & Marienau, C. (1993). Self-assessment: A source for individual and organizational learning. *Contemporary Education, 64*(3), 166–169.

Written self-assessments are also frequently an ongoing guide to what learners as a group are experiencing and understanding—or not. **Urusa Fahim** finds that reviewing their self-assessments enables her to ask questions or in other ways respond to what is happening with them in terms of both content acquisition and their affective experience of learning in ways that are novel and sometimes disconcerting. Hearing from someone who feels anxious or insecure—sometimes reading between the lines—permits appropriate intervention, allowing ALFAS to express compassion in ways that encourage the adult during rough patches.

There are no hard-and-fast rules about the how-tos of reflection and self-assessment; it depends on the intended outcomes. Most ALFAS advise that reflections are more effective if adults are provided with prompts, at least initially, until they develop a sense of what self-assessment entails. Without guidance, adult reflections easily devolve into a "dear diary" entry (I did this, then I did that), or the "postcard from summer camp" (Having a great/awful time; hope it's going to continue/change).

It is important that adults not feel their self-assessments are judged or evaluated, else, as **David Boud** points out, they are unlikely to risk being forthright about their lack of engagement or what they do not understand. Many ALFAS choose to not point out compositional errors in an adult's self-assessment, do not grade it, and instead focus their responses on affective and affirming comments—though they may also highlight areas where a self-assessment has been particularly effective, as a way to encourage improvement by catching the adult doing something right (as **Larry Daloz** so memorably puts it). **Janise Hurtig**'s approach, which does involve grading their self-assessments, is unusual in that self-assessment is also part of the content of the course.

Self-Reflective Self-Assessment Essays

Janise Hurtig's graduate course is about assessing learning. An important demonstration of their learning is adults' self-assessment of their own learning in the class. At the outset, each adult identifies initial objectives for her own learning. At the end, her task is to use those objectives as the focus of a final two- to three-page self-assessment. Janise instructs them to "draw on your own experience and the readings" and provides detailed narrative prompts for that paper:

> For the first self-assessment, I ask them to be sure to describe the evidence of their learning. I suggest that they draw on the portfolio of their work, meaning their collection of their work for the course since we began, such as drafts and redrafts of assignments, reading responses, and the like. Or they may draw on other kinds of evidence—things they have said or thought, discussions with classmates, maybe dreams they have had about assessment—whatever they recognize as clear evidence of that learning. In other words, I want them to avoid a laundry list. I ask them to be sure to identify how they know they have acquired new skills and knowledge.

For the second self-assessment assignment, a "narrative reflection on yourself as an 'assessor,' Janise requires that adults draw on materials and sources they have been introduced to during the course:

> In this case, this include results on the Teaching Preference Inventory (TPI), readings from Pratt and Associates' *Five Perspectives on Teaching in Adult and Higher Education,* and Wiggins and McTighe's *Understanding by Design,* especially chapter 7, "Thinking Like an Assessor," and whatever other course readings they found especially relevant to their professional practice as an assessor.

Janise again provides a detailed narrative prompt:

> I ask them to now think of themselves as an assessor, not as a teacher. I suggest that they explore their assessment

> priorities, how they deal with the power dimensions of assessment and the cultural issues they consider when they assess their learners. I ask: "How will you or do you assess the learners/participants in your offering, in light of your teaching perspective? Are there any inconsistencies between your teaching perspective and your assessment approach? How might you reconcile these?," and so on.

In aligning the prompts with the rubric Janise provides at the start of the course, she identifies the criteria for each element of the two assignments (exhibit 8.1): "Each of the two essays can earn seven points. In handing out and going over both the rubric and the criteria, I help them understand what is expected and how I will allocate those points."

Exhibit 8.1 Self-Assessment, Self-Reflective Criteria, and Rubric Alignment

Completeness: Is the assignment complete? Are all materials/written products in each section complete? Have all the assignments and each element for the section been addressed?

Thoroughness, Depth, and Creativity: Is the content addressed thoroughly and deeply? Do you explore the content in unique ways from your distinct perspective?

Supported by the Literature/Research/Experience: Do you draw on multiple resources (course readings, other readings, legitimate on-line sources, your own experience) to support your positions, critiques, and analysis about the various components of your assessment plans or your reflections on your learning or yourself as an assessor?

Relevance to Applied Practice: Is it clear how the content of the deliverable relates to your own professional practice as an educator of adults?

Deliverables	Completeness 1 = Complete .5 = Half done 0 = Less than half done	Thoroughness, Depth, Creativity 2 = Thorough and creative 1 = Thorough or creative or a bit of each 0 = Neither thorough nor creative	Supported by the Literature 2 = Uses the literature to inform or support insights 1 = References the literature but connection is not clear OR draws connections that do not reflect content of literature referenced 0 = Does not draw on literature	Relevance to Applied Practice 2 = Makes several or encompassing connections to own practice 1 = Makes only one or a superficial reference to own practice 0 = Does not relate the content to own practice	Total Points
Reflection on your learning	/1	/2	/2	/2	/7
Reflection on self as assessor	/1	/2	/2	/2	/7

By providing detailed prompts, a rubric that emphasizes what constitutes an effective self-assessment and clarifies her expectations, and consistent feedback, Janise scaffolds both the content and process of a learning experience that effectively requires growth in adults' capacity for personal and professional self-reflection—a major step toward greater self-direction in all areas of life.

Feedback

The word *feedback* is a twentieth-century invention. It emerged along with the development of microphones to amplify sound. What some people think of as feedback is the shriek when the sound system receives more input (called "feed") than it can handle. In fact, feedback is a process, not a product. It is such a ubiquitous aspect of ALFAS' practice that it is part of nearly every approach in this book and a primary feature of many. Rather than overload the system, feedback can also be calibrated to regulate it, thus enhancing the amplified product rather than detracting from it. This is a helpful analogy to have in mind when providing feedback to adults.

Another important factor is what the brain thinks of feedback. Feedback is a social interaction, and the brain is hard-wired to care deeply about how people respond to us. Positive feedback floods the brain with pleasure-inducing dopamine. Negative feedback can trigger a painlike response, and the parts of the brain that respond to social pleasure and pain also respond to physical pleasure and pain. Social pain interferes with cognitive performance and memory formation, whereas social reward can have lasting positive effects (Lieberman, 2013).

When adults are anxious—a fairly consistent aspect of their learning process, especially when the topic is breaking new ground—effective feedback can be a major factor in how their brains respond. If there's too much feedback, especially about what went wrong, a learner may be overwhelmed. If there's too little feedback, especially about what went right, the learner's brain will not have a chance to focus on something she or he clearly can do (the evidence is there) but is not yet entirely secure in. Most important, effective feedback focuses on developing adults' capacity to revise their own thinking rather than on directing (fixing) their behavior. In short, feedback without the brain in mind can be counterproductive.

We used to read adults' papers with a red pen at the ready. (This was B.C.—Before Computers.) It was automatic to immediately point out and correct the writer's mistakes and make critical marginal notes about many areas that needed further attention. At the end of the paper, we would add an encouraging comment about the overall effort and then a synopsis of the various problems for the writer to focus on. We questioned the wisdom of this approach when we overheard adults talking about marked papers we had just returned. "I'm afraid to read it," one woman said. "She must have hated it, because she hemorrhaged all over it."

Melanie Booth notes that there are different kinds of feedback, and each should be used with intention. "Directive feedback is largely instructive: 'add more here' or 'don't use passive voice.' It's not about learning as much as it is telling the writer what to do." She contrasts this with corrective feedback, which is essentially editing. Editing not only takes a lot of ALFAS' time, but it rarely helps adults learn how to spot and correct their own mistakes. (These two approaches to feedback account for most of our story of ineffective feedback described above.) More effective is minimal marking: highlight a few prominent errors that are patterns, "not too many at once because overload overwhelms," and in a marginal note point out what needs to be changed and ask the learner to find and fix these throughout the rest of the writing sample.

Facilitative is the most effective feedback for encouraging a writer's growth and development. When ALFAS ask carefully crafted questions that require the adult to rethink rather than just retype, we also invite her brain to create new connections.

Feedback that both affirms what the adult is trying to accomplish and encourages her to expand her perspectives and skill set is an ideal balance of support and challenge. (See "Further Reading: Writing to Learn.") It's also important to focus on specific recommendations for improvement rather than generalizations, Melanie says:

> "More analysis" and "greater clarity" don't explain much. Also, it's best to use a constructive rather than critical tone—reinforce the adult's strong points. For instance, it's great when the first thing the adult reads is an honest appraisal of something done well, followed with, "and this would be even better if you tried . . . ," and then add those suggestions. If there's a rubric for the assignment—always a good idea—that can help to structure the specific feedback.

Ideally, feedback is used formatively—to guide ongoing progress—rather than only summatively—at the end, as part of grading. In fact, conflating feedback with grading is likely to diminish its value as an adjunct to learning.

Further Reading: Writing to Learn

Bean, J. C. (2011). *Engaging ideas: The professor's guide to integrating writing, critical thinking, and active learning in the classroom.* San Francisco, CA: Jossey-Bass.

Hodges, E. (1997). Negotiating the margins: Some principles for responding to our students' writing, some strategies for helping students read our comments. *New Directions for Teaching and Learning,* no. 69, 77–89.

Straub, R. (2000). *The practice of response: Strategies for commenting on student writing.* Cresskill, NJ: Hampton Press.

Zinsser, W. K. (1988). *Writing to learn.* New York, NY: Harper & Row.

P-Q-P Peer Feedback Guide

Melanie Booth notes it is often easier for adults to recognize their own writing problems in someone else's draft. In addition, having to intently review another adult's written perspective on a topic often broadens the reader's viewpoint.

When introducing adults to peer feedback, Melanie first creates a sense of community and confidentiality. Adults need to feel safe in sharing their vulnerability about being judged. She then provides structure, guidance, and practice in how to have those conversations successfully. The structure each adult follows in offering feedback is one that Melanie also uses, and she provides a brief P-Q-P (praise-question-polish) rubric with examples.

Her first step is to put the writer at ease (praise), then ask about a few particular content areas that might need clarification (question), and finally offer specific suggestions on areas that would benefit from additional polishing (polish). Praise involves noting specific things the writer did well, not just global comments—for example, "I think the example about the human resources manager was well connected to the importance of accountability and what happens when that principle isn't followed." With that reassurance, the writer is likely to be more open to—perhaps curious about—questions that suggest ways to rethink aspects of that work—for example: "When you describe miscommunication between the two executives, I'm not clear how to relate to your subtopic heading on nonverbal communication. I think I would understand it better if you added some explicit connection."

The polish phase builds on the support provided thus far and encourages the writer to go even further—for example: "I see you've used the phrase, 'at this point in time,' in several places. I think some alternative ways to make the timing clear would be preferable."

An additional safety net when peers are first trying to develop peer feedback skills is to initially provide a nonpeer's paper for everyone to work on. When they exchange their feedback with a peer who has read the same paper, they imagine themselves as the paper's author and can reflect: Does this feedback help me? Do

I now understand what part of my writing was effective? Do I see where and how I might improve?

PQP guidelines are an excellent scaffold toward developing peer feedback skills. Adults' brains are far more receptive to both giving and getting peer feedback if they have been provided safety, structure, and opportunities for practice.

Iterative Writing and Feedback Cycles

As writing instructor **Michelle Navarre Cleary** sees it, scaffolding requires facilitators or instructors to have "a full sense of what you are asking adults to do. You may have tacit knowledge about your course or training that you have not made explicit even to yourself." She emphasizes the importance of ALFAS themselves understanding how to fit together the pieces of an assignment or course in order to achieve both intermediate and ultimate goals. When it comes to writing, something that many instructors have done well for years, it can be hard to realize that the writing strategies that they take for granted might be unknown to their learners:

> I offer adults choices and impress on them that there are multiple ways to get to the same goal or outcome. Having choice is also important to counter the myth that there is one right way to write. As I model different approaches to the process of writing, I give them a variety of tools they can use, and time to practice using these tools on their own and with each other.

Michelle explains that the tools offer various ways to generate, organize, develop, and revise their ideas and that it is important that participants practice while still in class. "If adults leave without having a start on their first paper," she says,

> many will freeze up and produce little, or wait until the last minute and hand in a brain dump. So while we

> are there, I show them how to use tools such as generic questions, timed writing, listing and mind mapping, and dialog to help them generate ideas.

Once adults have produced some samples of their own work, Michelle also has them learn to identify and critique various rhetorical constructions, first by analyzing published papers and then by exchanging drafts with peers: "We follow a cycle of try it on, try it out, share and get feedback from others, do minicorrections of your own work, give feedback to a peer, and so on. They repeat that cycle several times."

Michelle's learners eventually write first drafts on four different topics, using the various tools she introduced earlier. Then they select two of those topics for a second draft, again trying out different tools as they focus on revising for clarity and coherence. Finally, they complete two final drafts in which they practice editing not only to meet their audience's expectations of correctness but also for rhetorical effect. Because the brain wants to be right, is cautious, and tends to follow established patterns, the careful scaffolding and continuous feedback—from instructor, peers, and self (self-assessment)—along with the requirement that they experiment with alternatives in a low-stakes way gives adults' brains a chance to be curious and still safe.

No matter how well meaning our comments are, most adults initially experience feedback as critique—not just critique of how they performed on a particular assignment but of *them*—their entire being. The first reaction is nearly always to feel that we are telling them what they've done wrong—that *they* are wrong—rather than guiding them to what they might do better. We compound this when our feedback is too detailed and too directive. When ALFAS overload the system, the adult's response is a silent, internal shriek. Nevertheless, well-constructed, measured, thoughtful feedback can improve adults' skills, enhance their sense of well-being, as well as encourage greater self-responsibility.

Rubrics

When used effectively, a rubric is an excellent adjunct to scaffolding and provides effective support and challenge. Detailed descriptions of what a learning activity is about and how it will be assessed makes ALFAS' expectations transparent; it also requires adults to reflect on their own understanding of what is being asked of them. "If adults are beginning to learn or practice something new," **Melanie Booth** says, "it gives them something to hang onto until they can go beyond the rubric, when they have developed the capability to do so"—the essence of scaffolding. Ideally, rubrics are not just given as a handout; the process of reading through, discussing, clarifying, and perhaps questioning parts of the rubric can be a valuable reflective learning experience. Using rubrics along with modeling—such as samples of good, better, best—is even clearer. Melanie adds:

> If you are in a position to be evaluated, you need to know the criteria. If I don't share my criteria with you, it doesn't help you meet the criteria or *learn* to meet the criteria. It's a mystery that you're somehow just supposed to figure out and then perform. That shuts people down. Rubrics can be a communication tool *and* an enlightenment tool.

Breaking particulars of an assignment into manageable, perhaps more familiar, parts and describing different levels of achievement helps adults learn to distinguish between acceptable, very good, or excellent work. Both chunking the assignment and providing comparative categories are aspects of scaffolding. Melanie also underscores the importance of properly aligning the rubric with the assignment:

> In my faculty development role, I've seen great assignments where the directions don't line up with the grading rubric. We're essentially asking adults to do *this* but evaluating them on *that*. So it's also a good thing that rubrics require *us* to be more deliberate about how we're structuring or scaffolding the learning experience. If we're asking adults to be at a masterful level the first time they tackle a new challenge, is that a reasonable expectation?

Rubrics vary widely in details and format. They need not be in columns, though that is an effective way to line up particulars of an assignment with gradations that represent increasing levels of accomplishment—for example, elements of superior, average, or insufficient products (exhibit 8.2). The language of the rubric should also be familiar enough that adults' brains can connect to meaningful and concrete examples, then use those connections to construct a clearer mental model of the assignment, and as a basis for dialogue among learners and facilitators about what constitutes "good work."

Exhibit 8.2 Rubric Excerpt: Columns and Gradations

Mastery of core ideas	Explanations of the theories are faithful to the source text and insightful. Main theoretical points are clearly summarized and not oversimplified.	Explanations are general, but consistent with the source text; major points are presented.	Explanations are inconsistent: some sections are clear while others are vague.

Other rubrics may include numerical ratings—perhaps keyed to a qualitative evaluation so adults know how well they did with a particular task, as in exhibit 8.3, an excerpt from a multipart rubric.

Exhibit 8.3 Structural Organization Keyed to Qualitative Assessment

Structural organization of paper						
A. Essay is effectively introduced with a clear, relevant thesis	0	1	2	3	4	5
B. Body paragraphs include sufficient support for main idea	0	1	2	3	4	5
C. Essay organization is logical and flows	0	1	2	3	4	5
D. Essay is effectively concluded	0	1	2	3	4	5

0 = Missing
1 = Off task
2 = Attempted but not successful
3 = Partially complete
4 = Complete, satisfactory
5 = Exceptional, insightful

The purpose and meaning of such assessments may require further explanation to avoid alarm. For example, a good first draft will probably have many evaluations near the middle of the scale. In such cases, adults need to know that the numbers do not equate to grades; rather they are formative cues about where they are on track to meet expectations and what needs more improvement. They may also be reassured to hear that even superior final papers may have few, if any, "exceptional" ratings.

Rubrics may be keyed to specific, one-time assignments or used to inform iterations toward mastery, as with write-revise assignments. A rubric can also be "developmental," as is the case with Roberta Liebler's Ethics Dilemma Investigation. She starts by describing a range of capacities starting with where adults are likely to be at the beginning of the learning experience and ends with the high-level expectations that are the final goal. At each level, the rubric sparks reflection on their process of accomplishment and growth.

Ethics Dilemma Investigation

In **Roberta Liebler's** graduate seminar, Developing a Personal Ethical Decision-Making Framework, adults investigate the question, "What is ethically right for me?" The course description explains further: "Though most people will agree what actions are wrong, dilemmas occur when a decision must be made between two rights. In a democracy, an honest person can respect different points of view, while remaining faithful to one's own convictions."

Roberta provides learners, who come from diverse professional settings, with a multilayered scaffold to support their decision making. She describes it as "a comprehensive decision-making loop within which are feedback loops that encourage learners to revise previous steps as new information comes in and detailed analysis develops."

Each adult chooses an ethical dilemma to explore, based on individual interests and settings. For each step of the analytical process, Roberta provides demonstrations and guidelines, various forms of case illustrations, and feedback on drafts of their work in progress. The following steps provide the context for the detailed rubric that follows:

Step 1: Each learner identifies an *ethical dilemma*; clarifies her unexamined response, including examination of her core values; reveals biases; identifies all the stakeholders; and explores information (literature and other sources) that illuminates the issue.

Step 2: Learners outline the *options.* They explore their chosen ethical issue from at least two dilemma paradigms (e.g., justice/mercy; short term/long term; truth/loyalty; individual/community).

Step 3: Learners build their ethical arguments. They discuss the options using at least two resolution principles (e.g., Kantian, utilitarian, care based, social contract) that make sense for the perspectives they are highlighting. They also identify opposing perspectives and compare and contrast them.

Step 4: Learners evaluate the ethical options. Here they examine their chosen ethical dilemma from two or more contextual perspectives, such as personal, family, work, community, nation, world.

Step 5: Learners make a decision that involves arriving at and supporting a solution to their ethical dilemma.

Step 6: Learners reflect on their own ethical development. They contemplate questions such as: "How has your ethical view changed (or strengthened) since you began your investigation? What did you learn about how different people view this controversial issue? What surprised you? What new evidence might change the decision? What have you learned about yourself? What more would you like to know?"

The ethics dilemma rubric in exhibit 8.4 that Roberta created for this complex assignment enables her to take a formative approach, which includes providing feedback on multiple drafts of learners' incremental work during the seminar. The last two columns indicate Roberta's expectations for the final submission of the assignment.

Exhibit 8.4 Ethical Dilemma Rubric: Nested and Developmental

Trait	1 Beginning	2 Developing	3 Accomplished	4 Exemplary
1. Identify an ethical dilemma				
Ethical self-awareness	States own core ethical values or the origins of own core beliefs, but not both	Lists both own core ethical values and origins of own core beliefs	Provides details about own core ethical values and origins of own core ethical values	Analyzes clearly and in depth both own core values and origins of own ethical beliefs
Dilemma identification	Explains an ethical issue but not in terms of a dilemma	Imprecisely identifies an ethical dilemma and vaguely describes the ethical dimensions	Identifies ethical dilemma, but omits some of the ethically relevant dimensions	Clarifies an ethical dilemma in detail with all relevant dimensions, including defining the precise dimensions
Stakeholder awareness	Identifies only one stakeholder (usually self)	Considers a few of the potential stakeholders with uncertainty of who should be involved in the decision-making process	Identifies and considers most of the potential stakeholders but leaves out some of the relevant stakeholders	Identifies and considers all of the potential stakeholders relevant to the ethical decisions and clarifies each of their viewpoints
Relevant information investigation	Gathers some information about a few factors that impact the decision from only one disciplinary or cultural perspective	Becomes aware of information about a few factors that impact the decision from a few disciplinary or cultural perspectives	Lists factors that impact the decision from at least three disciplinary or cultural perspectives	Becomes knowledgeable of factors that impact the decision from several diverse disciplinary and cultural perspectives

(continued)

Trait	1 Beginning	2 Developing	3 Accomplished	4 Exemplary
2. Outline the options				
Ethical issue recognition	Recognizes basic and apparent ethical issues but is unable to see the complexity or interrelationships of components	Recognizes essential and apparent ethical issues but only incompletely sees the complexities or interrelations among the parts	Identifies ethical issues with recognition of either the complexity or the interrelationship among the issues	Discovers underlying ethical issues including the complex interrelationships among issues
Alternative actions and consequences probes	Identifies a few alternatives without evaluating the relevant assumptions and facts	Identifies a minimum of two alternative actions while mentioning some of the relevant assumptions and facts	Explains three or more alternative actions, along with an analysis of associated consequences	Explicates several alternative actions along with a detailed evaluation of each action's impact on each of the stakeholders
3. Build the ethical arguments				
Ethical perspectives/concepts, application	Limited display of major ethical theory such as only stating names with vague explanation	Names at least two major ethical theories with correct but cursory explanations	Explains at least three major theories with key points and only slight errors in accuracies	Provides the names and accurate, detailed explanations of at least three major ethical theories and how they apply to the dilemma
Relevant facts and assumptions, assessment	Ignores most of the relevant facts	Cursory review of information presented as facts	Judges information presented as facts by looking for ambiguous, illogical, and dubious information	Wisely appraises the relevant facts with careful notation of unsupported assumptions and ambiguous information
Ethical option, arguments appraisal	States the options but does not rate them	Cursory rating of the ethical arguments for the options	Rates most of the options for ethical reasoning and arguments	Appraises in detail the ethical reasoning and arguments for all options

Trait	1 Beginning	2 Developing	3 Accomplished	4 Exemplary
Options' impact on stakeholders' evaluation	Little suggestion of reflection on the impact of the options	Some suggestion or reflection of the impact of some of the options on some of the stakeholders	Evidence of reflection on how each of the options will impact the main stakeholders in the short term	Extensive evidence on the impact of each of the options on the well-being of all the stakeholders in the short and long term
4. **Evaluate the ethical options**				
Ethical perspectives, application	With support from instructor or classmates, can apply a cursory ethical perspective to a situation but is unable to make the application independently	Independently can apply an ethical perspective to an ethical question with only slight inaccuracies	Independently can apply to a new example an ethical perspective to an ethical question with limited specific implications of the perspective	Independently can apply ethical perspective to a new situation with accuracy, including detailed explanation of the implications
Ethical reasoning	Uses only legal or personnel considerations	Applies only one ethical decision-making framework in process of resolving the ethical dilemma	Applies two ethical decision-making frameworks in process of resolving the ethical dilemma	Applies and compares/contrasts three ethical decision-making frameworks in process of resolving the ethical dilemma
Various ethical perspectives evaluation	States two ethical perspectives but does not state the objectives, assumptions, and limitations of the different perspectives to the dilemma	States at least two ethical theory perspectives, including stating the objectives, assumptions, and limitations of the different perspectives to the dilemma	Explains at least three ethical theory perspectives, including analyzing the implications of the perspectives on the dilemma	Details the assumptions and implications of at least three ethical theory perspectives, including a comparison and contrast of how each perspective applies to the issue being analyzed

(continued)

Trait	1 Beginning	2 Developing	3 Accomplished	4 Exemplary
5. Make a decision				
Effect of ethical decision on stakeholders	Only considers the impact of proposed ethical stance on self	Takes an ethical stance, but considers the impact only on a few stakeholders	Takes a stance that coherently addresses the considerations of most of the stakeholders in the short run	Arrives at an insightful, coherent decision that comprehensively and realistically addresses the ramification on all stakeholders immediately, intermediately, and long term
Ethical decision-making framework choice analysis	Vaguely considers the ethical decision-making process	Recognizes a single decision-making framework for considering an ethical dilemma	Ponders two decision-making frameworks for assessing an ethical dilemma	Explores in depth more than two decision-making frameworks for evaluating an ethical dilemma
Ethical action definitively explained	Does not conclusively select an action	Selects an action that is not appropriate for the dilemma and/or is not supported by ethical reasoning	Offers an implementation plan with brief ethical support of the entire plan and its component parts	Articulately conveys an implementation plan that demarcates the decision-making process while providing evidence of the advantages and perils of the selected action in comparison with the alternatives
Counterarguments response	No attention to counterarguments	Justifiable argument does not identify or respond to plausible counterarguments	Reasonable argument identifies and responds to a few of the plausible counterarguments	Justifiable arguments carefully respond to plausible counterarguments

Trait	1 Beginning	2 Developing	3 Accomplished	4 Exemplary
6. Reflect on one's ethical development				
Ethical development appropriate for a graduate student demonstrated	Considers only own immediate needs	Shows preconventional level of ethical development such as limitation to only own perspective or deferring to authority	Demonstrates conventional level of ethical development such as stereotypical roles in the social order and impact of decision only on the immediate stakeholders in the short term	Displays postconventional level of ethical development, including considering implications on the larger society in the long term
Reflection on how solution(s) will demonstrate ethical responsibilities	Does not mention the rights and responsibilities the individual has to others	Identifies and accepts in a general way how will exercise ethical responsibilities to intimates	Identifies and accepts in a general way how will exercise responsibilities to others	Identifies and freely accepts specific and wide variety of ways will exercise rights and responsibilities to others and the larger community
Chosen individual ethical view articulated	Describes a partial or not individualized ethical worldview	Describes an incomplete ethical worldview	Articulates a generalized individual ethical worldview, including application to at least one specific case	Enunciates precisely a coherent individual ethical worldview that demonstrates deep reflection, including application to several specific cases

Roberta's seminar illustrates how scaffolding can support deep approaches to learning (see Marton & Booth, 1997). The topic—ethical dilemmas—and the decision-making process Roberta has structured fully engage learners' cognitive and affective faculties as they imagine and describe ethically justifiable actions and behavior. Recognizing the challenges inherent in this seminar, Roberta strives for early investment by inviting learners to select an ethical issue of significance to them—one that is situated in their own worlds.

Roberta anticipates that adults will initially be overwhelmed when she introduces the six-step process and the rubric at the beginning of the seminar. She therefore works through individual case examples with the entire group and offers one-on-one guidance as needed. She also has adults practice the six-step analytical process with cases gleaned from readings or current news. As the rubric illustrates, Roberta makes the developmental process visible so that learners can see their progress and appreciate the outcomes of their hard work.

Experienced ALFAS use several ways to engage adult learners in different kinds of reflection processes, typically without saying, "Now, it's time to reflect!" a command that can hit the anxious brain button and inhibit curiosity. ALFAS can alert the curious brain with question prompts, feedback, and rubrics that support adults to connect their experience to the current matters and invite deeper considerations.

(?) Pause for Reflection

1. Are there ways of engaging adult learners in reflection that would you like to add to your repertoire?
2. How might you fine-tune the way you offer feedback, in the spirit of fostering reflection for meaning making?
3. How might you whet the appetite of adult learners in your setting to try out various ways of reflecting on their own practice?

Part III

Reflecting on Practice

HAVING EXPLORED approaches that experienced ALFAS (adult learning facilitators in any setting) use when facilitating with the brain in mind, we now turn to theories and models that illuminate these practices. The authors featured in chapter 9 are well known in their various fields of endeavor, though not always in the field of adult learning. In addition to learning theorists, broadly defined, other areas of expertise are adult development, psychology, and philosophy. In briefly exploring these theories, we highlight aspects that link to how the adult brain learns.

Chapter 10 extends both the conceptual and practical implications of brain-aware facilitation to the larger question of why developmental growth and complexity of mind are essential for our individual and collective well-being, and underscores the role symbolic and analogic learning may play.

Finally, in the Epilogue, we describe aspects of our own journey of revising our practice toward more brain-aware approaches. Though we were enthusiastic and committed, doing so required us to challenge many of our own assumptions in ways we had not anticipated—an experience we imagine many colleagues share.

9

Enhancing Brain-Aware Practice with Theory

There is nothing so practical as a good theory.

— VARIOUSLY ATTRIBUTED

TWO BRILLIANT minds are associated with this evocative quote: Albert Einstein, the theoretical physicist who changed our understanding of the system called the universe, and Kurt Lewin, the Father of Social Psychology, who changed our understanding of human systems. Though little was known about how brains learn when theories of adult learning and development were being formulated in the mid-twentieth century, the theories we now explore have for decades been compatible with ALFAS' (adult learning facilitators in any setting) practice. We focus primarily on those most relevant to how we have portrayed the brain and learning.

We chose to back into theories (you may have noted several contributors do also) in order that they better inform practice-based questions and concerns. Since our purpose is to emphasize theoretical aspects we see as brain-aware, rather than go into depth for each theory, we refer you to other sources for fuller descriptions and further analysis.

That said, the links we propose between these theories and how the adult brain learns are of our own devising. Few of these theorists referred explicitly to the brain in any substantive way. In making these connections, we relied on recent works by well-regarded neuroscientists, many of whom we cited in chapters 1 through 3.

Learning from Experience

An essential premise of adult learning is that it begins with and proceeds from experience. A quarter-century ago, John Heron, from England, and David Kolb, from the United States, authored theories of experiential learning still widely used in the field.

Both were influenced by John Dewey's (1933, 1938) distinction between noneducative and educative experiences, the latter being those transformed into learning. The most educative experiences involve a person's substantive interpretations of subsequent experiences, and transactional exchanges between individual and environment. In both Heron's and Kolb's models, reflection serves as a bridge from reflexive, unconscious thinking to reflective consciousness. Bringing such tacit knowledge into awareness is a critical element of each theory's description of constructing knowledge; both processes of knowledge construction are also informed by and applicable in the real world. Heron's model has from the outset explicitly emphasized the role of the embodied and analogical in learning; these have lately become more visible in Kolb's updated model. (See "Further Reading: Other Models of Experiential Learning.")

John Heron's Modes of Psyche and Ways of Knowing/Facilitation

John Heron (1992), whose background is transpersonal psychology and philosophy, identifies four modes of functioning that are continuously interwoven in everyday living: affective, imaginal, conceptual, and practical. His model of the human psyche arranges these modes in a pyramid-shaped up-hierarchy, that is, one that "works from below upwards, like a tree: something that has roots, a trunk, branches, and fruit" (p. 20). This contrasts with the more familiar hierarchy, where higher positions control and rule those below.

Heron's modes of psyche pyramid has similarities with our *Theatre of Knowing* visual metaphor (see part II, introduction). He positions the affective mode—in our theatre, where learning occurs—at the base of the pyramid, because it "is the root and fundament of all the other modes and contains them in tacit or latent form" (p. 20). Feelings and emotions fuse with the imaginal to form the next level of the hierarchy, where intuition and imagery live. The next higher mode in Heron's pyramid, conceptual, is where reflection and discrimination occur. According to Whybrow (2015), intuition is a "preconscious [right hemisphere]

> **Further Reading: Other Models of Experiential Learning**
>
> For a brief orientation to other models of experiential learning see Merriam and Bierema's *Adult Learning: Linking Theory and Practice* (2014). In addition to Kolb, they reference "Jarvis' types of learning model, Tennant and Pogson's four levels of experiential learning, and Fenwick's five perspectives on experiential learning" (pp. 108–114). See also chapter 2 and appendixes A to C in Taylor, Marienau, and Fiddler's *Developing Adult Learners: Strategies For Teachers and Trainers* (2000).

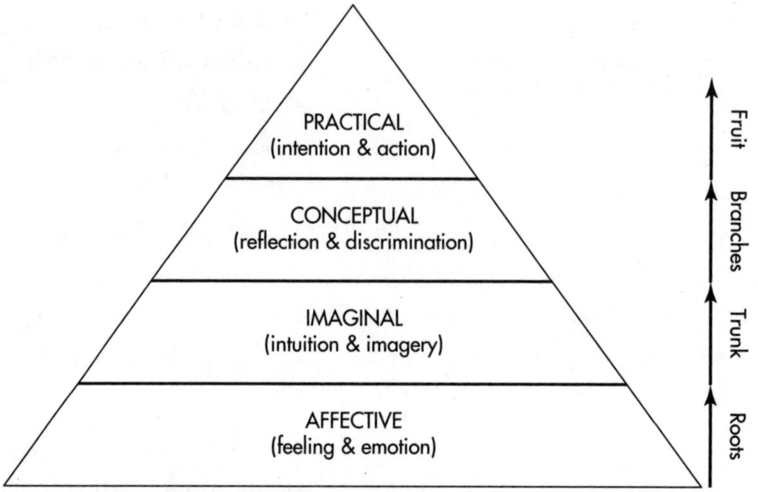

Figure 9.1 Heron's Modes of Psyche
Source: Adapted from Heron (1999) and Paxton (2003).

network of *reflexive* self-knowledge" (p. 50), whereas conceptual is a reflective [that is, left hemisphere] capacity, "the conscious mind at work" (p. 49). At the top of the hierarchy is the practical mode where informed and intentional action in the real world takes place.

In figure 7.2 of this volume, Heron reframes the modes of psyche as ways of knowing that ideally can guide approaches to group facilitation. Learning begins with direct experience—*experiential*—which calls on the affective and imaginal (RH). (For purposes of facilitation, experience could be current, in the moment, or explicitly recalled with the intention of learning from it anew.) The next movement, *presentational,* picks up imaginal and connects it with conceptual, to capture the essence of the experience in symbolic (not yet verbal) form (also RH-centered activity). Only after a nonverbal expression of this connection would the adult move to the *propositional* mode, where she picks up (LH) conceptual framing and begins to entertain (LH) practical aspects. In the uppermost part of the pyramid, *practical,* application is joined with affective, and the cycle begins anew. Heron's model of facilitation offers ALFAS an astute rationale for why the integrated ("center stage") approaches in chapter 7 are especially effective with adult learners.

A striking difference between typical facilitation methods and Heron's model is his emphasis on explicit presentational—symbolic, nonverbal, embodied, analogical—knowing. Though he refers to what is now decades-old research, Heron's analysis of the neurological implications of his facilitation model is still largely in line with current findings and many of our own assessments. For example, he underscores starting with positive emotional attitudes and also approvingly cites Gardner's framework of multiple intelligences as supportive of facilitators using diverse experiential modalities. Heron then highlights the importance of interweaving symbolic and imaginal expression, as well as group interaction, discussion, and feedback, to achieve meaningful and lasting learning.

> The point about imaginal presentations is that they contain within their patterns the latent concepts and propositions—which may precipitate themselves spontaneously into the [adults'] minds. This kind of unforced generation of conceptual learning is the rationale for taking the learning process, in a deep and sustained way, into the affective and imaginal modes. Of course, there is still explicit cultivation to do at the conceptual level itself. *But the seedling is already above ground* [our emphasis, Heron, 1992, p. 230].

In Heron's view, conventional approaches to teaching and learning have vastly overlooked the crucial role of the first two stages of this cycle: initial positive arousal and creative, imaginal, and symbolic treatments of material to be learned.

David Kolb's Theory of Experiential Learning and Integrative Development

David Kolb (1984), whose field is social psychology, explores the complex connections between and among experience, learning, and development, including a theory of experiential learning, a model of the learning cycle, and a self-report instrument that reveals learning styles and preferences. He also extends his learning theory to a developmental theory he calls integrative development.

Two functions are at the core of Kolb's theory of experiential learning: how we take in information and what we do with it. Each function is the subject of a dialectical choice or intrinsic preference ("style"), which varies with the situation. We grasp information either directly through the senses or indirectly through intuiting concepts and their connections. We transform that information through reflection or action. Kolb stresses that being in greater command of these choices makes for a more flexible—hence, a more effective—approach to learning and creating knowledge. Although Kolb's current model does not directly address RH/LH issues, his emphasis on dialectical balance echoes the need for hemispheric balance. His central aim, explained in the updated version of *Experiential Learning* (2015), is "to explain how individuals learn and to empower learners to trust their own experience and gain mastery over their own learning" (p. 53).

Kolb's four adaptive learning modes in figure 9.2 depict the two dialectical functions. At the upper end of the grasping function (vertical axis), concrete experience (CE), such as data or information, stimulates the senses; at the lower end, abstract conceptualization (AC) evokes intuition about concepts. In the transforming function (horizontal axis), the individual's attention is toward either reflective observation (RO) on the experience (left side) or active experimentation (AE) in response to the experience (right side). Learning profiles, or learning styles, are determined by where individuals' widely varying preferences fall on each axis.

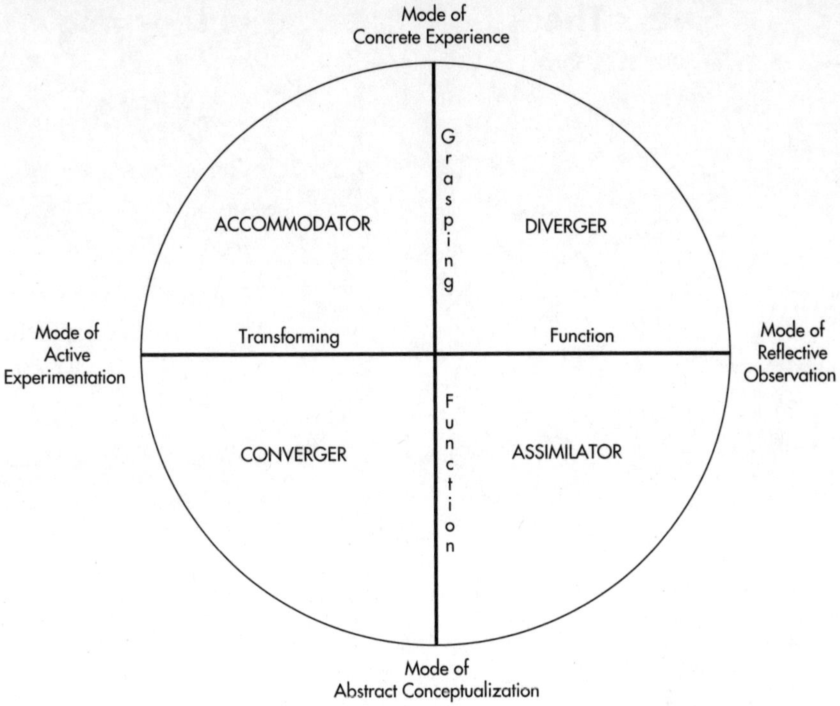

Figure 9.2 Kolb's Learning Cycle
Source: Adapted from Kolb (1984).

In addition to identifying the four adaptive learning modes of the cycle (CE, RO, AC, and AE), each quadrant—the transaction between two modes—is described in terms of the dominant learning style it represents. *Diverging* (upper right) emphasizes the space between experience and reflection; thus, people with a diverging style prefer to brainstorm ideas and keep options open. *Converging* (lower left) is the opposite of diverging, thus emphasizes the space between abstraction and experimentation; those with a converging style prefer to focus on established methods and steps. The other two terms are drawn from Piaget (1955). *Assimilation* describes incorporating new information into one's existing schema (the space between reflection and abstraction); *accommodation* refers to changing one's existing

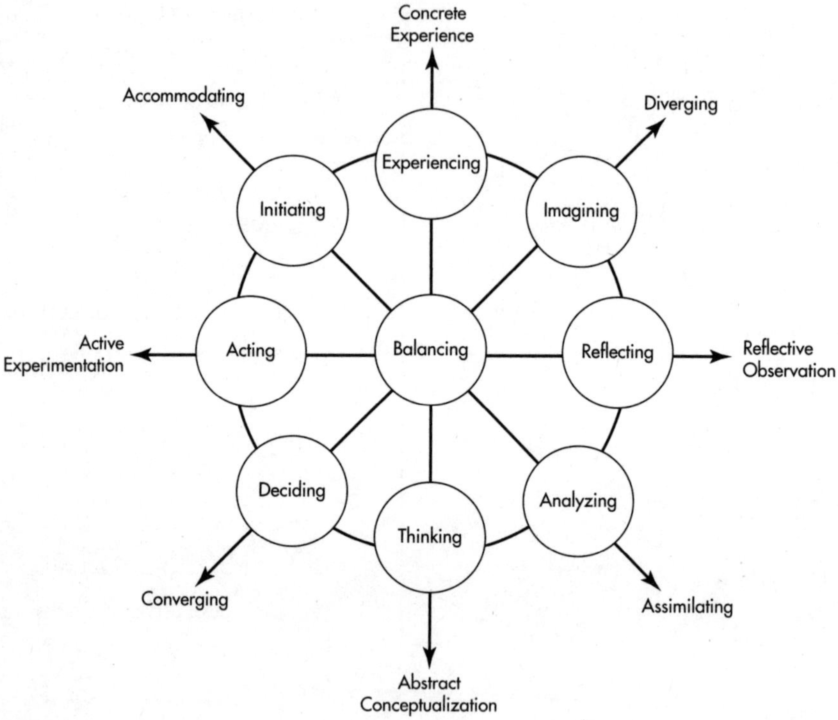

Figure 9.3 The Nine Learning Styles and the Four Dialectics of the Learning Cycle

Source: Kolb (2015, ch. 4, p. 147).

schema and actions in response to new information (the space between experimentation and concrete experience).

The expanded learning cycle, revised in 2013 (figure 9.3), is designed to encourage the development of greater adaptability and flexibility in how people approach and engage in learning, thereby expanding their repertoire. The four adaptive learning modes have grown to nine typologies in order to represent a more dynamic flow through the learning process. A precursor to experiencing is now *initiating*, to reflecting is *imagining*, to thinking is *analyzing*, and to acting is *deciding*. In the center is the new ninth adaptive capacity, *balancing*. Taken as a whole, these nine typologies are "dynamic traits that can be 'flexed' to meet demands of different learning situations" (see "What Is the KLSI 4.0?" on www.learningfromexperience.com).

From a brain-aware perspective, Kolb's model helps us appreciate individual differences and the various ways people enter and engage the learning process. Not unlike the difference between those who take whatever-it-is out of the box, undo the packaging, and start assembling it right away, versus those who leave all the interior packaging intact until thoroughly reading the directions and checking for all the pieces, some learners actively delve into experience—immediately trying something out to figure out how it works—while others take action only after careful consideration and planning.

As well, some adults move easily among the modes, while others, entrenched in what is familiar and comfortable, are unlikely to find that other approaches could be more effective. By helping them become more aware of their learning preferences, ALFAS can develop adults' capacity to adapt to different demands and situations, avoid the tempting groove of their learning Broadways, and thus to learn more effectively in the face of greater complexity.

Zull's Anatomy of Kolb's Model James Zull (2002), a biologist and educator, proposed explicit connections between Kolb's learning cycle and the architecture of the brain.

What Kolb calls *concrete experience*, Zull calls *gathering data,* meaning reception in the sensory cortex (near the back). Zull next refers to *reflection,* involving integration of data and memories in the association areas (midbrain). A *hypothesis* (abstract concept) is then generated in the frontal integrative cortex (front). *Testing* the hypothesis follows in the motor cortex (midbrain), as it involves physical activity (writing and talking are also forms of testing). Motor activity leads to new experience and new sensory input, and the cycle continues. This, according to Zull, is the brain's own cycle of learning, including those things learned below the level

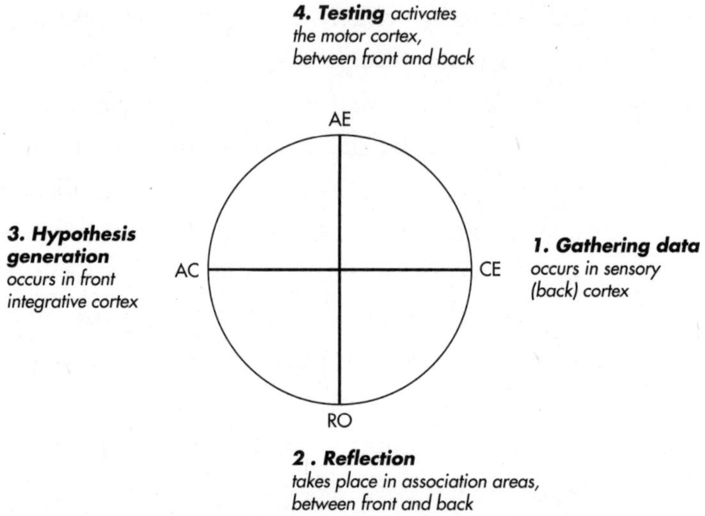

Figure 9.4 Zull's Anatomical Schematic of Kolb's Learning Cycle

Note: The numbers follow the typical order of Kolb's learning cycle. Kolb's cycle thus is rotated one position to the right to better approximate the orientation of areas of the brain. Zull's sketch is "not meant to be precise or anatomically accurate, but to help convey [his] general ideas" (p. 28).
Source: Adapted from Zull (2002).

of awareness. Specific meanings flow from association areas to the frontal cortex, to become the basis for conscious thought and planning, involving images, language, intent, recall, feelings, decisions and judgments.

To be effective, according to Kolb (1984) learners need to exercise all abilities represented in the four modes: "Involve themselves fully, openly, and without bias in new experiences (CE) . . . reflect on and observe their experiences from many perspectives (RO) . . . create concepts that integrate their observations into logically sound theories (AC), and . . . use these different theories to make decisions and solve problems (AE)" (p. 30). Meeting such challenges at higher levels of integration is key to Kolb's theory of *integrative development*—"learning as a holistic process of adaptation to the world" (p. 31).

Integrative Development Looked at from a brain-aware facilitator's perspective, Kolb's theory of integrative development involves being alert to feelings and their effects (affective dimension), seeing things differently and in new ways (perceptual), gaining new understandings (symbolic), and acting appropriately for the situation (behavioral)—activities we have identified as being on both sides of the Curtain of Awareness. Kolb appears to focus these four dimensions of complexity on an adult's conscious activity; we infer that more is going on behind the scenes than can be articulated and made visible. In any case, he sees the overarching developmental task as integrating as many of the four capacities as possible that are most germane to the situation (environment). Whether an adult is likely to always be conscious of these dimensions, ALFAS can have them in mind when devising assignments. Several approaches in part 2 include activities explicitly or implicitly based on Kolb's model. For example, see Reflecting on Practice in chapter 8.

Reflection

Reflection plays a major role in both Kolb's and Heron's models of learning from experience. To Kolb, reflection is a process that fosters "internal transformation of experience" (2015, p. 49). The LSI (Learning Styles Inventory) 4.0 intentionally includes "more specific reflective processes that vary by learning style and developmental level . . . and that define a continuum of reflection" (p. 58). There is a spiral-like flow between and among the styles. For example, the imagining style (associated with reflective observation) engages RH activity, where images get shaped and transformed, while still enfolded in the "concrete experiences [CE] of sensation and affect." Conversely, reflection in the analyzing style seems to deal more with LH-type activities—"systematic manipulation of abstract symbols fully independent of experience and context." Between these, the reflecting style "explores deeper meanings to *integrate* [our emphasis] image and symbol" (p. 58).

As with Kolb's updated model of the learning cycle, Heron's (1999) model of fourfold knowing does not confine reflection to just one mode or phase. Heron integrates four discrete cognitive modes or ways of knowing with stages of the inquiry cycle to guide group facilitation:

> Experiential knowing—imaging and feeling the presence of some energy, entity, person, place, process or thing—is the ground of presentational knowing. Presentational knowing—an intuitive grasp of the significance of patterns as expressed in graphic, plastic, moving, musical and verbal art-forms—is the ground of propositional knowing. And propositional knowing—expressed in statements that something is the case—is the ground of practical knowing—knowing how to exercise a skill. (Heron, 1999, p. 122)

Contributor **Doug Paxton** (2015, p.c.) explains that when facilitating a group, the ALFAS would include a reflection pause between each of the four phases.

Nonetheless, in Heron's model, reflection is most pronounced in the phase between expressive (presentational) and verbal (propositional). As adults move between these ways of knowing, the Curtain of Awareness becomes more translucent as they start to articulate their newly emerging meaning to themselves and one another. It is important that ALFAS remain sensitive to adults' vulnerabilities and fear of judgment. As David Boud cautions in chapter 8, the experience belongs to the learner, and she or he must have the authority to decide what and how much to share with others.

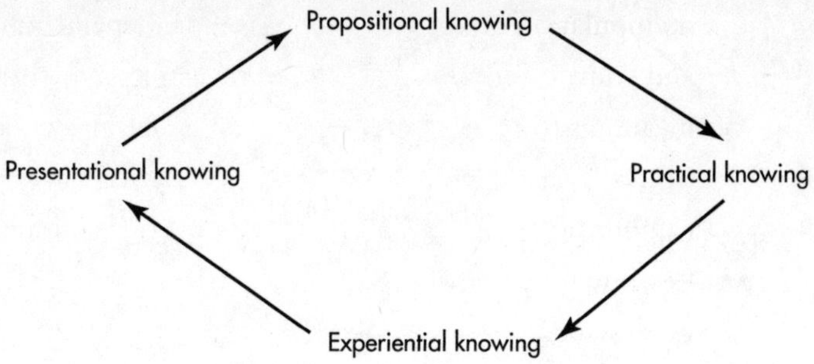

Figure 9.5 Heron's Fourfold Circuit of Experiential Knowing
Source: Adapted from Heron (1999, p. 123).

David Boud's Reflective Learning Model

Shortly after David Kolb described his model of learning from experience, Australian David Boud was working on his reflective learning model. For Boud, whose research background is in adult and higher education, "It is only when we bring our ideas to our consciousness that we can evaluate them and begin to make choices about what we will and will not do" (Boud, Keogh, & Walker, 1985, p. 19). Boud focuses in particular on individuals' reflections on complex experiences, including attention to feelings, in preparing for application in the real world. Without sufficient reflection, the potential of adults' experience may go unrealized and may yield little that they can apply to new situations or use as a foundation for deeper understanding. From a *Theatre of Knowing* perspective, the spotlight of reflection may illuminate initial associations and newly established connections behind the Curtain of Awareness, thus permitting reconsideration and adjustment.

Because reflexive thinking is automatic and ongoing, much goes unnoticed. Although ALFAS may intentionally engage adults in a new learning experience, each brain is still subject to its filters born of prior experience. These may include positive

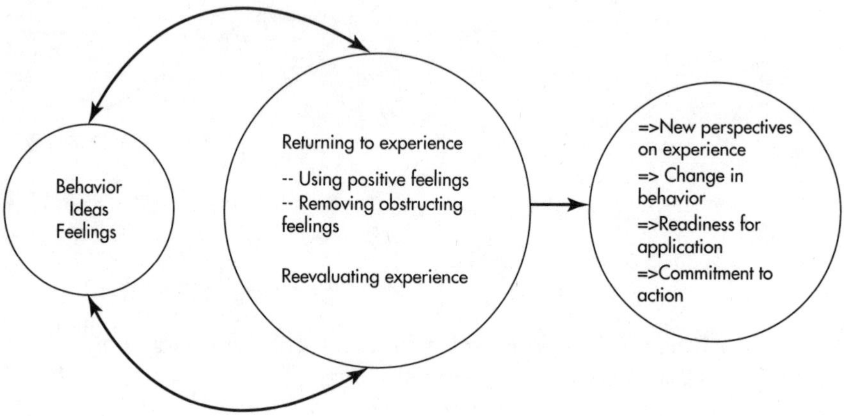

Figure 9.6 Boud's Reflective Learning Model
Source: Boud, Keogh, and Walker (1985, p. 20).

or negative attitudes toward learning itself, one's capacities as a learner, and the content or objective of the learning experience. In the absence of conscious reflection on and acknowledgment of such contradictory—and largely hidden—assessments and responses, current learning can be very much curtailed. Boud notes that we all bring our embodied life history with us on every occasion, which profoundly affects our perceptions of what does and does not count as important. It also sensitizes us to some features of our world and blinds us to others as it shapes the intent we have that guides our priorities.

Boud's model outlines a three-phase process that includes attention to what comes before and after the experiential learning event. Prior to the event, the preparation phase (*anticipatory reflection*) takes into account the adult's motivations, expectations, and skills, as well as characteristics of the learning environment. Reflective processes after the event focus on aspects of the event itself, paying particular attention to emotions and feelings that may color what is remembered, hence the meaning being made. Without this step, which is easily overlooked or truncated, the potential for learning that can change minds is diminished.

For example, after-the-fact reflection done in isolation, rather than in conversation, may reconfirm what adults believe they already know rather than promote critical reflection.

Boud also stresses the need to establish confidentiality about the personal content of adults' reflections, thus creating safety. Another aspect of safety—and good practice—is to not use personal reflection as a basis for grading or other assessment. If adults feel their personal revelations will be judged, forthright disclosure of their real feelings and reactions is likely to be subordinated to what they believe the ALFAS wants or expects. (See Boud's Managing Self-Reflection in chapter 8, which enables adults to focus on their feelings and reactions with regard to highly personal experiences, without having to describe details or the content of the experience, itself.)

Both Boud and Kolb emphasize the importance and potential empowerment of encouraging adults to reflect in ways that promote their own choice making and meaning making. They therefore caution against overly formalized, facilitator-directed reflective activities that may enhance cognitive learning (as measured by traditional exam-based assessments), but inhibit the kind of learning that ultimately promotes greater self-direction. In learning situations, it is necessary to promote sufficient conscious reflection to turn experience into learning. As many of the approaches in part 2 illustrate, experienced ALFAS value activities that promote reflection, and they often incorporate them in many segments, assignments, and deliverables.

Social Learning

Three main theoretical frameworks contribute to social learning theory: Bandura's early formulation, which continues to enjoy wide application in the social sciences; Vygotsky's insight that all learning is ultimately social learning; and Lave and Wenger's ideas concerning situated learning and communities of practice.

Bandura's theory (1977, 1986) posits that people learn from watching other people. Seeing the consequences of others' actions, we either emulate or avoid what they modeled, thus saving ourselves from having to experience everything directly. Watching also reminds us which behaviors to employ and when, and it provides a constantly expanding repertoire.

Social learning theory also describes how people learn with and from each other. Early in the twentieth century, Lev Vygotsky (1978) found that children working in pairs could often solve a problem that neither could solve alone. He proposed that all learning is ultimately social learning and that the most effective learning environments encourage interaction, collaboration, and dialogue. The gap between what people can do entirely on their own and what they find difficult or impossible to do on their own Vygotsky called the *zone of proximal development*, or ZPD. (See "Extended Mind.")

Wenger (2000) defines social learning as "a dynamic, two-way relationship between people and the social learning systems in which

Extended Mind

Vygotsky's focus on social learning effectively contradicts what has been called the "vertical sandwich" theory of cognition—essentially, that between the "bread" of sensation (perceptual/sensory input) and the "bread" of action (motor output), the brain provides the cognitive, information-processing "filling." In including the social surround, Vygotsky's perspective appears to support philosopher Mark Rowlands' (2010) notion of the "extended mind" (p. 37). Rowlands describes a wide range of artifacts, processes, and mechanisms that extend the brain: things that take the place of memory and storage, such as writing, reading, and sticky notes; the Arabic numbering system, and computing devices, from the abacus to those used to plot interstellar voyages, that make possible simple to high-precision computation; and so on. Such extensions allow our brains to engage in more of the complex activities that, so far at least, cannot be otherwise accomplished, such as interpretation, creativity, and meaning making.

they participate. It combines personal transformation with the evolution of social structures" (p. 227). Framing the issue from a systems rather than an individual level, Lave and Wenger (1991), known for their formulation of situated learning, ask: What social contexts are most conducive to learning?

Situated learning examines how groups of people with common interests and issues participate in structuring frameworks that help their members understand their particular world of practice. Three elements define communities of practice: members are connected through a "joint enterprise" to which they are able to contribute; they establish mutual, trustworthy relationships; and they share and use resources appropriately (Wenger, 2000, p. 229). That said, Wenger cautions that communities of practice "are born of learning, but they can also be its cages" (p. 230), a Broadway-following reality for ALFAS to keep in mind when emphasizing social learning approaches.

From the brain's perspective, it's straightforward: we are "wired to be social" (Lieberman, 2013, p. ix). As our earlier visit with Mr. Oog pointed out, social learning systems enabled successful human engagement and developed early; cognitive abilities rely on the more recently developed frontal and prefrontal cortex. Moreover, although "the entire brain participates" in social learning, the right hemisphere, seat of empathy and nonverbal connection, "appears to be dominant" (Cozolino, 2014, p. 41). At every opportunity, RH will work on connecting with and understanding other people. It is always engaged in social learning, unless we specifically attend elsewhere.

Lieberman (2013) concludes that a major reason for humans' relatively larger brain size, compared with other primates, is our need to solve social problems; living successfully in groups requires keeping sufficient track of complex social cognition. More specifically, Terrence Deacon (1997) points to "close cooperation in mother-infant relationships, passing on tricks for extractive foraging, organizing hunts, manipulating reproductive competitors, attracting mates, recruiting groups for warfare and collective defense, or providing a sort of efficient social glue" (p. 350).

This premise is further supported by evolutionary anthropologist Robin Dunbar (1998), who suggests that the need to mediate social issues was more pressing, in terms of survival and therefore brain development, than needing to problem-solve more general environmental problems. It is not surprising, then, to find that the social learning system is always on, unless the adult makes a concentrated effort to switch to the logic-based, problem-solving system. Furthermore, when either system is highly engaged, the other is largely disengaged—another good reason to pay sufficient initial attention to adults' emotional state while they are trying to learn.

An additional aspect of the social brain relevant to ALFAS' practice is our species' craving for others' positive regard. Approaches such as "welcome the body into the room" and "provide sufficient support" are likely to trigger the same dopamine-fueled reinforcement systems that prompt positive feelings and contribute to learning how to solve problems (Lieberman, 2013, p. 78).

Assuming that activities are structured with awareness of the need to establish safety before asking people to rely on one another in meaningful ways, group interdependence is another important contributor to an adult's learning process. Many ALFAS featured in part 2 organize small groups, form teams, and foster community. Many also focus on social learning as a way to encourage adults to be open to seeing, relating to, and learning from those who are different from themselves.

We are geared for cooperation as a way of life. The brain has spent millions of years perfecting various systems that draw us to others, make us aware of how they think and feel, and sometimes lead us to aid them in preference to ourselves—all of which happens without conscious cognition. The downside of this desire for connection is the tendency to want to harmonize with the group (our brains flocking together along some collective Broadway). ALFAS need to account for this by providing the supports and challenges that encourage adults to develop and uphold their own criteria for decision making, while still being open to thoughtfully considering, and possibly integrating, other perspectives. In essence, social learning is predicated on the fact that learning and development take place in a social context of environmental prompts as people act on the world and it, it turn, acts on them.

Multiple Intelligences

Howard Gardner's theory of multiple intelligences (1999) asks us to shift what we believe about the nature of intelligence and to revalue individual learning differences. Gardner underscores the drawback of framing "intelligence" (as typically measured on an IQ test) almost entirely in terms of an individual's capacity for verbal/linguistic and mathematical/logical expression—primarily an LH orientation. Though valuable in certain contexts, notably typical formal education, it devalues brains (and the people they belong to) that draw more heavily on RH capacities and appear to learn differently.

Gardner (1999) instead defines *intelligence* as a "biopsychosocial potential to process information that can be activated in a cultural setting to solve problems that are of value in a culture" (pp. 33–34). He suggests that recognizing multiple intelligences may help ALFAS better appreciate learners who "possess different kinds of minds, with different strengths, interests, and modes of processing information" (p. 106). Bruce Williams (2002), a contributor to this book and experienced adult facilitator, who has also made a study of learning and the brain, emphasizes the need for

Further Reading: Sources on Multiple Intelligences

For a condensed review of major perspectives on intelligence, see Merriam and Bierema's *Adult Learning: Linking Theory with Practice* (2014) and Williams's *Multiple Intelligences for Differentiated Learning* (2002). For an appreciative critique of MI, see Smith's "Howard Gardner and Multiple Intelligences" (2008).

differentiated approaches to facilitating learning—that by varying methods to address the multiple intelligences present, the facilitator can use learners' "intelligence strengths" as well as strengthen their "intelligent weaknesses" (pp. 15–16). (See "Further Reading: Sources on Multiple Intelligences.")

Gardner posits eight intelligences (Williams, 2002):

Verbal/linguistic—ability to use language for a particular aim

Logical/mathematical—ability to analyze problems carefully, manipulate mathematical processes skillfully, and use the scientific method rigorously

Intrapersonal—ability to grasp the inner workings of one's self in such a way as to understand one's own life and operate well individually

Interpersonal—ability to grasp the inner workings of others in such a way as to connect with them and work with them

Visual/spatial—ability to conceptualize and use patterns in space

Musical/rhythmic—ability to appreciate, create, or perform rhythmic or musical patterns

Bodily/kinesthetic—ability to find or to create solutions through the use of the body

Naturalist (added in 1990)—ability to distinguish varieties of plants and animals and to amass knowledge of the workings of the external world

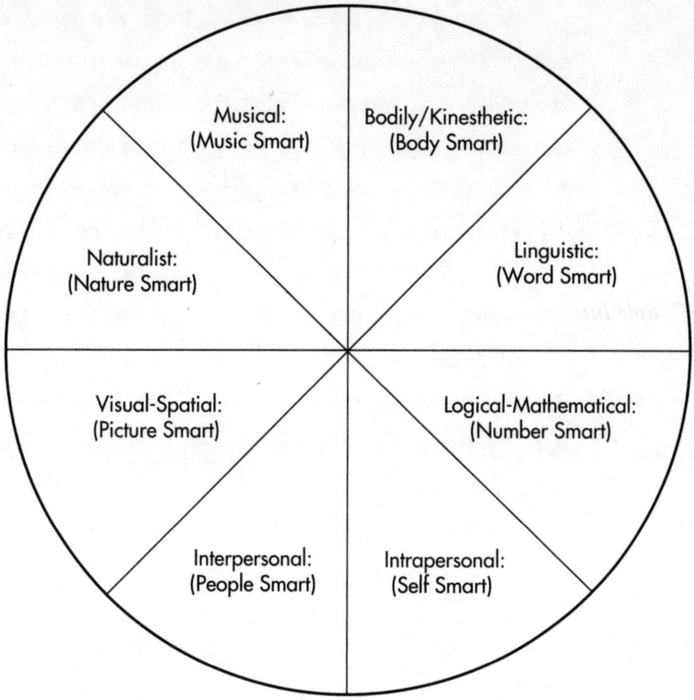

Figure 9.7 Multiple Intelligences Wheel

These cannot be slotted neatly into left and right hemispheres because each may involve both LH and RH activities to varying degrees, depending on the context and purpose of the activity (figure 9.7).

Gardner cautions practitioners against labeling individuals according to their apparent preferred intelligence as these rarely operate independently and are used in combinations unique to each individual. Rather, a preference can be considered an "initial encounter or entry" (Williams, 2002, p. 25) to the material, thus affording facilitators better choices in engaging diverse learners. Once adults have gained entry, ALFAS may be able to help them strengthen those areas in which they are less developed by providing the appropriate balance of support and challenge.

Although the notion of separate *intelligences* is an open question from a neurological perspective (Smith, 2008), they are useful as a way for ALFAS to frame practice. Even if MI is not a literal description of brains processing differently, it alerts ALFAS to think more carefully about responding to individual differences with varied approaches. Moreover, Gardner's emphasis on multiple entry points accords with what is known about how emotions influence learning. For example, facilitation that acknowledges adults' initial anxiety and then builds on their experience, wise starting points for ALFAS in almost any instance, may be particularly effective with those whose learning orientations are more aligned with symbolic than verbal mediums. Many approaches in part 2 illustrate how facilitators can create a hospitable climate for learning and more effectively connect the individual to the content.

Gardner's notion of telling analogies also echoes the brain's reliance on metaphor as its fundamental means of making meaning. We interpret "telling" as not limited to verbal analogies, but also including approaches that emphasize embodied learning. Many contributions highlighted in part 2 also support learners in reaching for greater complexity of analysis and understanding, which Gardner has termed *approaching the core* (see "Further Reading: More from Gardner").

Further Reading: More from Gardner

See Gardner (1999), *Intelligence Reframed: Multiple Intelligences for the 21st Century* and Gardner reprint, *Multiple Approaches to Understanding* in Illeris (2009), *Contemporary Theories of Learning: Learning Theorists—in Their Own Words*; Williams (2002), *Multiple Intelligences for Differentiated Thinking*; and Smith (2008), "Howard Gardner, Multiple Intelligences and Education" for more detailed examples and discussion of approaches that align with multiple intelligences and that bring learners more deeply into issues, such as through entry points, telling analogies, and approaching the core.

Constructive-Development Theory and Transformative Learning

With the groundbreaking publication of William Perry's (1968/1999) study of epistemological development in the college years, the field of adult learning found itself intersecting at many points with constructive-developmental theories. (See "Epistemology 101.")

> **Epistemology 101**
>
> Derived from the Greek words for knowledge or understanding (*episteme*) and study of (*logos*), epistemology is the study of how we come to know, what knowledge is, and what constitutes knowledge as different from, say, belief. Though this has been a largely philosophical question, it has real-world consequences when applied to learning and research, which are all about coming to know something. For most of the last two hundred years, the dominant paradigm (framework of belief) about knowing was positivism, which assumed that there is an external reality that we can attempt to know only through rigorous application of the scientific method. Constructivism, by contrast, which slowly gained traction in the latter part of the twentieth century, claimed that people create (construct) reality based on their interpretation of what they experience. Constructivism is therefore in line with emerging research on the brain. (For more on this and how variations in epistemological assumptions affect research methods, see Gray, *Doing Research in the Real World*, 3rd ed., 2014.)

Constructive-development theories (as opposed to those based on, for example, age or life stages) claim that how we know changes throughout the life span in qualitatively different ways. These paradigm shifts in how we understand ourselves and the world around us are, according to various theorists, the wellspring of psychological, ego, moral, and faith development. Based on careful longitudinal studies of children and adolescents, Piaget's (1955, 2008) model of cognitive development assumed that capacities usually achieved in late adolescence—abstraction and logical thinking, or *formal operations*—continued throughout adulthood. Expanding on Piaget's research and insights, others have described further potential changes in adulthood (Sinnott, 1998; Magolda, 1992, Loevinger & Blasi, 1976). Meanwhile, adult educators have also explored approaches to learning that appear to achieve what developmental theorists characterize as developmental goals of adulthood (Tennant & Pogson, 1995; Brookfield, 1989, 2012). We briefly explore in greater detail only three: how Belenky, Clinchy, Goldberger, and Tarule (1986, 1997) describe such developmental changes in *Women's Ways of Knowing*; Jack Mezirow's (1991, 2000) theory of *transformative learning;* and Robert Kegan's (1994) orders of consciousness model of development. We chose these because each explicitly links learning and development. (Kolb's notions connecting learning and development were described earlier.)

Women's Ways of Knowing

Nearly 30 years ago, Mary Field Belenky, Blythe McVicker Clinchy, Nancy Rule Goldberger, and Jill Mattuck Tarule (1986/1997), psychologists and educators, struggled with the implications of William Perry's (1968/1999) well-known scheme of intellectual (cognitive) development, which had been based on research with young, white males attending a highly selective college. Applied to women, his findings suggested that females are less cognitively developed than males. When Belenky and her colleagues subsequently interviewed 135 women of varying ages, social class, and ethnic and educational backgrounds, they found a developmental progression that paralleled Perry's but with substantive differences. The overarching metaphor of learning that emerged from the interviews was progressive development of "voice," which referred to women's growing sense of their own right to be heard as well as choose who to listen to—interwoven with development of "self" and "mind." The authors named these positions, (which were seen as gender-related though not gender-specific ways of knowing), *silence* (for which there was no comparable stage in Perry's model), followed by *received*, *subjective*, *procedural*, and *constructed knowing*. Though not initially deemed hierarchical, the authors later framed this as progressive progression as signaling development toward engaging the world with increasing capacity for complexity. (See "Five Perspectives on Knowing.")

Five Perspectives on Knowing

Subsequent to the first publication of *Women's Ways of Knowing*, these authors edited *Knowledge, Difference, and Power*, which examined their earlier work from various vantage points, some affirming and some critical (Goldberger et al., 1996).

Looking more closely at the characteristics of subjective, procedural, and constructed perspectives gives us deeper insight into how the brain learns. Subjective knowing is an important and valuable achievement as part of the early adult's life process. We come to "just know" our own minds, hence begin to establish a clearer sense of self, no longer unconsciously seeking others to tell us what to know. However, what appears as our own "gut sense" or "inner voice" turns out to be highly influenced by our (invisible) Broadways and Grand Canyons.

The move to procedural knowing signals development of the voice of reason—a more complex capacity to examine any idea using thoughtfully designed procedures (often in accord with established academic methods) as an antidote to the limitations of subjective knowing; it is not, as was the case before subjective knowing, simply to shift with the prevailing wind. An enduring and significant finding of *Women's Ways of Knowing* (Belenky, et al., 1986) is the discovery of two kinds of procedural knowers—separate and connected—as described below: A separate knower might say, for example:

Separate and Connected Knowing

I never take anything someone says for granted. I just tend to see the contrary. I like playing devil's advocate, arguing the opposite of what somebody's saying, thinking of exceptions to what the person has said, or thinking of a different train of logic. (A separate knower.)

When I have an idea about something, and it differs from the way another person is thinking about it, I'll usually try to look at it from that person's point of view, see how they could say that, why they think that they're right, why it makes sense. (A connected knower.) (p. 100)

In many settings, however, the preference for "logic, analysis, debate," which is in line with an LH orientation, is regarded as more rigorous and appropriate than the preference for "empathy, collaboration, careful listening," which is in line with an RH orientation (Stanton, 1996, p. 31). Separate knowing also appears to be consistently preferred by more men than women. This may contribute to the assumption that the separate voice of propositional and procedural logic is intellectually or morally more developed than the connected voice of empathetic experiential logic. (Kegan's model, below, also addresses this fallacy.) *Women's Ways of Knowing* findings are explicit that this is not the case: both voices are rational processes. The authors write, "Connected knowing [is also] a rigorous, deliberate, and demanding *procedure*, a way of knowing that requires *work*... [It is] not effortless intuition" (Clinchy, 1996, p. 209).

Constructed knowing, not to be conflated with connected knowing, is the most complex and inclusive of the knowing perspectives, integrating heart and mind, thinking and feeling, debate and dialogue, as well as the separate and connected modes. From this perspective, one has the capacity to engage in formal argument while also leading and listening with empathy and care. From an ALFAS perspective, explicitly integrating embodied and analogic knowing with analytical and abstract knowing, as is the case with several approaches in part 2 is an invitation to constructed knowing.

Mezirow's Transformative Learning

For Mezirow, the overriding issue is emancipatory learning, which strives to liberate adults from distorted perceptions, beliefs, and assumptions that effectively limit their freedom to be responsible actors in the world. What we call Broadways and Grand Canyons he calls constricting meaning schemes, acquired "unconsciously in childhood through socialization" (1991, p. 33) and often reinforced throughout adulthood. As such, they represent identity, culture, and the status quo in a self-referential LH-oriented "reality" that is difficult to counter or dislodge.

Although such norms are valuable signposts to community acceptance in traditional societies, the changing requirements in most modern societies demand greater adaptability and awareness of the limits of one's own perspectives. "Culturally prescribed values and belief systems acquired through socialization may no longer be adequate" (Mezirow, 1991, p. 34), nor are traditional authority structures that establish themselves as the arbiter of how things "ought" to be. Instead, adults must take greater responsibility to address a wider range of issues with more complex ways of thinking. (Kegan, whom we examine next, calls this a hallmark of self-authorizing consciousness.)

Mezirow's notion of transformative learning (in contrast with largely instrumental informative learning) emphasizes enabling adults to more fully experience the benefits of autonomy, rationality, and voice. Ideally this leads not only to their own self-empowerment but also the betterment and potential liberation of society as a whole. Mezirow (2000) voiced his vision: "Transformative learners, with social or organizational change as objectives, seek out others who share their insights to form cells of resistance to unexamined cultural norms in organizations, communities, families, and political life. They become agents of cultural change" (p. 30).

This echoes the commitment and care for others that the authors of *Women's Ways of Knowing* describe as central to the position of constructed knowing. "Constructivist women aspire to work that contributes to the empowerment and improvement in the quality of life of others.... [They] feel a part of the effort to address with others the burning issues of the day and to contribute as best they can... integrating feeling and care into their work" in such people-oriented areas as social services, antipoverty, environmental protection, and city planning (Belenky et al., 1986 p. 152). (In chapter 10, we further contrast informational and transformational knowing and include examples of those who appear to demonstrate the complexity and commitment of constructed knowers.)

Given the adult brain's commitment to what it already "knows," achieving such outcomes requires ALFAS' intentional effort and guidance—merely providing more or better information does not dislodge or reroute Broadways. "Dramatic personal and social changes become possible when we become aware of the way that both our psychological and our cultural assumptions have created or contributed to our dependence on outside forces that we have regarded as unchangeable" (Mezirow, 1991, p. 88).

Mezirow's approach to creating conditions that foster such changes begins with the challenge of a *disorienting dilemma*—an experience that runs counter to expectations or deeply held beliefs and assumptions. (See "Mezirow's Ten Phases of Perspective Transformation." Many embodied experiences in part 2 incorporate several of these phases.) Adults then need ongoing support as they contend with the awkwardness, anxiety, and even

Mezirow's Ten Phases of Perspective Transformation

1. A disorienting dilemma
2. Self-examination with feelings of guilt or shame
3. A critical assessment of epistemic, sociocultural, or psychic assumptions
4. Recognition that one's discontent and the process of transformation are shared and that others have negotiated a similar change
5. Exploration of options for new roles, relationships, and actions
6. Planning of a course of action
7. Acquisition of knowledge and skills for implementing one's plans
8. Provisional trying on of new roles
9. Building of competence and self-confidence in new roles and relationships
10. A reintegration into one's life on the basis of conditions dictated by one's new perspective

Source: Mezirow (1991, pp. 168–169).

guilt that may ensue. When trying on new perspectives, roles, and understandings, while also considering what implications for action might be, it is encouraging to engage with others navigating similarly uncharted waters. Such experiments can ultimately lead to fully incorporating the new perspectives into one's self-understanding and way of being in the world. (In practice, these phases are more flexible than the list suggests.) Occasionally change occurs as a sudden paradigmatic shift. More commonly, small, incremental shifts in awareness, perhaps over many months, and even well beyond the limits of a specific learning occasion, finally lead to new ways of seeing and understanding: a transformed perspective.

Although Mezirow's (1991) primary attitude favors what he considers rational activity—validity testing, argumentation, critical reflection, hypothesis testing, rational assessment of evidence (discourse and dialogue)—he also notes, "Often understanding comes from finding the right metaphor to fit the experience analogically into our meaning schemes, theories, belief systems, or self-concept" (p. 80) and that "metaphors rather than hypotheses play a central role in the logic involved in communicative learning" (p. 64). Even so, he later acknowledged as "partially justified" the criticism that his interpretation of transformative learning may have neglected "the role of imagination, intuition, and emotion" (2009, p. 27).

We underscore his suggestion that at times, "intuition may substitute for critical reflection" and his acknowledgment that "because transformation is often a difficult, highly emotional passage, a great deal of additional insight into the role of imagination is needed and overdue" (p. 27). Mezirow's theory of transformative learning provides meaningful guidance for ALFAS as they invite and encourage learners to get off their Broadways and explore ways to change their minds toward development of greater complexity and commitment.

Kegan's Orders of Consciousness Model

We have several times in preceding chapters referred to "mental complexity" or "complexity of mind." In briefly describing Robert Kegan's constructive-developmental model, we illuminate those concepts and why we find them central to ALFAS' practice.

In 1982, Kegan extended to adults Piaget's insight that children and adolescents know in markedly different ways identified as developmental stages. As a psychologist, Kegan first emphasized ego development, that is, how people understand themselves in relation to the world. In 1994, he expanded his theory (which had in the interim been subject to empirical testing) to look more closely at issues omnipresent in most adults' lives: parenting and partnering, working, healing (psychological growth), learning, and dealing with diversity. In each of these notably different arenas of adult life, the same trajectory of development emerged:

incremental growth toward greater self-knowledge, flexibility, inclusiveness, and complexity.

Kegan identified five *qualitative* transformations along the way—paradigm shifts—that fundamentally change how adults perceive, understand, and interact with their inner and outer worlds.

To maintain our focus on adult learning and the brain, we examine more closely only two of Kegan's five orders of consciousness, as these are the major developmental transformations of modern adulthood. (Past childhood and adolescence, development is only tenuously related to age; see "Maturity Is Not Development.")

Maturity Is Not Development

Many development theories are age based; that is, development is presumed to track with the calendar. This is not the case with constructive development theory. That said, fewer than 10 percent of chronological adults continue to operate primarily from second order, which is more typically associated with adolescence. Most adults fully achieve third order, which is normative in most societies as it means the individual has "grown up" and "joined the tribe." Most adults do not reach the threshold of fourth order, regardless of age, as it would mean the capacity to question and contradict or reframe third-order rules and expectations. Currently, so few people achieve fifth-order consciousness that we will not examine it further. However, the fact that people are both more long-lived than at any other time in history and increasingly seeking opportunities for ongoing learning and development may be changing that statistic. (See figure 9.8.)

Socialized Mind: Third Order of Consciousness The end of psychological adolescence is marked by transformation to the *socialized* or *socializing* mind. Adults operating from third-order consciousness have internalized the rules and expectations of their tribe with regard to the various demands of adulthood, such as those described above. The everyday, invisible furrow that marks one's Broadways and Grand Canyons directs and limits how one

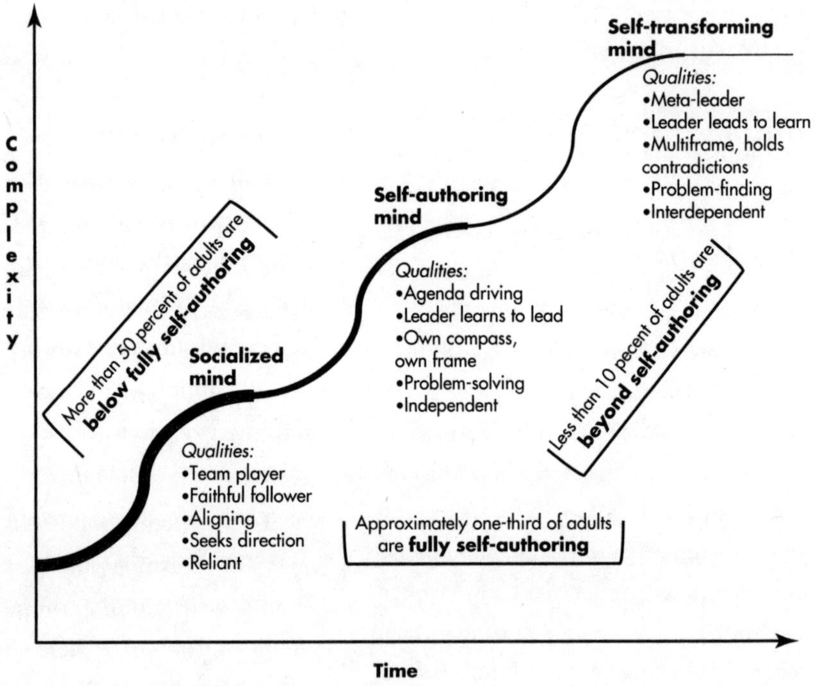

Figure 9.8 Kegan: Adult Mental Complexity
Source: Adapted from Kegan and Lahey (2009, pp. 16, 28).

understands self and others—and even what knowing, itself, means.

The socialized way of knowing is comparable to Mezirow's meaning schemes constructed in childhood and elaborated in adolescence and adulthood, thus largely in accord with the beliefs and assumptions of those "like us." This traditional worldview is well suited for living in homogeneous societies where people explicitly frame their life choices according to established rules. In the pluralistic modern world, this mind-set is most visible among members of closely knit religious communities, such as the Amish or Orthodox Jewry, whose rules for living sharply contrast with those of the dominant culture. Less obvious, since most people share these assumptions, are the dominant culture's similarly fixed prescriptions and interdictions with regard to what constitutes appropriate behaviors and choices.

Self-Authorized Mind: Fourth Order of Consciousness

Mezirow's description of potential outcomes of transformative learning—autonomy, rationality, empowerment of self and others, capacity to question one's own assumptions/Broadways and cultural beliefs/Grand Canyons—and *Women's Ways of Knowing*'s description of the development of voice beyond subjective toward procedural knowing are akin to Kegan's description of the developmental transformation to self-authorizing consciousness. (See table 9.1 for a comparison of three constructive-developmental models: Kegan's *Orders of Consciousness,* Perry's *Moral and Intellectual Development,* and Belenky, et al. *Women's Ways of Knowing.*)

Here is a concrete example of such a perspective shift. Implicit (third-order) agreement to obey the law is essential to maintaining a functioning society. Even so, a more complex view recognizes law as a system that codifies assumptions about what a functioning society is and should be, and can therefore be a matter of conscience. Fifty years ago, Martin Luther King Jr. and others asked, Should a democratic society disenfranchise and otherwise discriminate against a group of its citizens? After many failed attempts to work within the legal system, those who thoughtfully answered that question in the negative proceeded to (nonviolently) break the law, a consciously values-based decision that accepted the consequences (such as being brutalized and jailed). This points toward a more complex construction of the meaning of law-abiding. Whistle-blowers—people who break laws or rules of confidentiality because they see a more complex picture of what constitutes appropriate and principled behavior—may also be in this category. Adults making this shift can no longer unquestioningly rely on others' guidance. They must instead reflect on and evaluate the world as it is—and is rapidly

Table 9.1 Three Constructive-Developmental Models, Compared

Perry (1999) Moral and Intellectual Development	Kegan (1982, 1994) Orders of Consciousness	Belenky, Clinchy, Goldberger, and Tarule (1986) Ways of Knowing
Dualism • Right/wrong, we/they, black/white (rather than gray), either/or (also: my group is "righter" than those not like me/us) • Knowledge can be acquired • Source of knowledge is Authorities, who either have right answers now or eventually will • Expectation to someday become an Authority	Instrumental • Identifies with own interests, needs, and desires • Social contract is, "What can you do for me?" • Lack of empathy • Characterized by dualistic thinking • Needs concrete directions; step-by-step procedures [Second order: community-influenced Broadways and Grand Canyons are slowly being formed, typically during adolescence]	Received knowing • Knowledge comes from others (e.g., friends, family, teachers, TV) • No expectation to become an authority • Listens, has few opinions, remembers and reproduces knowledge • Conventional moral judgments (but potentially vulnerable to cult leaders)

Multiplicity/Relativism • Early: Everyone is entitled to his or her own opinion • Late: Some opinions are more justifiable than others — one must develop criteria for evaluation • Even Authorities do not know everything	Socializing • Values and sense of self are derived from others • Uneasy with disagreements that suggest conflict and therefore threaten underlying connection • Needs clear expectations and unambiguous directions about what should be done [Third order: exemplified by the filters of Broadways and Grand Canyons]	Subjective/*Procedural* knowing • "I know what I know" — "private" knowledge comes from inner voice or gut feelings but may apply only to oneself • Discomfort with ideas that contradict one's own • May use appropriate academic forms and procedures, but is following the rules • *Recognizes underlying purpose of and uses appropriate methods, procedures, and rules for evaluating and creating knowledge*

(*Continued*)

Table 9.1 (*Continued*)

Perry (1999) Moral and Intellectual Development	Kegan (1982, 1994) Orders of Consciousness	Belenky, Clinchy, Goldberger, and Tarule (1986) Ways of Knowing
Commitment • Knowledge is contextual; values are situational • To live meaningful lives, one must make and commit to decisions in the face of Relativism (i.e., absence of certainty) and be open to reconsidering those decisions as new circumstances warrant	Self-authorizing • Knowledge is consciously constructed • Values and ethics are situational • Ideas can be challenged and changed without loss of self • Awareness of and concern for the greater good [Fourth order: Broadways and Grand Canyons can be illuminated, hence may be challenged and changed]	Procedural/Constructed knowing • Recognizes own contribution to construction of knowledge. • Knowledge integrates voices of others and "procedural" process of knowledge creation and evaluation toward . . . • . . . Passionate involvement with the collective good

Source: Adapted from Taylor (2006, p. 202).

becoming—and construct their own value systems, which at times may mean contradicting others' expectations. Less than half the adult population has fully achieved the threshold of fourth order, yet developing such capacities may be essential for humanity as a whole to successfully navigate the demands of the culturally pluralistic, ecologically challenged, economically stratified global village we all live in.

As Mezirow also did, Kegan (2000) distinguishes between learning focused primarily on instrumental purposes and learning focused on being able to question how one understands—and what one assumes about—oneself and others. In-*form*-ative learning changes what we know by adding to the existing form of our awareness and understanding—a quantitative change. Trans-*form*-ative, by contrast, expands and elaborates on the form, itself—a qualitative change. The fourth-order, self-authorizing mind can know in a more complex way because it is no longer limited by the earlier, "tribal"-directed filters and patterns of behavior and understanding that marked the end of adolescence.

What role can we as ALFAS play in supporting development of such capacities? Kegan's (1994) description of self-authorized knowing echoes what many of our contributors have said about the focus of their practice: encouraging adults to think critically and appreciatively; to question the basis of their culturally endorsed feelings, values, and desires; to take greater responsibility for their roles and actions as learners and in other arenas of their lives; to acknowledge and embrace their roles in the construction of knowledge as well as their own value systems and cultural identities, and to commit to meaningful action toward the common good. From a brain-aware perspective, approaches that more explicitly involve attention to embodiment, analogy, and meaning making, plus an effective balance of support and challenge, are likely to encourage greater complexity of mind.

Key Ideas

- In Heron's view, conventional approaches to teaching and learning have vastly overlooked the crucial role of the first two stages of this cycle: initial positive arousal and creative, imaginal, and symbolic treatments of material to be learned.
- In Kolb's view, learning to learn from their own experience enables individuals to become knowledge co-constructors and prompts their development.
- An overarching developmental task is to integrate the four capacities of complexity (affective, symbolic, perceptual, behavioral) in context-appropriate ways.
- In Boud's view, the reflection process includes an anticipatory phase as well as an after-the-event phase.
- The potential empowerment of reflection is to promote each person's own choice making and meaning making.
- Our brains are always engaged in social learning unless we purposefully attend elsewhere.
- The notion of Gardner's multiple intelligences suggests that we have preferences for ways to enter into a learning encounter.
- The voices of connected and separate knowing are both rational processes; both are needed to engage effectively in the world.
- Mezirow's notion of transformative learning (TL) emphasizes enabling adults to more fully experience the benefits of autonomy, rationality, and voice. Ideally this leads not only to their own self-empowerment but also the betterment and potential liberation of society as a whole.
- Mezirow's theory of TL provides meaningful guidance for ALFAS as they invite and encourage learners to get off their Broadways and explore ways to change their minds toward development of greater complexity and adaptability.

- Since most people share them, the dominant culture's prescriptions and interdictions with regard to what constitutes appropriate behaviors and choices are virtually invisible.
- While most adults become participating members of their tribe, far fewer develop the capacity to question, contradict, or reframe the predominant rules and expectations of that tribe.
- We feel modeling our willingness to be vulnerable and insecure while developing a new capacity or skill (such as facilitating embodied learning), is a meaningful contribution to our adult learners' process of learning, regardless of how the activity, itself, turned out.

? Pause for Reflection

1. How might you use any of the theories and models described in this chapter in your work with adult learners?
2. Which theories and models do you want to learn more about?
3. Are there other theories and models you draw on in your work with adult learners that seem now to also be brain aware?

10

Toward Complexity and Commitment

When you become aware that something is *in a certain way, then you also become aware that it* could *be in some other way.*

— FERENCE MARTON and SHIRLEY BOOTH

FOR MUCH of this book, we have focused primarily on how brain-aware facilitation may support individual adults toward more effective engagement with learning in various formal and informal settings. We now return to our long-standing interest in the intersections between adult learning and adult development, first introduced in the Preface. Brain-aware facilitation can also encourage adults to further develop their capacities for complexity as they seek to make more informed choices and act in more thoughtful and deliberate ways with regard to the greater good. As Elizabeth Minnich, philosopher and author of *Transforming Knowledge* (2005), wrote:

> We are creatures and creators of meaning.... [These meanings] can sustain us in peaceful, caring, just relations with others and with the earth we share. They can divide

> and rank us within systems of dominance. They can open us to love, friendship, respect, justice, nurture. They can enable us to enslave, exploit, rape, kill those who have been defined as less than fully human. We are called . . . to keep thinking, to hold horizons open. We . . . remain responsible (p. 1).

In the final analysis, when we ask ourselves what is adult learning *for*, we see its potential to meet a wide array of responsibilities at differing levels of complexity. We accept as a given the need to achieve the learning objectives of a course, training, or program, to meet workplace challenges, and to enhance individual and group capacities. More important, we want to enable adults to engage more effectively as caring and courageous citizens within an increasingly globalized village. Ultimately, we hope to encourage their engagement with the multifaceted and interlocking political, social, economic, and ecological systems that lead to major social ills such as poverty and war, which may threaten the viability of our species. This requires leadership—not necessarily formal, positional leadership, but the capacity and commitment to act within one's own spheres of influence.

We accept Kegan's (1994) claim that such awareness and commitment require complexity of mind beyond the limitations of socialized consciousness. From a brain-aware perspective, that means challenging long-established and largely invisible assumptions—our neural Broadways and Grand Canyons—that inform every aspect of our lives, often including a sense of incapacity or nonresponsibility for things that seem beyond our control.

Purpose and reason matter. The learning environment matters too, not just as a spur to behavior but as a spur to development. We maintain that ALPHA's practice can support and develop what is inside the black box: complexity of mind. We concur with the constructive-developmental perspective that such complexity also informs meaningful behavior. To have the capacity to perceive in a new way precedes the capacity to respond in a more effective way.

Successfully engaging adults to explore such new ways of thinking and feeling can be more than a little problematic. The movement toward greater self-awareness may be fraught with the potential for loss of what one has known and believed. Heifetz, Linsky, and Grashow (2009), however, describe such loss as an opportunity to reframe existing "priorities, beliefs, habits, and loyalties" (p. 19) and a step toward creating new and more powerful options that can enable individuals and communities to flourish during times of change and challenge. Successfully managing the disruption requires keen awareness of one's existing assumptions as well as the capacity to envision other possibilities.

Awareness involves perception and conscious knowledge. Just as the brain initially perceives only through the portals of the five senses, the meaning the brain makes of these perceptions emerges only through the filters of existing assumptions. To the extent that our filters keep us from seeing the larger context, we are less aware than we might be. As Mary Catherine Bateson (1994) notes, "Family systems, the organization of institutions, the way we run our country, the way we respond to other cultures, the uses of political and military power—all these things are based on interlocking sets of metaphor" (p. 142). Having built layer upon layer of embodied metaphors that are the root of everything we perceive, know, or understand, we not only have our metaphors, but our metaphors have us.

Our filters are also the subject of continual interplay between our individual embodied experiences and the external environment. Especially in younger learners, this interplay establishes the neural networks that define expectations and parameters for growing into adulthood. In this way, communities we identify with—our "tribes," as it were—create and ordain rules for appropriate feelings, attitudes, behaviors, and ideas, such as the roles elders or authority figures play; what is most highly valued and sought after; appropriate gender roles; display or inhibition of emotions; who is deemed "other"; how sexual activity is perceived; how to decide conflicts (see "Supreme Morality"). Though such injunctions are important to socializing the self-involved adolescent, as adulthood progresses, these Grand Canyons, often felt as inviolable, can act as barriers to effective communication and collaboration across tribal boundaries.

Ironically, one nearly universal norm is belief in the ultimate truth and rightness of our own group's worldview. Also affecting awareness is the brain's tendency to seek certainty and avoid ambiguity. "Losing the certainty of a particular worldview can make you feel sick, bewildered, dizzy" (Bateson, 1994, p. 91). We are drawn to those who are like-minded—an apt metaphor—thus continually reconfirming our assumptions. And since these *assumptions* operate behind the Curtain of Awareness, we cannot know when, in fact, they are making the decisions.

Supreme Morality

As Joshua Greene noted in *Moral Tribes* (2013):

> Some tribes grant special authority to specific gods, leaders, texts, or practices.... For example, many Muslims believe that no one—Muslim or otherwise—should be allowed to produce visual images of the prophet Muhammad.* ... Many American Christians believe that the Ten Commandments should be displayed in public buildings and that Americans should pledge allegiance to "one nation under God." (And they're not talking about Vishnu.) (p. 11)

*A belief that was violently enforced at the Paris offices of the French satirical magazine, *Charlie Hebdo*, in 2015. Google *Je suis Charlie*, for example: https://en.wikipedia.org/wiki/Je_suis_Charlie

Two Ways of Knowing/Learning

To explore awareness from another perspective, we examine a metaphor that contrasts two lenses representing different ways of knowing and learning. Both are valuable and worthy approaches; however, to support adults in developing greater complexity of mind, we ALFAS need to emphasize the second.

Knowing More

This way of knowing provides access to a broader range of information. Using the lens metaphor, *knowing more* involves looking through a series of increasingly wider-angled lenses that, bit by bit, broaden the field of vision. This is analogous to a camera's panoramic lens. With each increment, one can see more of what there is to see. This kind of knowing is based on accretion: increasing one's fund of knowledge. Over our lifetimes, we develop skills of observation that enable us to acquire new information; in so doing, we come to know, and can presumably do, more—still within the boundaries of our familiar world.

As ALFAS, we are committed to facilitating such foundational learning. A pilot needs a sophisticated understanding of how planes respond to different mechanical and environmental conditions; a historian requires detailed knowledge of who, when, and why, as well as what other historians have said over time; a physician needs thorough grounding in chemistry, anatomy, and biology; and an effective manager must command flexible communication styles and have skills in motivating employees and directing work flow.

Seeing Differently

By contrast, the second way of knowing, which empowers one to see and think differently, is comparable to a three-dimensional lens. Currently, 3-D cameras use dual lenses to imitate the spacing of our two eyes; what is closest to the camera or observer appears more prominent. The lens we describe, however, can never exist in a mechanical object. Rather than taking an ever wider view, our imaginary 3-D lens reveals a scene that has not only dimensional depth but also nuance and variation. Instead of a flat panoramic view, certain parts of the scene become clearer and take on significance and meaning. These differences are not simply a matter of distance; they arise from a different kind of interpretation. Rather than acquiring new information, one's intention is toward constructing meaning. "Human intelligence is not just knowing more, but reworking, recategorizing, and thus generalizing information in new and surprising ways" (Rosenfield, 1988, p. 193). The premise of this second kind of learning is not *quantitative* (seeing more) but *qualitative* (seeing differently). Heifetz and others (2009) might say that this kind of *adaptive learning* requires new and different interpretations of experience.

When we reframe our colleagues' questions and concerns (listed in the preface) from this perspective, we see our overarching task as encouraging adults to learn and know in a qualitatively different way—which means facilitating with developmental intentions. For brain-aware ALFAS this suggests a powerful role in explicitly fostering skills and capacities adults need to engage in more complex awareness. As Proust famously wrote, "The real journey of discovery consists not in seeking new landscapes, but in having new eyes."

Enabling the first kind of knowing is more in line with what Pratt (2005) describes as the transmission perspective, where adults expect the teacher or facilitator "to possess the knowledge" they need and then to "dispense and defend that content as accurately, efficiently, and completely as possible" (pp. 219–220)—essentially to convey to them the requisite skills and content that will widen their panoramic lens. Kegan

(2000), Mezirow (2000), and others in chapter 9 refer to this as informational learning.

Facilitators focused on the second kind of knowing—knowing differently—find it an even more demanding task. When "changing one's mind" refers primarily to adding information or skills, the convey-and-transfer approach is likely to be sufficient. However, when the changes refer to knowing in more multifaceted ways—including the possibility of contradicting what one already "knows" and creating an as yet unimagined, more complex vision of what might be—information accrual doesn't cut it. It requires transformative learning—awareness that emerges not from incorporating more information into a current framework of understanding but from perceiving a larger context that was previously unseen (or only dimly seen), thus requiring a reconfigured, more comprehensive framework (more concretely, neural network). Marton and Booth's (1997) observation about becoming aware that something *is* in a certain way alludes to this second kind of awareness—a new appreciation of systemic interdependence—which can be difficult to achieve, as evident in figure 9.8, Adult Mental Complexity. As Bateson (1994) notes, "Our habits of attention work against seeing, and the connections in the system are invisible.... Focusing on the pursuit of particular, narrow goals, we pay attention to a fraction of the whole" (p. 138). Yet only when we have developed the capacity to see the larger, more complex context and our own relationship to it can we approach some other way of addressing the issues that increasingly bedevil modern life.

Heart, Hemispheres, Heron, Heifetz

As we neared the end of writing this book, we felt it was important to simplify and synthesize the major take-aways. What might we say to interested colleagues who casually asked, "so, what is your brain book finally all about?" without going into more detailed explanations than their question probably intended to elicit? We lit on four alliterative stand-ins for core ideas: heart, hemispheres, Heron, and Heifetz, which we could elaborate on more or less quickly, depending on our colleague's curiosity (and patience).

The first two descriptors, heart and hemispheres, signify aspects of brain function of particular interest to ALFAS—those involving emotion and metaphor. Heron and Heifetz, by contrast, denote concrete frameworks that inform practice in what we find are especially relevant ways. Clearly, these are not logical or categorical distinctions. All four overlap and intertwine. Emotions and feelings involve hemispheres in terms of how and where they are processed. Some aspects of hemispheric lateralization (ways the RH and LH work differently) are relevant to metaphoric and symbolic processing. Presentational knowing, which specifically requires metaphoric and symbolic expression, is an essential element of Heron's model of facilitation. And when Heifetz and his colleagues describe how to exercise leadership—"If you are not engaged with your own heart, you will find it virtually impossible to connect with [others']" (2009, p. 38)—we find ourselves back at emotions. As we briefly examine each of these, we also point to ways they correspond.

Heart

For most of 2014 and 2015, the violent displacement of millions of people in the Mideast and northern Africa made almost daily international news headlines as tens of thousands risked their lives and their children's lives to escape the horrors of war. Desperate migrants continued to cross the Mediterranean in unseaworthy vessels even as thousands perished in the attempt. Though caring individuals around the globe donated to aid agencies, most governments discussed and dithered while harrowing reports and images multiplied.

A major turning point was the photograph of a toddler whose little body had washed up on a beach in Turkey still clothed, lying in the casual pose of a child who had fallen asleep at a picnic ("Syrian migrants, including toddler, drown off Turkey," 2015). In a tragedy of massive proportions, a single child's death—an image that every parent and grandparent recognized as one of their own—broke through. Public response shifted from what had seemed concerned helplessness, "It's terrible, but what can we do?" to the moral epiphany, "something must be done, now!" This also marked a shift on the part of many governmental leaders toward greater empathy and decisive action.

Current brain research helps us understand why that photo had such impact. In their article titled, "We Feel, Therefore We Learn," Immordino-Yang and Damasio (2007) describe *emotional thought* as contributing to the "neurobiological underpinnings of morality, creativity, and culture" by providing an "*emotional rudder* to guide judgment and action" in the real world (original italics, p. 3). The heart-breaking image of the dead child steered several nations toward moral resolutions that had earlier eluded them. Societal transformations, Leonard Joy (2011) reports, are based on shifts in values—and without emotions to alert us, we don't know what we value.

Emotions are also at play in far less dramatic contexts in classrooms and training settings. As John Dirkx (2008) points out, adults' feelings about any learning environment and the activities they encounter there are both "unavoidable by-products" of learning and "constitutive of the very learning process" itself (p. 7). Even so, some facilitators avoid emotion based on Cartesian suspicion that it impedes rather than promotes learning. We align with Dirkx in seeing emotions as embodied experiences that can promote the "fundamental change or shift in our understanding of ourselves or our relationship with the world in which we live" (p. 15) associated with transformative learning and increasing complexity of mind.

Emotions also fuel commitment. What we care about is what we are likely to act on, if we can get off the Broadways that may limit our sense of our own capacities. As Heifetz and colleagues note (2009), the *heart* (their word) of adaptive leadership emerges from the desire to "serve purposes that matter to you deeply" and that give greater meaning to life than can be achieved through personal ambition (p. 221).

Hemispheres

Although both left (LH) and right (RH) hemispheres are involved in processing emotions, they do so with different agendas. Except for anger, which is largely activated in the LH, the RH is more involved in emotional interpretations of all kinds: facial expressions, spoken language intonations, assessing context and social meaning, and emotions that increase connection and bonding, such as empathy and trying to understand another's mind. Furthermore, the RH focuses broadly on the natural world, living beings, and the subtle demands of closeness and connection.

The left hemisphere by contrast has a narrowed focus that more readily attends to the artificial, mechanical, and technological world. It is the seat of manufactured, intentional emotional expression—more likely a calculated than unconscious and spontaneous response. The LH is also more optimistic in general than the RH, though that may be because it limits its sphere of attention to what it already is comfortable with. Rather than cooperation, it prefers competition, lacks empathy, and revels in knowing its *own* mind.

Both hemispheres also deal with symbolic processing, again with a difference. The LH tends toward the concrete and iconic—as one example, quickly mapping *red* onto *stop*. To the RH, red could be metaphorically associated with *anger*, *love*, *sunset, flowers* (as in, "My love is a red, red rose"), and so on.

Though each hemisphere needs the other to perform at its best, the LH "appears to be in denial about this" (McGilchrist, 2010, p. 437). In keeping with its self-referential and competitive values, it insists that its formalized, rational approaches to knowledge are the only ones worth having. Indeed, the LH is so enmeshed in its own approach that "*evidence of failure does not mean that we are going in the wrong direction, only that we have not gone far enough in the direction we are already headed*" (our emphasis, p. 235). LH sees the RH's embodied and symbolic knowing as either delusionary or incomprehensible—a perspective it isn't bashful about articulating.

One of the clearest distinctions between the hemispheres is their awareness of and engagement with the body—and by extension, with the natural world as a whole. The RH not only sees connections in nature but cannot ignore them, while the LH analyzes individual natural elements as if from a great distance. Ecological issues, whether local or global, are a case in point. The LH frames these as problems with technical solutions, rather than acknowledging the systemic nature of the myriad interacting factors and our own participation in those systems. Although McGilchrist (2010) acknowledges the LH's many achievements and contributions to humankind, "the left hemisphere's assault on our embodied nature is not just an assault on *our* bodies, but on the embodied nature of the world around us" (original emphasis, p. 440). Given that current societal assumptions have allowed the LH nearly free rein in many learning environments, it may be incumbent on those of us who recognize the problem to try to correct the imbalance.

Stroke of Insight

Jill Bolte Taylor had been a brain scientist for a dozen years before suffering a massive hemorrhagic stroke on the left side of her brain (J. B. Taylor, 2006). Her YouTube TED talk about the four hours between waking up to a debilitating headache before finally being able to summon help has been viewed over three millions times (https://www.youtube.com/watch?v=UyyjU8fzEYU). The fact that she brings the mind and training of a neuroanatomist to her observations and interpretations gives her subjective descriptions considerable weight.

She did not realize that morning, as she tried to figure out what was happening to her and what to do, that her inability to concentrate was due to increasing loss of function as the blood seepage impacted her LH. In the absence of typical LH interjection, however, she discovered how the RH experiences itself and the world. As she describes:

> Instead of finding answers and information, I met a growing sense of peace. In place of that constant [LH] chatter that had attached me to the details of my life, I felt enfolded by a blanket of tranquil euphoria.... As the language centers in my left hemisphere grew increasingly silent and I became detached... I was comforted by an expanding sense of grace. In this void of higher cognition and details pertaining to my normal life, my consciousness soared into an all-knowingness, a "being at *one*" with the universe. (p. 41)

This awareness continued, though less intensely, during much of her decade-long neurological healing process. As Taylor observed herself slowly regaining her LH capacities, she wondered what would become of the RH values she now preferred. Could she retain her "newfound sense of connection with the universe...? How much... would I have to sacrifice in order to recover the skills of my left mind?" (p. 132).

Taylor's unique perspective appears to confirm McGilchrist's (2010) observation that the RH's emotional expressivity, deep sense of embodiment, capacity for metaphor and inference, openness to experiencing the world anew, tolerance of ambiguity, power of compassion and empathy, and sense of ultimate connectedness with all living things are among its great assets—and greatly needed in the current reality. Much that ails modern society may be traced to the dominance of LH values and attitudes combined with its firmness of purpose in the absence of concern for the natural world or empathy for other human beings.

Heron

Heron's (1992, 1999) model offers a partial antidote to those ills. He provides a comprehensive rationale for including symbolic, imaginal, and embodied learning as an essential aspect of whole person learning. People engaged in *presentational knowing* communicate experience tacitly, artistically, and figuratively—the RH's métier—before bringing it to explicit awareness through language (See figure 7.2, Stages of Inquiry/Facilitation). Directly engaging what's behind the Curtain of Awareness can effectively give voice—at least metaphorical voice—to aspects for knowing that are otherwise unavailable. In effect, Heron makes a point of shining a spotlight behind the scrim (see figure II.1, *Theatre of Knowing*).

He also details an integrated, flowing—dare we say, logical—process and structure so that tacit activity does not become merely a palate-cleansing appetizer or spicy add-on to the main dish of *text and talk*, or *demonstrate and do*. A facilitator new to ideas of symbolic or imaginal learning is supported in visualizing whole-person engagement. Moreover, Heron's model of facilitation practice is supported by "a theory of the person . . . [with some] practical implications for learning" (p. 1, 1992). For advanced practitioners, he and Peter Reason also describe a model of action learning, or collaborative inquiry designed to encourage movement toward commitment and change (Reason, 1989).

Heron's characterization of the differences between feeling and emotion do not always precisely align with current neuroscience. Even so, more than two decades before Damasio's conclusion that we feel, therefore we learn, Heron observed that "Feeling determines the sweep of a person's imaginative vision and thus provides the imaginal material out of which intellectual thought proceeds and upon which it gets to work . . . [and it] alone brings us into relation with the distinct yet interconnected other" in a way that is welcoming and open rather than dismissive or defensive (1992, pp. 94–95). This calls to mind McGilchrist's (2010) description of how the RH—the imaginal hemisphere—is attracted to and desires to be "present" to the Other, since it finds that being in the ebb and flow of relationship energizes and enlivens it. This contrasts with the unimaginative LH's primary attention to relationship that is fixed and predictable, and therefore more easily manipulated.

At the same time, Heron's language in describing the kind of knowing most valued in our culture, *propositional knowing*, seems to align with what McGilchrist identified as the LH's preferences: propositions, facts, generalizations, laws, theories, measurement, and language- and logic-based concepts. The problem arises, Heron says, when we realize that this means "the sort of world we are examining is thus a product of the chosen tool, the concept, which we use for the purpose" (p. 169). This example of the LH's self-referential logic is akin to physicist Werner Heisenberg's (1958) well-known precept that what we observe is not nature herself, but nature exposed to our method of questioning. The LH knows what it knows—especially about what it means *to know*—and is therefore unable to see that this limits what it *can* know. By contrast, symbolic and imaginal knowing extend beyond the limitations of verbal and conceptual form. As such, they open to possibilities that LH cannot entertain—movement beyond what *is* to what *might* be.

Imaginal and embodied experiences are a source of creativity and fulfillment, whether or not they are subsequently expressed in words and concepts. When they are expressed, as is the case with Heron's facilitation model, feeling lays the groundwork for more richly engaging with the world of experience and propositional knowledge. Heron (1992) also notes that fully engaging the feeling dimension for what it is, "packed with meaning prior to any explicit formulation of this meaning in verbal and conceptual terms" (p. 138), is substantively different from the "bare, spare, mere and dumb kind of apprehension" that treats feeling and symbolic, tacit knowing as it if were "a primitive, necessary evil on the way to the real business of the day, which is propositional knowledge" (p. 163).

Though it has meant rethinking aspects of our own practice, we could not ignore Heron's conclusion about how, as ALFAS, we can better facilitate meaningful learning:

> If we agree that presentational symbolism [nonverbal, artistic, feeling expression] is indeed a mode of knowing, then we can no longer conveniently distance ourselves from its use by delegating it to the artistic community. We need to bring it right back into the mainstream knowledge quest. (1992, p. 176)

As we interpret it, integration of analogical and embodied learning moves mainstream learning beyond information or skill acquisition. As such, it is a foundation for the kind of changes in feeling and understanding that lead toward greater complexity and commitment.

Heifetz

As noted earlier, changes in awareness associated with knowing and behaving *differently* can be disorienting. For most people most of the time, their brains would rather not go there, so adept are we at avoidance: "If it ain't broke, don't fix it." We also do a good job of deflecting the possibility that something actually is broke; in some instances, powerful stakeholders—with conflicting agendas—help muddy the waters. With regard to serious issues that might require significant effort, "more studies are needed," "the facts are not all in," and "the experts disagree," many people are relieved to feel absolved of responsibility.

But Ronald Heifetz, Marty Linsky, and Alexander Grashow (2009) *are* the experts. As leadership consultants in today's fast-moving world, where markets are changing, new technologies are disruptive, organizations seem dysfunctional, and globalization has arrived, they deal with people who want answers *now*. Although Heifetz and colleagues don't discuss brain function, their description of the adaptive leader's capacity to see himself or herself in context, both as an individual and as part of the system, aligns with the RH's ability to recognize and interpret connection and context:

> Exercising adaptive leadership is about you (an individual system) making interventions in a social system of which you are a part. You have to understand not only the larger system you step into . . . but also yourself in its full complexity, multiplicity, and inconsistency. And then you have to think about how the two systems interact. (p. 183)

In the absence of this awareness—seeing differently and framing issues and situations differently—we are left with the LH's self-referential, decontextualized, reductionist, and ultimately misguided analysis. The LH sees current challenges as technical problems for which authorities can provide answers (if not now, then eventually). Its driving assumption is that how things have been done is what will be done in the future, with some improvements. That said, technical problems do exist and they may require considerable time, effort, and resources to resolve. But technical problems are ultimately addressed by *knowing more*, which is essential using the *same* kind of thinking that created them.

When, instead, the backdrop to the visible problem is a systemic, values-based (therefore emotion-laden) issue that is invisibly keeping the system as it is, a technical approach won't work. The Broadways and Grand Canyons of individuals and groups resist change partly because it is unfamiliar and uncomfortable, and also because the LH cannot see—actually, *imagine*—another way to respond. Heron's focus on presentational knowing, however, provides an entrée to that imaginal resource and, in so doing, contributes to the capacity for *agility*: self-leadership based on understanding "the way we experience and respond to the world around us" (Meyer, 2015, p. 57). Such value-focused awareness and greater self-knowledge are elements of what Heifetz and colleagues term *adaptive leadership*.

Their adaptive leadership approach is not limited to organizational change; it can be brought to bear on any system, including the individual system. Many of the tools Heifetz and colleagues identify sound very much like what the brain does on its way to greater complexity. However, before these tools can be used effectively, people must have developed the capacity to know differently, which often means framing the entire issue differently.

Drought may be a provocative example. Current—mostly technical—responses focus on some combination of accessing more water and using less of it: low-flow shower heads and toilets, efficient water-using appliances, deeper wells, new desalinization approaches, better water management systems, bigger water transportation pipelines, more effective sewer water reclamation systems, and so on.

These are clearly necessary and useful strategies, but might there be a more systemic perspective lurking in plain sight? What are our implicit values in terms of what has seemed to be (at least in some countries) an infinite, always available resource? Turn on the tap: there it is. Need to dispose of liquid waste: go ahead. Want to build new cities or farms in what are essentially deserts: can be done.

Is the problem drought, or is it how we think and feel about water? Is this a problem *we have*, and can therefore observe, deconstruct, and solve without changing our Broadways and Grand Canyons? Or does it *have us*—and is therefore almost impossible to perceive. If the latter, we might first have to try to uncover our hidden assumptions about access, criteria, and cost (not just monetary)—but we cannot uncover them simply by knowing more. Before we can imagine—operative word—adaptive approaches, we have to reframe the question, which means knowing differently.

This example is meant to provoke deeper reflection about things that may at first seem obvious. Clearly, we are not attempting to directly engage the topic of drought. (Adaptive approaches don't work that way.) We are also mindful that this particular concern involves entrenched institutions with economic and political clout. That said, when issues are systemic and complex, the underlying approaches suggested by heart, hemispheres, Heron, and Heifetz may contribute to shifting individual and, ultimately, even institutional perspectives and commitment.

Complexity

The world we live in needs many more adults who can question the status quo and have the capacity to envision commitment to what Heron (1992) calls "human flourishing," which includes the rest of the biome, as well. Envisioning and acting on commitments to the greater good are hallmarks of an adult's developmental progression. As Daloz (1999) notes:

> the act of getting outside of one's own world and seeing through the eyes of another is of profound developmental significance. It demands that in some small way we cross the boundary between ourselves and the other person or idea or sensation.... In time, we come to recognize that those we may once have viewed as "them" have become part of a larger "us,"...commitment to a common good [replaces] defense of one's own private welfare,.... and we can begin to construct a reasonably compassionate world in which to resolve our differences without violence. (pp. 220–221)

Such developmental growth also means that we will be less vulnerable to the ways in which our anxious brains can be manipulated, as when they are temporarily calmed by the promise of greater security, even at the cost of demonizing others. In the absence of such growth, rather than responding to crises with more complex ways of knowing, we can find ourselves mired in the "xenophobia, paranoia, isolationism, and controlling/aggressive behavior" (Joy, 2011, p. 29) associated with the LH's perspective rather than the RH's desire to reach out and connect with the Other.

We also see as essential reconnecting with those who have been poorly served by excessively cognitive-focused or behavior-focused educational assumptions. Of necessity, this means challenging hegemonic assumptions about adult learning that have effectively silenced various cultural groups and dismissed nonconforming educational paradigms.

Much of what we have called *imaginal* and *symbolic* has deep connections to indigenous worldviews, philosophies, and learning. Matamonasa-Bennett (July, 2015) writes:

> In the indigenous approach, *feeling* and experiencing communal relationships through artistic and mythical dimensions, [including] ritual and ceremony . . . are the only viable means to wisdom and knowledge. Unlike Western approaches which emphasize *non-feeling*, rational, or linear approaches, these affective elements are not readily quantifiable, observable, or easily verbalized and are mostly ignored by mainstream academia.

This underscores the importance of Heron's facilitation approach, which specifically attends to emotional and symbolic aspects of learning. Moreover, emotions are the foundation for values and values fuel commitment.

Commitment

As ALFAS, we aspire to have our field, adult learning facilitation, adopt a more RH-oriented approach in both philosophy and practice. From the viewpoint of philosophy, that implies seeing adult learning as a journey toward greater awareness, connection, empathy, creativity, and courageous informed action. From a practice standpoint, it suggests more explicitly involving movement, metaphor, embodiment, and symbolic (expressive, artistic, non-verbal) activities.

We wish to encourage viewing our field of practice more from a perspective of a 3-D than a panoramic lens. The panoramic perspective on how to improve adult learning would focus primarily on adding new approaches to our toolkits—in effect, to elaborate on what we have been doing all along, just do it more and better. Granted, that is an important step in our process of change. However, more fundamentally, the 3-D lens would enable us to see, feel, know, and experience practice in a new, more complex, more *meaning-full* way. More than *additive*, that would be *transformative*. We realize that developing our own and others' capacities to bring more complex ways of knowing to current issues means we must also be willing to constantly review our own assumptions. Our personal commitment to continue to focus on facilitating such adult learning and transformation is further described in the epilogue.

"No one is born a good citizen; no nation is born a democracy. Rather, both are processes that continue to evolve over a lifetime".

—(Annan, 1998)

As Dewey (1938) noted decades ago, the democratic impulse may require a particular independence of mind and thought, based on the ability to question one's own—and, by extension, cultural and societal—beliefs and assumptions. Yet as we have seen, the adult brain does not readily engage in such self-questioning, preferring to maintain the safety and familiarity of what it already knows and avoid both the discomfort of not knowing and the additional effort of forging a more complex pathway. Even so, Paulo Freire's (1993) radical approach to teaching people living under severely oppressed conditions empowered them to "achieve a deepening awareness of both the sociocultural reality which shapes their lives and of their capacity to transform that reality through action upon it" (p. 27) by facilitating development of conscientization—the capacity for critical thinking and meaningful action that signal greater complexity of mind.

In *Common Fire: Leading Lives of Commitment in a Complex World*, Daloz, Keen, Keen and Parks (1996) studied over a hundred people who had "demonstrated capacities for reflective, creative, strategic response to suffering and tough problems" and "had sustained long-term commitments to work on behalf of the common good, even in the face of global complexity, diversity, and ambiguity" (pp. 4–5). These change agents share certain core characteristics, despite marked disparities in their historical backgrounds, current settings, and chosen activities. This point of view is further elaborated by Chickering (2008), who notes that change agents such as these are helping to create "involved communities.... An involved community is not a given... it is chosen" (p. 90). As a group, they embrace and feel at home in myriad situations, engage with others constructively and empathetically, can think critically and hold multiple perspectives, and see the world as it is and imagine what it could be—and commit to actions toward that vision. Such characteristics and capacities are illustrative of the complex way of knowing we metaphorically described as the 3-D lens.

Perhaps most demanding and disconcerting of all, this way of seeing and knowing requires tolerance for—indeed, embrace of—ambiguity and paradox: states of mind the brain much prefers to avoid. Not only must adults commit to the meaning they construct (assuming they have done so thoughtfully and with as much clarity as one can muster) but also remain open to revising those constructions as their capacities and understandings, described in chapter 9 as aspects of increased complexity of mind, develop still further.

Given that the most pressing issues of adult life are essentially adaptive challenges rather than technical questions, brain-aware ALFAS may have a crucial role to play in fostering such growth and transformation. Whatever the setting in which we practice, we are uniquely situated to activate heart, invite overt RH participation, and elicit adaptive approaches to leadership. Cultivating adults' capacity for complexity and commitment may be among ALFAS' highest aspirations and commitments.

Key Ideas

- We are all drawn to those who are like-minded—an apt metaphor—thus continually reconfirming our assumptions.
- Embodiment is at the root of everything we perceive, know, or understand—and therefore, ultimately of the choices we make or actions we take in response to our perceptions.
- Transformative learning emerges not from incorporating more information into a current framework of understanding but from perceiving a larger context that was previously unseen (or only dimly seen), requiring a reconfigured, more comprehensive framework (or, more concretely, neural network).

- We see our overarching task as encouraging adults to learn and know in a qualitatively different way, which means facilitating with developmental intentions.
- Where the RH focuses broadly on the natural world, living beings, and the subtle demands of closeness and connection, the LH focuses narrowly on the created world—that which is mechanistic and technological.
- RH's emotional expressivity, deep sense of embodiment, capacity for metaphor and inference, openness to experiencing the world anew, tolerance of ambiguity, power of compassion and empathy, and sense of ultimate connectedness with all living things are among its great assets—and greatly needed in the current reality.
- We see as essential to reconnect with those who have been poorly served by excessively cognitive-focused or behavior-focused educational assumptions. This means challenging hegemonic assumptions about adult learning that have effectively silenced various cultural groups and dismissed nonconforming educational paradigms.

? Pause for Reflection

1. From the perspectives of the adults whose learning you facilitate, how does complexity play out in their lives and learning?
2. How might enhancing adult learners' RH-oriented capacities help them to influence change and betterment in their communities?
3. What are some key implications, personally and professionally, for you as an ALFAS?

EPILOGUE

Or, a funny thing happened on the way to the (meta-) forum.

— KEN MILLER

FOR MILLENNIA, mathematicians, astronomers, philosophers, and later, theologians shared a worldview that placed the earth at the center of the universe. Doubters were largely ignored. For several centuries, the mathematical model of that system could predict with considerable accuracy the movement as various celestial bodies and even account for oddities such planets seeming to move backward. Over the longer term, disparities emerged that could no longer be reconciled; meanwhile, new analytical and mechanical tools (such as the telescope) made new data available. But by then, what had begun with the Greeks as inquiry had become for Christianity a matter of dogma.

Though our well-functioning cosmology was based on years of experience, we didn't think of ourselves as dogmatic. True, our earlier researches into the brain and learning caused us to affirm rather than question the movement of the stars as we perceived them. But as we studied the heavens more deeply, we started to find patterns we hadn't noticed before or that hadn't appeared entirely relevant to us. As we integrated emerging suppositions and recent findings in far-flung fields not ordinarily associated with adult learning, we realized that our cosmological map was up for question. We had even begun to minimally integrate imaginal and symbolic aspects into our practice, having seen how central they are to the brain's way of learning. Yet almost before we knew it, the earth moved.

The sun is now at the center. Metaphor cannot be separated from the body. At first, it seemed as if embodiment might just be an interesting side issue, but it kept turning up in unexpected places from cognitive science to theories of mind. Several neuroscientists quoted throughout this book also explicitly describe the importance of the body to learning, and not just as a stimulus receptor. We were especially influenced by McGilchrist's (2010) view that as a society, we tend to "discount and marginalize the importance of our embodied nature, as though it were something incidental about us, rather than essential to us: our very thinking, never mind our feeling, is bound up with our embodied nature, and must be, and this needs to be acknowledged" (p. 439).

With growing awareness comes responsibility. After years—decades!—of a fairly consistent and successful approach to practice, we went back to beginner's mind. We were now convinced that working with embodiment was an exciting and important new way to think about facilitating adult learning—but, as fifteenth-century cartographers anxiously wrote at the edges of maps of the known (flat) world, "This way be dragons."

As new opportunities arose—trainings and workshops planned, courses scheduled—we realized we could no longer carry on business as usual. In encouraging ourselves to break through our accustomed patterns, we reminded (re-minded) ourselves that we didn't have to jettison everything, but we did have to shift our rhythms and develop new material and activities. We shared our fears and occasional moments of clarity—and our commitment to see it through.

Some confessions. We had to reconsider our initial sense that certain activities might be silly or fluff (because we didn't know how to do them authentically) and acknowledge their brain awareness. We had to overcome our discomfort with wordlessness (we're *good* at words) as well as our inhibitions about embodiment (We're supposed to do *what*?). Fortunately, as we reappraised the dozens of approaches our colleagues contributed, we saw each time new possibilities to adapt them in light of our own growing body-brain awareness.

Having listened to colleagues describe these approaches and sometimes having observed them in action, we finally had to step off the edge of the map. A couple of early examples: opening a three-day gathering of adult educators by getting them up out of their chairs to create a physical timeline of project milestones and later having them create a physical bar graph of various groups' accomplishments; having midcareer professionals draw (i.e. sketch) their own metaphors to capture their feelings about being newly admitted to a graduate program. Despite our anxieties and misgivings, participants reported a level of awareness and energy from engaging in these activities that we would never before have anticipated.

Armed with what we now understand about the *why* behind embodied-analogical facilitation and our attempts at toe-in-the-water practice, our curious brains are on full alert. If something doesn't work well enough, we vow not to retreat to our anxious brain but to be radically curious about the experience, as Peet and others (2011) have said.

At times, we simply engage adult participants in the new approach; at others we invite them into our process. We may ask: "How was it for you? What worked or didn't work? How might it be improved? Is it worth trying out with another group?" Our fears of losing our aura of competence seem unfounded. Adults are almost unfailingly supportive and appreciate the fact that we, like they, are embarked on a journey of learning and development. In the end, though it had not been our intention, we feel that modeling our willingness to be vulnerable and insecure while developing a new capacity or skill is a meaningful contribution to their process of learning, regardless of how the activity itself turns out.

There is no ending to this story about how ALFAS may choose to engage with brain-aware facilitation of adult learning. Much is yet to be discovered in the rapidly emerging neurological understanding of how the adult brain learns. Theories of adult learning and development will no doubt need to catch up. Practices will need to be expanded and enriched. Our hope and intention is to contribute to the growing conversation about how best to facilitate deep and meaningful adult learning as we join with you on this journey. Please see our website www.embodiedbrains.org.

We shall not cease from exploration
And the end of all our exploring
Will be to arrive where we started
And know the place for the first time.
—T. S. Eliot, *Four Quartets*

REFERENCES

Ambrose, S. A., Bridges, M. W., DiPietro, M., Lovett, M. C., & Norman, M. K. (2010). *How learning works: Seven research-based principles for smart teaching*. San Fransciso, CA: Jossey-Bass.

Annan, K. (1998). Speeches/statements: "A society that cuts itself off from its youth severs its lifeline," secretary-general tells world conference. Retrieved from http://www.un.org/events/youth98/speeches/sgyouth2.htm

Akyol, Z., & Garrison, D. R. (2011). Assessing metacognition in an online community of inquiry. *Internet and Higher Education 14*(3), 183–190. doi:10.1016/j.iheduc.2011.01.005

Bandura, A. (1977). *Social learning theory*. Englewood Cliffs, NJ: Prentice Hall.

Bandura, A. (1986). *Social foundations of thought: A social cognitive theory*. Englewood, Cliffs, NJ: Prentice Hall.

Bateson, M. C. (1994). *Peripheral visions*. New York, NY: HarperCollins.

Baynes, K., & Gazzaniga, M. S. (2000). Consciousness, introspection, and the split-brain: The two minds/one body problem. In M. S. Gazzaniga (Ed.), *The new cognitive neurosciences* (2nd ed., pp. 1355–1363). Cambridge, MA: MIT Press.

Bean, J. C. (2011). *Engaging ideas: The professor's guide to integrating writing, critical thinking, and active learning in the classroom*. San Francisco, CA: Jossey-Bass.

Belenky, M. F., Clinchy, B. M., Goldberger, N. R., & Tarule, J. M. (1986). *Women's ways of knowing: The development of self, voice, and mind*. New York, NY: Basic Books.

Belenky, M. F., Clinchy, B. M., Goldberger, N. R., & Tarule, J. M. (1997). *Women's ways of knowing: The development of self, voice, and mind*, 10th anniversary edition. New York, NY: Basic Books. (Original work published 1986)

Berns, G. (2008). *Iconoclast: A neuroscientist reveals how to think differently*. Boston, MA: Harvard Business Press.

Boud, D. (1992). The use of self-assessment schedules in negotiated learning. *Studies in Higher Education, 17*(2), 185–200. doi:10.1080/03075079212331382657

Boud, D., Keogh, R., & Walker, D. (Eds.). (1985). *Reflection: Turning experience into learning*. New York, NY: Nichols.

Bransford, J. D., Brown, A. L., & Cocking, R. R. (Eds.). (2000). *How people learn: Brain, mind, experience and school*. Washington, DC: National Academies Press.

Brookfield, S. D. (1989). *Developing critical thinkers*. San Francisco, CA: Jossey-Bass.

Brookfield, S. D. (1999). *Discussion as a way of teaching*. San Francisco, CA: Jossey-Bass.

Brookfield, S. D. (2009). *The power of critical theory*. San Francisco, CA: Jossey-Bass.

Brookfield, S. D. (2013). *Powerful techniques for teaching adults*. San Francisco, CA: Jossey-Bass.

Buonomano, D. (2011). *Brain bugs: How the brain's flaws shape our lives*. New York, NY: Norton.

Burton, R. A. (2008). *On being certain: Believing you are right even when you're not*. New York, NY: St. Martin's Press.

Campbell, T. H., & Kay, A. C. (2014). Solution aversion: On the relation between ideology and motivated disbelief.

Journal of Personality and Social Psychology, 107(5), 809–824. doi:10.1037/a0037963

Candy, P. C. (1991). *Self-direction for lifelong learning: A comprehensive guide to theory and practice*. San Francisco, CA: Jossey-Bass.

Chickering, A. W. (2008). Strengthening democracy and personal development through community engagement. In S. Reed & C. Marienau (Eds.), *Linking adults with community: Engagement through community based learning* (pp. 87–95). New Directions for Adult and Continuing Education, no. 118. San Francisco, CA: Jossey-Bass.

Chiron, C., Jambaque, I., Nabbout, R., Lounes, R., Syrota, A. & Dulac, O. (1997). The right brain hemisphere is dominant in human infants. *Brain, 120*, 1057–1065.

Clark, A. (1997). *Being there: Putting brain, body, and world together again*. Cambridge MA: MIT Press.

Clinchy, B. M. (1996). Connected and separate knowing: Toward a marriage of two minds. In N. R. Goldberger, J. M. Tarule, B. M. Clinchy, & M. F. Belenky (Eds.), *Knowledge, difference, and power*. New York, NY: Basic Books.

Commons, M. L., & Miller, P. M. (2001). A quantitative behavioral model of developmental stage based upon the model of hierarchical complexity. *Behavior Analyst Today, 2*(3), 222–240. Retrieved from http://www.baojournal.com/BAT%20Journal/BAT-Journals-2009.html

Cozolino, L. J. (2014). *Attachment-based teaching: Creating a tribal classroom*. New York, NY: Norton.

Daloz, L. A. (1999). *Mentor: Guiding the journey of adult learners*. San Francisco, CA: Jossey-Bass.

Daloz, L. A., Keen, C. H., Keen, J. P., & Parks, S. (1996). *Common fire: Leading lives of commitment in a complex world*. Boston, MA: Beacon Press

Damasio, A. (1994). Descartes' error: Emotion, reason, and the human brain. New York, NY: Penguin.

Damasio, A. R. (2000). *The feeling of what happens: Body and emotion in the making of consciousness*. New York, NY: Harcourt.

Deacon, T. (1997). *The symbolic species: The co-evolution of language and the human brain*. London: Allen Lane.

Dewey, J. (1933). *How we think, a restatement of the relation of reflective thinking to the educative process*. Boston, MA: Heath.

Dewey, J. (1938). *Experience and Education*. New York, NY: Macmillan.

Dirkx, J. M. (2008). The meaning and role of emotions in adult learning. In J. M. Dirkx (Ed.), *Adult learning and the emotional self*, 2008(120), 7–18. doi:10.1002/ace.311

DiSalvo, D. (2011). *What makes your brain happy and why you should do the opposite*. Amherst, NY: Prometheus.

Dunbar, R.I.M. (1998). The social brain hypothesis. *Evolutionary Anthropology*, *6*, 178–190. doi:10.1002/(SICI)1520-6505(1998)6:5<178::AID-EVAN5>3.0.CO;2-8

Edelman, G. M. (2006). *Second nature: Brain science and human knowledge*. New Haven, CT: Yale University Press.

Edelman, G. M., & Tononi, G. (2000). *A universe of consciousness: How matter becomes imagination*. New York, NY: Basic Books.

Fauconnier, G. (2001). Conceptual blending and analogy. In D. Gentner, K. J. Holyoak, & B. N. Kokinov (Eds.), *The analogical mind: Perspectives from cognitive science* (pp. 255–285). Cambridge, MA: MIT Press.

Fiddler, M., & Marienau, C. (2008). Developing habits of reflection for meaningful learning, (pp. 75–85). In, S. Reed & C. Marienau (Eds.). *Linking adults with community: Promoting civic engagement through community-based learning.* New Directions for Adult and Continuing Education, no. 118. San Francisco, CA: Jossey-Bass. doi:10.1002/ace.297

Flavell, J. H. (1979). Metacognition and cognitive monitoring: A new area of cognitive-developmental inquiry. *American Psychologist, 34*(10), 906–911. doi:10.1037/0003-066X.34.10.906

Flavell, J. H. (1987). Speculations about the nature and development of metacognition. In F. Weinert & R. Kluwe (Eds.), *Metacognition, motivation, and understanding* (pp. 21–29). Hillsdale, NJ: Erlbaum.

Freire, P. (1993). *The pedagogy of the oppressed*. (M. B. Ramos, Trans.). New York, NY: Continuum.

Gardner, H. (1999). *Intelligence reframed: Multiple intelligences for the 21st century*. New York, NY: Basic Books.

Geary, J. (2012). *I is an other: The secret life of metaphor and how it shapes the way we see the world*. New York, NY: Harper Perennial

Gelertner, D. (1994). *The muse in the machine*. New York, NY: Free Press.

Genter, D., Bowdle, B., Wolff, P., & Boronat, C. (2001). Metaphor is like analogy. In D. Gentner, K. J. Holyoak, & B. N. Kokinov (Eds.), *The analogical mind: Perspectives from cognitive science* (pp. 199–254). Cambridge, MA: MIT Press.

Gilman, C. P. (1973) *The yellow wallpaper*. New York, NY: Feminist Press.

Goldberger, N. R., Tarule, J. M., Clinchy, B. M., & Belenky, M. F. (Eds.). (1996). Knowledge, difference, and power: Essays inspired by *Women's Ways of Knowing*. New York, NY: Basic Books.

Goswami, U. (2001). Analogical reasoning in children. In D. Genter, K. J. Holyoak, & B. N. Kokinov (Eds.), *The analogical mind: Perspectives from cognitive science* (pp. 437–470). Cambridge, MA: MIT Press.

Gray, D. E. (2014). *Doing research in the real world* (3rd ed.). Thousand Oaks, CA: Sage.

Greene, J. D. (2013). *Moral tribes: Emotion, reason, and the gap between us and them*. New York, NY: Penguin Press.

Guba, E. G., & Lincoln, Y. S. (2005). Paradigmatic controversies, contradictions, and emerging confluences, revisited. In N. K. Denzin & Y. S. Lincoln (Eds.), *The Sage handbook of qualitative research* (pp. 191–215). Thousand Oaks, CA: Sage.

Haskell, R. E. (Ed.). (1987). *Cognition and symbolic structures: The psychology of metaphoric transformation*. Norwood, NJ: Ablex.

Heifetz, R. A., Linsky, M., & Grashow, A. (2009). *The practice of* adaptive leadership: *Tools and tactics for changing your organization and the world.* Boston, MA: Harvard Business Press.

Heisenberg, W. (1958). *Physics and philosophy; The revolution in modern science*. London: G. Allen & Unwin.

Heron, J. (1992). *Feeling and personhood: Psychology in another key*. Thousand Oaks, CA: Sage.

Heron, J. (1999). *The complete facilitator's handbook.* Philadelphia, PA: Kogan Page

Hodges, E. (1997). Negotiating the margins: Some principles for responding to our students' writing, some strategies for helping students read our comments, 77–89. New Directions for Teaching and Learning, no. 69. San Francisco, CA: Jossey-Bass. doi:10.1002/tl.6907

Hofstedter, D. (2001). Analogy as the core of cognition. In D. Gentner, K. J. Holyoak, & B. N. Kokinov (Eds.), *The analogical mind: Perspectives from cognitive science* (pp. 499–538). Cambridge, MA: MIT Press.

Horton, M., & Freire, P. (1990). *We make the road by walking.* Philadelphia, PA: Temple University Press.

Illeris, K. (2009) *Contemporary theories of learning: Learning theorists—in their own words.* New York, NY: Routledge.

Immordino-Yang, M. H., & Damasio, A. R. (2007). We feel, therefore we learn: The relevance of affective and social neuroscience to education. *Mind, Brain and Education, 1*(1), 3–10

Johnson, S. & Taylor, K. (Eds.) (2006). *The neuroscience of adult learning.* New Directions for Adult and Continuing Education, No. 110. San Francisco, CA: Jossey-Bass.

Joy, L. (2011). *How does societal transformation happen?: Values development, collective wisdom, and decision making for the common good.* Quaker Institute for the Future Pamphlet 4. Caya Caulka, Belize: *Producciones de la Hamaca.*

Kahneman, D. (2011). *Thinking fast and slow.* New York, NY: Farrar, Straus, and Giroux.

Kegan, R. (1982). *The evolving self: Problem and process in human development.* Cambridge, MA: Harvard University Press.

Kegan, R. (1994). *In over our heads: The mental demands of modern life*. Cambridge, MA: Harvard University Press.

Kegan, R. (2000). What "form" transforms? A constructive-developmental approach to transformative learning. In. J. Mezirow & Assoc. *Learning as transformation*. San Francisco, CA: Jossey-Bass.

Kegan, R., & Lahey, L. L. (2009). *Immunity to change*. San Francisco, CA: Jossey-Bass.

Kolb, D. A. (1984). *Experiential learning: Experience as the source of learning and development*. Englewood Cliffs, NJ: Prentice Hall.

Kolb, D.A. (2015). *Experiential learning: Experience as the source of learning and development*, 2nd ed. Upper Saddle River, NJ: Pearson Education, Inc.

Kuhn, T. S. (1962). *The structure of scientific revolutions*. Chicago, IL: University of Chicago Press.

Lakoff, G., & Johnson, M. (1999). *Philosophy in the flesh: The embodied mind and its challenge to Western thought*. New York, NY: Basic Books.

Lakoff, G., & Johnson, M. (2003). *Metaphors we live by*. Chicago, IL: University of Chicago Press. (Original work published 1980)

Lamoreaux, A. J., & Taylor, K. (2011). Prior learning assessment and the developmental journey: From "mapless" to cartographer. In C. Hoare (Ed.), *The Oxford handbook of reciprocal adult development and learning* (pp. 80–100). New York, NY: Oxford University Press.

Lave, J., & Wenger, E. (1991). *Situated learning: Legitimate peripheral participation*. Cambridge, MA: Cambridge University Press.

Lieberman, M. D. (2013). *Social: Why our brains are wired to connect*. New York, NY: Crown.

Llinás, R. R. (2002). *I of the vortex: From neurons to self*. Cambridge, MA: MIT Press.

Loacker, G., & Alverno College Faculty (Eds.). (2000). *Self assessment at Alverno College*. Milwaukee, WI: Alverno College Press.

Loevinger, J., & Blasi, A. (1976). *Ego development*. San Francisco, CA: Jossey-Bass.

MacGregor, J. (Ed.). (1993). *Student self-evaluation: Fostering reflective learning*. New Directions for Teaching and Learning, no. 56. San Francisco, CA: Jossey-Bass.

MacLean, P. D. (1990). *The triune brain in evolution: Role in paleocerebral functions*. New York, NY: Plenum Press.

Magolda, M. B. (1992). *Knowing and reasoning in college: Gender-related patterns in students' intellectual development*. San Francisco, CA: Jossey-Bass.

Marienau, C. (1999). Self-assessment at work: Outcomes of adult learners' reflections on practice. *Adult Education Quarterly, 49*(3), 135–146. doi:10.1177/074171369904900301

Marton, B., & Booth, S. A. (1997). *Learning and awareness*. Mahwah, NJ: Erlbaum.

Matamonasa-Bennett, A. (2015, July). Tribal cultures, ancient minds & modern science. Second Global Conference: Making Sense of the Animal and Human Bond. Mansfield College, Oxford UK.

Mayer, R. (2011). Applying the science of learning. Indianapolis, IN: Pearson.

McGilchrist, I. (2010). *The master and his emissary: The divided brain and the making of the Western world*. New Haven, CT: Yale University Press.

Merriam, S. B., & Bierema, L. L. (2014). *Adult learning: Linking theory with practice*. San Francisco, CA: Jossey-Bass.

Meyer, P. (2010). *From workplace to playspace: Innovating, learning, and changing through dynamic engagement*. San Francisco: Jossey-Bass.

Meyer, P. (2011). How to create an agile organization. *Chief Learning Officer, 10*(2), 36–39. Retrieved from http://www.clomedia.com/

Meyer, P. (2015). *The agility shift: Creating agile and effective leaders, teams, and organizations*. Brookline, MA: Bibliomotion, Inc.

Mezirow, J. (1991). *Transformative dimensions of adult learning*. San Francisco, CA: Jossey-Bass.

Mezirow, J. (1996). Contemporary paradigms of learning. *Adult Education Quarterly, 46*(3), 158–173. doi:10.1177/074171369604600303

Mezirow, J. (2000). *Learning as transformation*. San Francisco, CA: Jossey-Bass.

Mezirow, J. (2009). *Fostering critical reflection in adulthood: A guide to transformative and emancipatory learning*. San Francisco, CA: Jossey-Bass.

Minnich, E. K. (2005). *Transforming knowledge*, 2nd edition. Philadelphia, PA: Temple University Press.

Ozman, H., & Craver, S. M. (2003). *Philosophical foundations of education*. Upper Saddle River, NJ: Prentice Hall.

Paxton, D. (2003). Facilitating transformation of white consciousness among European-American people: A case study of a cooperative inquiry. *Dissertation Abstracts International*, *64*(01), 297A. (UMI No. AAT3078796)

Peet, M. (2013). *The integrative knowledge portfolio process: Identifying your capacities, discover your purpose, demonstrate your difference*. Detroit, MI: University of Michigan.

Peet, M., Lonn, S., Gurin, P., Boyer, K., Matney, M., Marra, T., . . . Daley, A. (2011). Fostering integrative knowledge through eportfolios. *International Journal of ePortfolio, 1*(1), 11–31

Perry, W. G., Jr. (1999). *Forms of intellectual and ethical development in the college years: A scheme*. San Francisco, CA: Jossey-Bass. (Original work published 1968)

Piaget, J. (1955). *The child's construction of reality*. London: Routledge.

Piaget, J. (2008). Intellectual evolution from adolescence to adulthood. *Human Development, 51*(1), 40–47. Retrieved from http://search.proquest.com/docview/224016422?accountid=25334

Pink, D. H. (2005). *A whole new mind*. London: Marshall Cavendish.

Polanyi, M., & Grene, M. (Eds.). (1969). *Knowing and being; essays*. Chicago, IL: University of Chicago Press.

Pratt, D. D., & Associates. (2005). *Five perspectives on teaching in adult and higher education, updated edition*. Malabar, FL: Krieger.

Ratey, J. J. (2002). *A user's guide to the brain*. New York, NY: Vintage Books.

Rosenfeld, I. (1988). *The invention of memory: A new view of the brain*. New York, NY: Basic Books.

Rowlands, M. (2010). *The new science of the mind: From extended mind to embodied phenomenology*. Cambridge, MA: MIT Press.

Safire, W. (2004, March 24). Of God and the flag. New York Times. Retrieved from http://nytimes.com

Schmidt, G. L., Cardillo, E. R., Kranjec, A., Lehet, M., Widick, P., & Chatterjee, A. (2012). Not all analogies are created equal: Associative and categorical analogy processing following brain damage. *Neuropsychologia, 50*(7), 1372–1379. doi:10.1016/j.neuropsychologia.2012.02.022

Schön, D. (1984). *The reflective practitioner: How professionals think in action*. New York, NY: Basic Books.

Shermer, M. (2011). *The believing brain: From ghosts and gods to politics and conspiracies; how we construct beliefs and reinforce them as truths*. New York, NY: Times Books.

Siegel, D. J. (1999). *The developing mind: How relationships and the brain interact to shape who we are*. New York, NY: Guilford Press.

Sinnott, J. D. (1998). *The development of logic in adulthood: Postformal thought and its applications*. New York, NY: Plenum Press.

Smith, M. K. (2008). Howard Gardner, multiple intelligences and education. In *The encyclopedia of informal education*. Retrieved from http://infed.org/mobi/howard-gardner-multiple-intelligences-and-education/

Squire, K. (2011). *Video games and learning: Teaching and participatory culture in the digital age*. New York, NY: Teachers College Press.

Stadsklev, R. (2012). *Handbook of simulation gaming in social education/Constitution today*. Author. (Originally published 1975)

Stanfield, R. B. (Ed.). (2000). *The art of focused conversation: 100 ways to access group wisdom in the workplace*. Gabriola Island, BC: New Society.

Stanton, A. (1996). Reconfiguring teaching and knowing in the college classroom. In N. R. Goldberger, J. M. Tarule, B. M. Clinchy, & M. F. Belenky (Eds.), *Knowledge, difference, and power*. New York: Basic Books.

Straub, R. (2000). *The practice of response: Strategies for commenting on student writing*. Cresskill, NJ: Hampton Press.

"Syrian migrants, including toddler, drown off Turkey," 2015. http://www.timesofmalta.com/articles/view/20150902/world/syrian-migrants-including-toddler-drown-off-turkey.582933

Sue, D. W. (2010). *Microaggressions in everyday life: Race, gender, and sexual orientation*. Hoboken, NJ: Wiley.

Taylor, J. B. (2008). *My stroke of insight: A brain scientist's personal journey*. New York, NY: Viking.

Taylor, K. (1995). Sitting beside herself: Self-assessment and women's adult development. In, K. Taylor and C. Marienau (Eds.) *Learning environments for women's adult development: Bridges toward change*, 21–28. New Directions for Adult and Continuing Education, no. 65. San Francisco, CA: Jossey-Bass. doi:10.1002/ace.36719956505

Taylor, K. (2006). Autonomy and self-directed learning: A developmental journey. In C. H. Hoare (Ed.). *Handbook of adult development and learning* (pp. 196–218). New York, NY: Oxford University Press.

Taylor, K., & Marienau, C. (1993). Self-assessment: A source for individual and organizational learning. *Contemporary Education, 64*(3), 166–169.

Taylor, K., & Marienau, C. (2008). Effective approaches to fostering developmental growth in women learners: A view from neurophysiology. In J. K. Allen, S. J. Bracken, & D. R. Dean (Eds.), *Most women are students: Implications for college faculty and policymakers* (pp. 55–74). Sterling, VA: Stylus.

Taylor, K., Marienau, C., & Fiddler, M. (2000). *Developing adult learners: Strategies for teachers and trainers*. San Francisco, CA: Jossey-Bass.

Tennant, M., & Pogson, P. (1995). *Learning and change in the adult years: A developmental perspective*. San Francisco, CA: Jossey-Bass.

Tompkins, C. A., Scharp, V. L., Meigh, K. M., & Fassbinder, W. (2008). Coarse coding and discourse comprehension in adults with right hemisphere brain damage. *Aphasiology, 22*(2), 204–223. doi:10.1080/02687030601125019

Varela, F. J., Thompson, E., & Rosch, E. (1991). *The embodied mind: Cognitive science and human experience*. Cambridge, MA: MIT Press.

Veenman, M. V. J., Van Hout-Wolters, B.H.A.M., & Afflerbach, P. (2006). Metacognition and learning: Conceptual and methodological considerations. *Metacognition and Learning, 1*(1), 3–14. doi:10.1007/s11409-006-6893-0

Vygotsky, L. S. (1978). *Mind in society: The development of higher psychological processes*. Cambridge, MA: Harvard University Press.

Wenger, E. (2000). Communities of practical social learning systems. *SAGE Social Science*, vol *7*(2), pp. 225–246.

Whybrow, P. C. (2015). *The well-tuned brain: Neuroscience and the life well lived*. New York, NY: Norton.

Wilbur, G., & Scott, R. (2013). Inside out, outside in: Power and culture in a learning community. *Multicultural Perspectives, 15*(3), 158–164. doi:10.1080/15210960.2013.809306

Wiggins, G. & McTighe, J. (2005). Understanding by design, 2nd ed. Alexandria, VA: Association for Supervision and Curriculum Development.

Willans, J., & Seary, K. (2011). "I feel like I'm being hit from all directions": Enduring the bombardment as a mature-age learner returning to formal learning. *Australian Journal of Adult Learning, 51*(1), 119–142. Retrieved from http://www.ajal.net.au/

Williams, R. B. (2002). *Multiple intelligences for differentiated thinking*. Thousand Oaks, CA: Corwin Press.

Williams, R. B., & Dunn, S. E. (2008). *Brain-compatible learning for the block*. Thousand Oaks, CA: Corwin Press.

Willingham, D. T. (2009). *Why don't students like school? A cognitive scientist answers questions about how the mind works and what it means for the classroom*. San Francisco, CA: Jossey-Bass.

Wilson, M. (2002). Six views of embodied cognition. *Psychonomic Bulletin and Review, 9*, 625–636. doi:10.3758/BF03196322

Wilson-Mendenhall, C. D., Barrett, L. F., Simmons, W. K., & Barsalou, L. W. (2011). Grounded emotion in situated conceptualization. *Neuropsychologia, 49*, 1105–1127. doi:10.1016/j.neuropsychologia.2010.12.032

Zhong, C., & Leonardelli, G. J. (2008). Cold and lonely: Does social exclusion literally feel cold? *Psychological Science, 19*(9), 838–842. doi:10.1111/j.1467-9280.2008.02165.x

Zinsser, W. K. (1988). *Writing to learn.* New York, NY: Harper & Row.

Zull, J. E. (2002). *The art of changing the brain.* Sterling, VA: Stylus.

ACKNOWLEDGMENTS

OUR DEEPEST appreciation goes to our long-time collaborator, colleague, and friend, Annalee Lamoreaux, who helped formulate the original vision of this book. Though she was unable to continue the journey with us to the end due to other responsibilities, she was an integral part of our formative conversations and pointed us toward aspects of research we might have overlooked. As the only one of us who had experience working with actual brains (as opposed to body-brains), she also kept us on track when our analogies and interpretations started going too far afield. This book is no doubt poorer for her departure, and we absolve her of any responsibility for how it ultimately turned out.

Dozens of ALFAS in diverse settings helped shape our thinking. Early on, we e-mailed many colleagues around the globe, asking them to share with us issues central to their practice. Thanks to all those who eventually contributed approaches; they are named in the contributor biographies. For others' insightful questions and comments, we acknowledge Tammy Appling-Cabading, Lorena Cassady, Ruth Gannon Cook, Laura Heid, Carrie Johnson, Carol Kasworm, Vishu Lalchandani, Chelsea Lazaridou, Alan Mandell, Renie McClay, Barbara McLaughlin, Cynthia Moore, William Moore,Vanessa O'Neil, Rebecca Proehl, Leodis Scott, Cynthia Stevens, Don Stone, Roy Whitmore, and Jacqueline Wright.

As we wrote and revised, Jerry Brunetti, Rick Halberg, and Ken Miller helpfully reviewed the manuscript more than once.

Others who provided feedback on one or more chapters include Dimitra Andritsakou, Andrew Cvitanovich, Deborah Gustlin, Leonard Joy, John Petroni, Irvin Roth, and Alissa Stolz. Victoria Howard helped us clarify many of the approaches. Doug Paxton's assistance in providing concrete examples of Heron's model of facilitation, both in conversations and through access to his 2003 doctoral dissertation, was much appreciated. For their constructive feedback and enthusiastic support, huge thanks to our external reviewers, Pamela Meyer and R. Bruce Williams. Their thoughtful questions and suggestions greatly enhanced the final manuscript.

Thanks also to those who offered special expertise: Josh Rosen for source finding and reference checking, Janice Enloe for scientific articles on physical movement, and Tova Diamond for help with logistics and manuscript preparation. Artist Jill Archer turned our scribbles and scrawls into creative, informative illustrations and helped us walk our imaginal talk.

We are most grateful to David Kolb for sharing a working draft of his manuscript for *An Update on Experiential Learning* prior to publication (2015) and for granting advance permission to quote from it. We also owe special thanks to Sandra Johnson (2006), whose dissertation linking brain function to adult development and learning sparked our initial interest and led to an early coauthored monograph.

Last, but also first, our heartfelt thanks go to our family and friends—you know who you are—who cheered us on through the many stages of writing this book. We look forward to spending time with you again.

ABOUT THE AUTHORS AND CONTRIBUTORS

ARCHER, JILL. An artist, designer, and entrepreneur who revels in turning words into shapes so they can reflect new meaning and lead to understanding, Jill knows that ideas are seen in new light when they're drawn, revealing new angles to any issue. She began her career as a commercial artist for advertising agencies and evolved into user experience and web development, and enjoys most when she can tell stories with pictures, getting messages across. She has extensive experience drawing for nonprofits, universities, corporations, authors, and small businesses.

Ben-Yoseph, Miriam.[a] To model learning through stories, Miriam shares her own life experiences: born in Romania, fluent in six languages, studied in Israel and the United States, leader in market research and training at Continental Bank, full-time college professor, and now professor emeritus. For her excellence in teaching adults, Miriam was named the 2006 Illinois Professor of the Year by the Carnegie Foundation for the Advancement of Teaching. Her teaching, research, and publications center on cross-cultural management and change management, as well as place and identity issues.

Booth, Melanie. Adult learners are Melanie's best teachers–hundreds of them since she began her career teaching English at a community college in Washington more than twenty years ago. Melanie is vice president of educational programming at WASC Senior College and University Commission. Prior to

[a] Affiliated full- or part-time with School for New Learning, DePaul University
[b] Affiliated full- or part-time with Saint Mary's College of California

this, she was the dean of learning and assessment and director of the Center for Experiential Learning and Assessment at Marylhurst University in Portland.

Boud, David. Early in his career, David became involved in experiential learning programs. Since then, he has taken great interest in learning-focused approaches in adult and higher education and has undertaken research and development on the role of reflection and the development of adult learners' judgment of their own work. He is professor and director of the Centre for Research in Assessment and Digital Learning, Deakin University, Melbourne, and research professor in the Institute for Work-Based Learning, Middlesex University, London, as well as professor emeritus at the University of Technology, Sydney.

Brookfield, Stephen. Stephen holds the John Ireland Endowed Chair, University of St. Thomas, Minnesota. The author of numerous books and articles on adult learning, teaching methods, critical thinking, and critical theory, his interests as a practitioner involve democratizing various settings to create inclusive learning spaces. He also helps people identify ways in which dominant ideologies, particularly racism and sexism, play out in daily life. He is the father of Molly and Colin, and the husband of Kim and leads a pop punk band, The 99ers, that has released five albums on Spinout Records.

Chen, Joseph. As a counseling psychologist in private practice, researcher, and faculty member in a competency-based degree program for adult learners, Joe focuses on the change process—internal, external, and cultural factors that can facilitate or impede successful change. He teaches courses and presents workshops on the multidisciplinary intersection of neuroscience, psychology, adult learning, and culture. He also consults and presents on these topics in corporate and faith-based settings and publishes in both psychology and education outlets.

Cleary, Michelle Navarre.[a] While a graduate student, Michelle got hooked on teaching adults when she taught writing to retirees in the morning and literature to workers in the evening. Having taught at community colleges, she now teaches, mentors, and administers in degree programs exclusively for adults. Michelle's scholarship focuses on two questions: How do adults develop as writers when they return to school? How can the teaching of writing to adults be improved? In addition, she is engaged in collaborative research projects on e-portfolios and on competency-based education.

Daloz, Larry. His forty-year career teaching, mentoring, administering, and writing about adult learning, coupled with the births of his grandchildren and growing dismay over environmental degradation, fueled Larry's commitment to combat climate change. Becoming active in the divestiture movement, Larry cocreated the Cascadia Climate Collaborative in the Pacific Northwest, bringing together climate leaders across realms, encouraging tough conversations about the moral and emotional dimensions of climate change, and welcoming others who care about climate change but don't yet see a way to become more deeply involved.

Elias, Dean.[b] Working in the War on Poverty in the 1960s and 1970s, Dean discovered and has since championed democratic education and case-in-point pedagogy. He has taught and served in leadership roles in four colleges that embodied these strategies (or at least permitted them). Dean consulted with community, national, and international organizations for thirty years; he now largely teaches and does research with radically democratic educational institutions. His current focus is experimenting with differentiated adult pedagogies that serve diverse populations.

Fahim, Urusa. Considering herself a reluctant teacher, Urusa did not plan on a teaching career that crosses borders between the United States and her homeland of Pakistan. Nonetheless, she found her way into academia because she could not refuse an offer to teach a new course or to develop one, so she stayed. Urusa developed her teaching techniques based on what helped her learn and made learning relevant and applicable. She values student feedback and uses it to adapt her syllabi and her teaching methods where appropriate.

Glenn, Dennis.[a] Over the past thirty-five years, Dennis has discovered the great joy of reinventing his career choices and himself. Having been an advertising photographer, commercial film director, and assistant dean for distributed education at Northwestern University, Dennis is currently chief learning officer of a company that creates virtual patient simulations for learning and assessment—what are now called serious games. In addition to teaching graduate students part time, Dennis is a life coach with his practice based on the principles of positive psychology.

Hurtig, Janise.[a] Since first applying ethnographic research to the development of community education programs in the 1980s, Janise has attempted to integrate her commitments to cultural understanding and emancipatory pedagogies in her educational practice, research, and writing. Trained as an educational anthropologist, she has spent the past twenty years seeking ways to incorporate those sensibilities into her work coordinating a community writing program, carrying out applied and participatory research and evaluation, and teaching part-time in academic settings in Venezuela and the United States.

Iler, Jim.[b] As a returning adult learner studying applied mathematics and tutoring students in math, Jim discovered he had a knack for helping others understand a topic that unnerved and confused many. His different approach attracted so many students that he found himself conducting professional development seminars on how to teach math. Jim has expanded his methods of teaching mathematics to other subject areas and for the past sixteen years has been teaching in the education department at University of California Berkeley Extension, passionately training future generations of teachers.

Kelly, James.[a] For twenty-five years, Jim conducted training-of-trainers programs in Peace Corps training centers throughout Central and South America, during which time he became fluent in Spanish. He has trained local professionals to employ learner-centered facilitation techniques and design engaging learning environments. Jim resided and worked for extended periods in El Salvador, Venezuela, and Chile and has significant working experience in Mexico, Central America, Peru, Paraguay, Haiti, and Jamaica. He coteaches seminars and workshops on facilitating adult learning for graduate students and professionals from diverse sectors.

Kisiel, Caroline.[a] Caroline has worked with adult learners in undergraduate and graduate programs for over eighteen years and in community settings for even longer. A certified leader in InterPlay improvisational practice, which helps adults reclaim their movement, stories, and voices through play, she offers workshops and trains leaders in the United States and abroad and applies tools in university courses on creativity, research, health and well-being, and educating adults. Caroline researches how play and improvisation can sustain the work of both educators and learners.

Kokkos, Alexis. Inspired by the work of Paulo Freire and the Frankfurt School, Alexis was one of the key founders of popular education in Greece in the 1980s. He later participated in founding the Hellenic Open University, where he is currently professor of adult education. Alexis has been the scientific coordinator of the Greek Train-the-Adult Educators national program, as well as the Train the School Teachers national program. His research and publications deal with transformative learning and the use of art in adult education.

Liebler, Roberta.[a] As an administrator, instructor, and curriculum developer in the continuum from high school to higher education (developmental studies, community college, undergraduate, graduate, through doctoral dissertation), Roberta contributes to the learning of adults of diverse interests, competencies, and backgrounds. She consults in adult higher education curriculum development and assessment, including in "greening-up" higher education programs. Roberta also devises and facilitates interdisciplinary curriculum, assessment and evaluation, prior learning assessment, teacher and trainer education, research design, cross-cultural ethics, sustainability, reading and technological literacy, and best practices in global education.

Loper, Paul.[b] Paul deeply believes that how we move forward is key to what our flourishing becomes. During his forty-plus years in the performing arts, his active support of empowered culture making was profoundly informed by his doctoral work on Chormmunity, his collaborative multi-epistemological workshops that empower and deepen a group's understanding of and creative access to itself. Integrating arts modes and sensibilities with other adult learning approaches, Paul facilitates transformative learning, participatory inquiry, embodied knowledge construction, and community building internationally in holistic health, education, arts, community, business, and social justice settings.

Marienau, Catherine.[a] As a returning adult learner and while directing an alternative degree program for adults in the 1970s, Catherine was inspired to reform higher education. She is still working toward this goal, having spent the last four decades as mentor, instructor, assessor, program designer, and academic administrator—primarily in individualized, competency-based degree programs for adult learners. She consults about adult learning and competency-based learning and assessment. Catherine's research, publications, and service deal with affecting optimal learning for adults across all levels of higher education.

Martin, Akilah.[a] Enhancing sustainability of environmental and natural resources and promoting science and engineering education are passions that drive Akilah's hands-on approach to full-time teaching of adult learners. She sees education as a vehicle for social change and conducts social action-oriented research on soil and water quality. Promoting conservation and preservation through her teaching, research, and advocacy, Akilah addresses issues locally, nationally, and globally.

Matamonasa-Bennett, Arieahn.[a] For the past sixteen years, Arieahn has been teaching adult undergraduate and graduate students with a particular focus on providing them with cross-cultural understanding, awareness and appreciation of diversity, and opportunities to examine multiple perspectives and paradigms. Arieahn is a licensed psychologist with expertise in multicultural psychology, women's psychology, Native American healing and teaching traditions, and the history, science, and psychology of human-animal relationships. Her goals are the integration of the philosophy and timeless wisdom of indigenous cultures with the current theories and practice of Western psychology and adult education.

Meyer, Pamela.[a] As a theatre director working in rehearsal halls and church basements, Pamela developed many of the strategies she now uses to help adults learn in a variety of contexts. Improvisation exercises have evolved to embodied learning strategies that Pamela now also uses with business leaders who want to be more agile and innovative. The author of four books on innovation, learning, and change, Pamela teaches courses in organizational change and adult learning theory and is director of the Center to Advance Education for Adults.

Otter, Ken.[b] As a lifelong wave rider, Ken lives life in motion more improvised than choreographed. Professionally, he designs and facilitates innovative and transformative learning experiences for people in both academic and practice settings. Linking traditional and contemporary knowledge as well as art and science, Ken promotes personal and social practices that cultivate health and wisdom in individuals, organizations, and communities globally. Always looking to partner, his current areas of focus include global leadership development, multistakeholder collaboration and innovation, and expanding relationality in organizational life and leadership through coaching and facilitation.

Paxton, Doug.[b] As a learner, educator, writer, and artist, Doug is passionate about what humanity has to learn from reconnecting to our values and the natural world. He brings to his teaching and facilitation over thirty years of leadership experience in the private, public, and nonprofit sectors. Doug worked at Business for Social Responsibility, Indochinese Housing Development Corporation, and as the founding program director of the Presidio MBA in Sustainable Management. He is an accredited values executive coach who has worked with hundreds of professionals across many fields.

Proby, Donald.[b] With gratitude and a definitive edge toward cultural humility, Donald is an aspiring social entrepreneur who teaches, researches, and writes about his passions. Since 1992, he has been a professional mediator, deeply committed to peace building, cross-cultural effectiveness, transformative adult learning, and social justice action. As a peace builder, he works with groups, institutions, and communities to bridge, not eliminate, differences. Donald's current research focuses on mainstreaming conflict in higher education.

Reed, Susan.[a] Dedicated to teaching and mentoring adult learners, Susan gives special focus to connecting students with community partners to promote community health. She is engaged in scholarship to determine how institutions of higher education can adjust service-learning practice to meet the needs of adult and other nontraditional students in order to develop skills of civic engagement and improve the retention of this population.

Rogers, Russ.[a] Fueled by the commitment that organizations (and their employees) deserve to be different from their past patterns, Russ has integrated organization behavior, performance engineering, and adult learning in the service of workplace and work-life progress and possibility. Through his research, university teaching, and organizational consulting and coaching, Russ's practice bridges the artificial gap between ideas and actions so that his clients at various levels of system (individual, team, organizational) derive ideas for action. His research focuses on processes for addressing the well-earned cynicism that inadvertently grows in nearly all work environments.

Saddington, Tony. As a "practical academic," Tony taught adult educators at the University of Cape Town for twenty-one years with a focus on experiential learning, adult learning, and educational design. In 2004 he was elected a life member of the steering committee of the International Consortium for Experiential Learning. Although retired, Tony continues to teach in the School of Education at the university on a program for school principals. His focus is the development of reflective practice as a critical part of leading and managing primary and high schools.

Sheckley, Barry. Now emeritus professor of education at the University of Connecticut, Barry has devoted over thirty-five years to exploring, through research and practice, how experience enhances learning. His many publications outlining how experience contributes to the skilled use of knowledge suggests that classroom–based instruction has limited impact on the development of proficiency. Barry advocates engaging adult learners in ongoing inquiry about problems they face in their daily life as the most effective way to help them learn successfully.

Stadsklev, Ron. Dedicated to improving learning through experiential techniques such as simulation gaming, Ron has presented professional development workshops for educators and trainers at all levels, including internationally, with primary focus on how to foster greater social awareness. His innovative use of gaming in employee selection was supported by the Fund for Improvement of Postsecondary Education. In 2014, Ron was acknowledged by the North American Simulation and Gaming Association for Lifetime Achievement for his many contributions to the field, including development of the EIAG debriefing system. Now semiretired, he still plays basketball on the Senior Olympic team.

Stanford, Ann Folwell. As a teacher of adult learners for over twenty-five years, Ann's passion for literature and writing shows up in various ways in her teaching and writing. She facilitated writing workshops at Cook County jail for nearly ten years and currently offers poetry workshops at a federal prison in downtown Chicago. Anne is a published poet and is currently writing a novel.

Taylor, Kathleen.[b] Twice a college dropout before it finally took, Kathleen has for over thirty years mentored and taught in noncredit and degree-granting adult-serving programs, both graduate and undergraduate. She consults internationally and facilitates professional development workshops on issues related to adult learning and development, transformative learning, and learning and the adult brain, areas in which she is widely published. Kathleen's research focuses on how to facilitate learning that can build adults' capacity to effect much needed change in the world, starting with themselves.

Tolliver Atta, Derise.[a] Describing herself as a psychologist by training and a healer by nature, Derise's life mission is to help people "remember" who they truly are. She facilitates this through her teaching, scholarship, and service. Derise has written and presented on African-centered education and psychology, spirituality and culture in adult learning, competence-based education, international education, wellness, and healing from racism and oppression. She takes adult learners on short-term study-abroad programs to West Africa and has directed a BA degree completion program for adult learners in Nairobi, Kenya.

Walden, Sue. Sue is founder of ImprovWorks!, an organization dedicated to applying the principles, skills, and tools of improvisation training to professional and personal development. Along with thirty-five years of teaching, performing, and directing improvisational theatre, she also has thirty years of designing interactive and engaging customized programs for organizations, coaches, and individuals. A published author, her current passions are training trainers, assisting facilitators to design deep-impact interactive learning programs, and helping people build the skills to navigate successfully in the current volatile, uncertain, chaotic, and ambiguous global climate.

White, Ken. Having devoted much of his career to enhancing opportunities for citizens and communities, Ken has worked with nonprofits and nongovernmental organizations on transformation at various scales, from the group and organizational up to the global. His work has taken him from indigenous communities north of the Arctic Circle to boardrooms north of the thirtieth floor, from church basements to Harvard Law School to the Massachusetts Supreme Judicial Court. Ken has worked with leaders and staff, activists and legislators, faculty and students in both traditional and nontraditional settings.

Wilbur, Gretchen.[a] With continuing curiosity about the culture of learning, Gretchen has built learning communities that actively engage diverse people in personally meaningful ways to achieve educational equity goals. She has not only modeled this for the past thirty-five years in her own practice as an adult educator, but also in education systems design and staff development leadership with K–12 teachers and administrators, university faculty, and community agency staff. Gretchen's research and publications focus on factors that influence student-initiated discovery and learning, thereby enhancing personal and social change.

Williams, R. Bruce.[a] With over forty years of international consulting experience, Bruce's specialty is facilitating participative, interactive group workshops, whether these are focused on strategic planning and consensus building or instructional methodologies for the classroom. His seven books deal with those areas. His facilitation skills led to his training health care workers in Kenya in community mobilization methods that would respond effectively to AIDS. Bruce led health professionals in Pakistan in leadership and management skills and is currently training high school principals in China in facilitation skills.

Wozniak, Kathryn.[a] Appreciation of the intersection of art and science in learning contexts is why Kathryn's studies have focused on writing and on computing and information sciences with concentrations in human-computer interaction and learning sciences. She has worked in both academic and corporate settings and enjoys engaging with adult learners in achieving their personal and professional goals in various contexts. Kathryn's research interests include adult learners' metacognitive development, educational technology, and social learning. She values the contributions that other disciplines have made to her field, including neuroscience, psychology, and education.

NAME INDEX

SUBJECT INDEX

C

T